Books by Milton Viorst

LIBERALISM: A Guide to its Past, Present and
Future in American Politics

HOSTILE ALLIES: FDR and Charles De Gaulle

THE GREAT DOCUMENTS OF WESTERN
CIVILIZATION

FALL FROM GRACE: The Republican Party and
the Puritan Ethic

FALL
FROM
GRACE

The Republican Party
and
The Puritan Ethic

BY MILTON VIORST

A TOUCHSTONE BOOK
Published by Simon and Schuster

To

My Mother and Father

A Touchstone Book
Published by Simon and Schuster
Rockefeller Center, 630 Fifth Avenue
New York, New York 10020

This edition is published by arrangement with
The New American Library, Inc.

First Touchstone paperback printing 1971
SBN 671-21076-9 Touchstone paperback edition
Manufactured in the United States of America

CONTENTS

INTRODUCTION   vii

PROLOGUE   xvii

CHAPTER 1   *The Yankee and His Faith*   1

CHAPTER 2   *Ancestors and Origins*   18

CHAPTER 3   *Metamorphosis by War*   41

CHAPTER 4   *The Yankee's America*   62

CHAPTER 5   *The Lost Constituencies*   87

CHAPTER 6   *Yankee and Immigrant*   115

CHAPTER 7   *The Lost Opportunities*   141

CHAPTER 8   *The Fall from Grace*   163

EPILOGUE   193

BIBLIOGRAPHICAL NOTES   203

INDEX   207

INTRODUCTION

IDEAS have consequences. Or so the Greeks at least believed. The conviction became an axiom of the Socratic revolution which led to the establishment of the Academy and to the operational link between knowledge and politics. Self-knowledge was at once the discovery and the instrument by which an inviolable order of truth and goodness became the foundation of the state.

From time to time in the story of western culture, however, the Socratic axiom has functioned as an edifying aphorism, reposing largely in the chronicles of historians, raising more eyebrows than eyewitnesses, owing to a widening credibility gap which surrendered illumination to doubt. The Augustinian-Carolingian vision and enterprise, which once formed a creative reciprocity between the Republic of Letters and the Republic of Freedom and contributed greatly to what Ernst Troeltsch has called, "the medieval unity of civilization," has been overtaken by events. The City, which the Greeks called, πολις (*polis*), as their way of saying, "space for freedom," has become a place of travail and torment, where the rupture of truth from power and power from truth goes on. There is laceration at the center, in the dark void left by the absence of a unifying perspective and a liberating purpose. "Indeed," as a contemporary observer has recently put it, "it is the constant complaint by all or nearly all city planners I have ever met that there is 'no meaning to city planning anywhere,' and that the whole enterprise as it presently exists is the greatest of hoaxes."[1] Thus, the "crisis of

---

[1] John Wilkinson in the *Introduction* to Jacques Ellul, *The Meaning of the City*, Grand Rapids, William B. Eerdmans, 1970, p. xii.

history" (Troeltsch) and the meaning of the city seem to have intersected at the pit of the void to provide a negative confirmation of the Socratic axiom that knowledge is power. We are all living under a "fall from grace." If, as Troeltsch painfully discerned yet vainly hoped, we are called to "the overcoming of history by history,"[2] there is an agenda of self-examination and of political wisdom, commitment and involvement on our hands.

Milton Viorst's account of the Republican party in the United States—its formative ideas and its history—is a précis of this broader, cultural and historical "fall from grace." "Grace" is a theological word. The word has a twofold meaning. One meaning is *relational,* and signifies the favor of God upon his creation and upon creatures with whom he is well-pleased. The second meaning is *operational,* and signifies the power to will and to achieve one's destiny, that is, the fulfillment of what one has been created to be and designed to achieve. Thus, to advert to a Calvinistic appropriation of John Wilkinson's, "the City, as the theater of the technological society"[3] is a theological phenomenon. The City presupposes a theological perspective and has a theological focus. A vision of truth and goodness, of righteousness, justice and peace as the matrix and foundation of a humane and humanizing order of life sustains or does not sustain, shapes or does not shape the responsible use of power and of policy at the center of the City, of its promise and possibility, its dynamics and achievement. We live by grace; or we fall from grace. The City of God is at once the goal and the model of the city of man, the heavenly city of the earthly city, the New Jerusalem of all the Jerusalems men build and re-build. Even the nonbelievers have taken to speaking of "the

[2] Ernst Troeltsch, *Der Historismus und Seine Probleme,* Aalen, Scientia, 1961, p. 772. [Translation mine.]

[3] John Wilkinson, *Ibid.,* p. xii. Calvin regarded the world as "the theatre of divine glory." *Institutes of the Christian Religion,* edited by John T. McNeill, translated by Ford Lewis Battles, Library of Christian Classics, Vol. XX, Philadelphia, the Westminster Press, 1960, Bk. I, 5, 2. Note 27, at this place suggests other passages.

desacralization of the city."[4] What Socrates identified as *piety*, Augustine and Charlemagne and their successors identified as *grace*. In 1893, the poetic and historical imagination of Katharine Lee Bates picked up the theme and enshrined it in a hymn for the story and the future of America:

> O beautiful for patriot dream
> > That sees, beyond the years,
> Thine alabaster cities gleam,
> > Undimmed by human tears!
> America! America!
> > God shed his grace on thee,
> And crown thy good with brotherhood
> > From sea to shining sea!

When the Republican party was founded in February of 1854, in Ripon, Wisconsin, this dream informed and formed its self-understanding and its commitment. More important still, this dream informed and formed its self-justification, for, as Mr. Viorst shows, the Republican party regarded itself as the instrument of the vision enshrined in the dream, favored of God with the will and the power to achieve its destiny.

The dream and its practice through self-justification! Therein lies the clue to the "grace" and the "fall" exhibited in Mr. Viorst's story. With a remarkable gift for narration, and an equally remarkable gift for combining insight with reportorial conscientiousness, the author of this account has offered us an invaluable documentary on the relations between theology and politics. Mr. Viorst has done his homework. The result is a tale told full: of chronicle and question, of data and decision-making, of achievement and failure, signifying the sense and subtlety, the promise and the peril of ideas in search of power and of power in search of ideas. The meaning of "grace" throughout the story is clearer than is the meaning of "fall." "Grace" refers to the self-understanding and self-justification

[4] John Wilkinson, *Ibid.*, p. xii.

through which the Yankees became "the most persistent ingredient in the American mixture" (Morison and Commager).
"The Yankee created the Republican party's ancestors—as he
did the Republican party itself—in his own image. . . . The
Yankee, time after time, has shown a willingness to risk his
party's existence rather than modify its Puritan goals." (p. 18)
The "fall from grace" refers expressly to a final failure of the
Republican party to win the power of the Presidency in the
crushing defeat of Senator Barry Goldwater in 1964. "The Republican party," writes Mr. Viorst, "is an organic institution,
with historical continuity and remarkable social constancy.
Though its policies and platforms may be transitory, it possesses
ideas, attitudes, and values that have been transmitted inviolate
through time. The Republican party pays homage to unchanging myths and symbols; at the same time, it remains dedicated
to coldly unchanging objectives which are often in marked contrast to these myths and symbols. The Republican party possesses, in short, a unique personality and character." (p. xx)
The defeat of Senator Goldwater turns out, upon careful analysis, to have been far more than a matter of electoral plurality.
"Goldwater did well enough capitalizing on racism in the South,
but in the North, save for Arizona, he could find no more
Yankee majorities. . . . He emerged from the election with the
hard-core Puritan vote, and no more. . . . Surely if Goldwater
had aspired to being the apostle of God's morality, the Republican party had fallen from grace. The long journey from Ripon
seemed to be over. The hope of the Yankee community to be
restored to political ascendancy now appeared dead." (p. 192)

This principal and *reportorial* meaning of the "fall from
grace" is accompanied by another and *iconoclastic* meaning.
This meaning seems to suggest that there is a "flaw" in the
Republican story rooted in a "taint" in the Republican character. . . . A brilliant playing of the "serpent-and-dove" (Matthew 10:16) game is going on; so brilliant and subtle that there
is no shadow even of the game of "the mote and the beam"
(Matthew 7:3, NEB). The reason is that Mr. Viorst is aware
that political analysis and interpretation arrive at "their most
meaningful" when they reach or cross the theological boundary.

On that boundary, "grace" and "fall" pass beyond metaphorical appropriation and point parabolically to the creative and fulfilling (one could also say, "saving") relation between power and truth, politics and piety. An iconoclastic report is possible because the reality of the relation between power and truth, politics and piety is not in question. The real question is whether there are eyes to see and ears to hear "what the spirit says to the churches" (Revelation 2:29, *inter alia*, NEB), what the God, "before whom the nations are as a drop in the bucket" (Isaiah 40:15, NEB) is saying to the peoples.

Whenever and wherever the consequences of ideas rise up to call the ideas to account, there ultimate meanings and issues are at stake. Whenever and wherever ultimate issues are at stake, "churches" are not confined to institutional aggregates of the baptized but are the saving remnant of humankind, the "communion of saints," that is, the company of iconoclasts who practice hope in the world. Whenever and wherever ultimate issues are at stake, the "nations" and the "peoples" are not confined to geographical and genetic aggregates of chauvinists but to "the whole human running race," as Sister Corita has put it. Whenever and wherever the consequences of ideas rise up to call the ideas to account, the word "God" breaks out of its ritualistic, creedal, dogmatic, and pietistic confinements and becomes an identifying Name for an originating, liberating and fulfilling sovereignty and power at work in the world giving human shape to human life. On the boundary where politics and theology meet, the line is drawn between idolatry and iconoclasm, between a self-understanding which is self-justifying and a self-understanding always "justified by grace" anew, between an ideology of power and the power of an ideology, between sinning that grace may abound and grace that abounds in every fall from grace, choosing "even things that are not, to bring to nothing things that are." (1 Corinthians 1:28b, RSV.)

In Mr. Viorst's story, the Puritan ethic is the critical, operational instance of the interrelation between politics and theology in American history. His exciting account makes more vivid than do most straight American histories, the range and depth of the Puritan formation of American experience and

of the American mind. "It is the triumph of the Puritan faith,"
he declares, "that it has succeeded, perhaps more than any other
religious doctrine man has devised, in eliminating the inherent
conflict between material ambitions and spiritual injunctions.
Puritanism's remarkable capacity to reconcile two fundamentally
antithetical forces—greed and abnegation—is, in fact, at the
base of the Yankee conquest of the North. It has been the
Yankee's strength—and perhaps his weakness, as well—that he
has been able to forge a society dedicated to the satisfaction of
man's avarice while sincerely believing it to be the expression
of his own virtue. As he moved westward, the Yankee built and
dedicated to the glory of God a stunningly materialistic civilization." (p. 5) This Puritan faith was focused upon man's direct
access to an intimate personal relationship with God; upon the
divine election with its corollary, a double predestination of
some souls to heaven and some to hell; a lively sense of the
commandments of God, set down in the Bible, as "the only
infallible rule of faith and practice," as the Westminster divines
put it; and faithfulness to one's baptismal and secular calling,
the behavioral way of making one's election sure. The step was
a natural and all but inevitable one from this faith to an ethic
of diligence in reverence and virtue, of hard work and thrift as
man's proper stewardship of the economy of God, and of material wealth as the clearest sign of divine favor.

Since Mr. Viorst has himself recognized that the "doctrines
that shaped the Yankee spirit" were "complex and subtle" (p. 5),
it is, perhaps, appropriate to note that at one or two points his
interpretation overstates the case. While rightly crediting John
Calvin as the theological and ecclesiastical patron of the Puritans, it is too much to say that "Calvin did not concede any
weakening of piety in commanding his followers to pursue their
worldly ends." (p. 5) In his own "Summary of the Christian
Life," Calvin majestically and movingly combines a "Meditation
on the Future Life" with a discussion on "The *Right* Use of
the Present Life and Its Supports," while pivoting the whole
argument upon a subtle connection between self-denial and
gratitude.[5] Again, the Puritans would have learned from Calvin

[5] John Calvin, *Op. cit.,* Book III, chapters 6-10. [Italics mine.]

less to think of the will of man as free, than to think of an obedient will as the gift at once of the divine election and of the only freedom worth having. Indeed, the reason Calvin could regard the doctrine of predestination as a "comfortable doctrine," and as a "consolation to the faithful," was that predestination delivered the faithful from worrying about whether the will was free, since they did not have to worry about their ultimate destiny. Yet, many a pioneer in theology and politics has been distorted by his followers. Calvin is no exception. And Mr. Viorst is certainly correct in regarding the rise and fall of the Republican party as a critical operational instance of the general correlation between Calvinism and Capitalism, widely known since Max Weber's perceptive essay on "Protestantism and the Spirit of Capitalism."

Something happened between the Yankee dream and the Yankee achievement. Mr. Viorst's awareness of this underlies his iconoclasm and points up a particularly illuminating and instructive facet of his story. This has to do with the slowly developing and gradually intensifying struggle within the Republican party between the "ideologues" and the "pragmatists." The "ideologues" are those members of the party for whom the Puritan ethic functioned at once as the test of integrity and the criterion of policy and program. The "ideologues" would rather fight than switch. They would rather lose than win, as the Yankee hold upon American formation and power began to be overtaken by events. The "pragmatists," on the other hand, were those members of the party whose adherence to the Puritan ethic was a matter of personal credo and of the general guidance and welfare of the party. But the "pragmatists" were also aware of the shifting dynamics of American society occasioned by the tensions between an agrarian and an industrial economy, between the coasts and the heartland, between original settlers and immigrants in a mushrooming and multi-ethnic population. "The pragmatists," Mr. Viorst writes, "insist on the primacy of the means, on winning the election; they ask of a candidate that he be able to get the votes. The ideologues insist on the purity of the end, on the candidate's orthodoxy; who fails their test they see as a heretic. Ostensibly, the dispute between means and ends might be thought of as easy to resolve. But in reality, it is between worldliness and piety, expediency and devoutness. Each side . . . in its Puritan fashion, heaps on the other a sectarian scorn. What appear to be differences over strategy are differences of moral conception applied to the realm of politics." (p. 173)

Mr. Viorst's iconoclasm, however, carries his assessment of the rise and fall of the Republican party beyond the relation between morals and politics. What appear to be differences over strategy are, indeed, differences of moral conception applied to politics. But the accent falls upon the *application* of the Puritan ethic to politics. The line between grace and fall, between promise and default, is drawn by ultimate issues at stake, and a theological understanding of what is going on is called for. "Idealogues" and "pragmatists" both shared Puritan values and Puritan expectations, as Mr. Viorst has noted. They also participated in a common idolatry. The intensity of the struggle over ends and means had indeed become a dispute between worldliness and piety, expediency and devoutness. But the fury of the dispute raised questions of orthodoxy and heresy, and this happens whenever differences over strategy expose the gap between ultimate commitments and behavioral dilemmas. Whenever and wherever that gap erupts, the presence or absence of a theological matrix for ethics and politics makes all the difference in the world. There is a world of difference between Calvin, following Augustine and Hobbes, following Cicero. It is the difference between a theocentric and a secularized view of providence, that is, of the relation between truth and power in the shaping of human possibilities and humanizing limits in the world.

The "ideologues" and the "pragmatists" in the Republican party fell apart over means and ends, worldliness and piety, expediency and devoutness because both had lost the sense for the creative distance which a theocentric providence maintains between the will and purposes of God and the values, strategies, and achievements of men. Consequently, there was no effective way of breaking in upon the self-justification by which the achievements of the party confirmed the truth and power of the Yankee dream. What the Yankees forgot to take with requisite seriousness was that the operational bond between truth and power in the world is forged by righteousness. The righteousness of God is God's active presence in the midst of his people as "help and salvation," on behalf of the fatherless and the widow, the stranger and the poor, breaking in upon and setting right what is not right in the world. The Yankees failed to discern in the providential favor of God a built-in pressure for justice upon the values and goals, strategies and policies by which men build and rebuild earthly cities in the image of the heavenly. Having failed of this discernment, the Republican story shows not only the paralyzing stalemate between ideology and power, but a lapse into a worldliness in which expediency serves no power but its own. The Puritan ethic had been de-theologized and functioned as a dehumanizing value structure.

Theologians have more often turned their attention to the problems and possibilities of politics than political analysts have turned their attention to the relation between politics and theology. Mr. Viorst's study ventures to redress the balance by pressing his "most meaningful" inquiries and findings to the boundary on which theology and politics meet. In so doing, he has raised—in a way as sobering as it is fascinating—the searching question of the relation between piety and secularity in the American future.

> Unless the Lord builds the house
> its builders will have toiled in vain.
> Unless the Lord keeps watch over a city,
> in vain the watchman stands on guard.
> (Psalm 127:1, NEB)

PAUL LEHMANN,
Charles A. Briggs Professor of Systematic Theology
Union Theological Seminary, New York City

March 1971

PROLOGUE TO

THE 1971 EDITION

AFTER the Presidential election of 1964, there were many who were ready to pronounce the Republican party dead.

This gloomy assessment was the consequence not simply of a severe defeat. Political parties had been beaten as badly before. What gave greater reason for pause was that the Republican nominee professed views which, for a politician pretending to appeal to a national constituency, were so totally unconventional. By the wildest stretch of the imagination, Senator Barry Goldwater could not have satisfied a majority of the voters. Yet the Republican party, knowing from the beginning that he was a loser, chose him anyway. The election itself determined not whether a Republican would be President, but only the margin by which the Presidency would be denied to him.

In mitigation of Goldwater's selection, one might say that the Republicans realized they could not have won in 1964, no matter whom they nominated. The circumstances of the moment —chiefly President Kennedy's assassination—created a climate highly favorable to the Democrats. But, conceding this climate, did not common sense then dictate a strategy designed to cut losses, while waiting for a more propitious year? The Republican strategy in 1964, however, was not to cut losses. The party, in fact, seemed to court them. It was as if the inevitability of defeat had made the Republicans positively suicidal.

But if not Goldwater, one may genuinely ask, what else were the Republicans to do? For years they had been nominating Presidential candidates from the pragmatic, or "moderate," wing of the party. For years—Eisenhower's excepted—they had been losing. The "moderates" themselves in 1964 seemed to recognize that they retained little claim on the nomination. They made no significant effort to capture it for one of their own. Quite reasonably, the party might have concluded that if it was going to lose anyway, it might as well experiment with a new approach, much as the Democrats had done with William Jennings Bryan in 1896 and Al Smith in 1928. And, were Goldwater such an experiment, one might acknowledge some logic in his choice.

Goldwater's nomination was not, however, meant as a step toward the future. The one significant bloc of non-Republican voters to which Goldwater appealed came from the South. But even with all the South's electoral votes, Goldwater needed substantial new support in the North and the West. Here the party sought few votes that were not already Republican, and actually drove away many that the Republicans had long considered safe. The Goldwater candidacy was not an investment in the future, any more than it was a gamble for victory. It was a gesture of frustration over the Republican future. It was an act of homage to the Republican past.

Thus there was, after 1964, a strong feeling throughout the nation that the Republicans were finished. A political party, after all, is an organization that seeks to control the machinery of government. The Republicans seemed to be admitting in 1964 that they were no longer able to play their part in the nation's historic two-party dialogue. They seemed to have surrendered their claim to being a political party. The evidence was strong that they had been reduced to a faction within the political system.

Yet, four years later, a Republican was firmly seated in the White House. Party leaders by then were buoyant, behaving as if the Republican party, putting behind it the catastrophe of 1964, had been restored to full vigor. They spoke of building a powerful new coalition under Republican leadership. The Grand Old Party, they announced, was rising again to become the force it was in generations past.

But such a contention must be evaluated with an eye to how the two-party system functions. A political party's electoral victory does not necessarily mean that it has received a mandate to implement a political philosophy. The electorate may vote for Party A as an endorsement of Party A's program; it may also vote for Party A, however, because it has become disenchanted with Party B, the party in power. The Republicans, it is true, won the Presidency in 1968. But surely the evidence indicates a profound popular disenchantment with a Democratic President and an impatience with the unpleasant consequences of his decisions, particularly in foreign pclicy. It is by no means clear that the Republican resurgence signified anything more than a temporary decline in confidence in Democratic leadership.

But if this argument suggests that the Republican restoration may be transitory, it does not hold that the Republican party is doomed to vanish. The Republicans are buttressed by a political system that makes the formation of new parties all but impossible. Election laws in most states serve as obstacles to the placing of third-party candidacies on the ballot. Television has raised the costs of any major challenge to the established party structure to an intolerable point. The problem of organizing in fifty states down to the ward-and-block level is all but impossible for a new group to solve. It would take an issue of the magnitude of slavery, the germ of the Republican party, to shake the current political system. Besides, the Republican party retains a large and loyal constituency, even if it can regularly obtain nationwide majorities no longer.

Despite rather consistent bad luck at the polls then, the Republicans continue to fulfill an important responsibility within the system. At the very least, the party serves as an alternative, available to administer the country whenever the electorate, for whatever reason, seeks to express its displeasure with the manner in which the majority party is running the government. As a second party, it must be on the alert to step in as a caretaker to assume the levers of the state when the principal party falls into disfavor. The Republicans, indeed, won in 1968. But there is scant evidence that the election returns meant anything more than that the voters wanted to be rid of the Democrats—and, fortunately, the Republicans happened to be standing by.

But if the public is indifferent to Republican philosophy and program, one may indeed wonder why the party does not change. Certainly, there is nothing either sacred or invulnerable about the Democrats. They possess inherent weaknesses, basic contradictions and profound divisions. They have not, in their many decades of power, manifested a consistent grasp of the country's problems or the ability to solve them. In fact, one might argue that, during the last Democratic administration their blunders intensified these problems. Surely there is ample reason to believe that another party could serve the country just as well, perhaps even better. Why should it not be the Republicans? One might assume, even on the basis of conventional self-interest, that the Republicans would gladly mend their ways to offer to the electorate a program and a philosophy that it could positively endorse.

There is, however, a fallacy in that assumption. The Republican party is not simply a group of politicians banded together to compete, on the most favorable possible terms, in election campaigns. The Republican party is an organic institution, with historical continuity and remarkable social constancy. Though its policies and platforms may be transitory, it possesses ideas, attitudes, and values that have been transmitted inviolate through time. The Republican party pays homage to unchanging myths and symbols; at the same time, it remains dedicated to coldly unchanging objectives which are often in marked contrast to these myths and symbols. The Republican party possesses, in short, a unique personality, an institutional character that is its very own. It is this character, far more than any compromise with electoral expediency, which determines the fundamental decisions that the party makes.

The Republican party's character—like that of any institution—is not static, but it changes only slowly. It is the product of its experiences, but each experience builds upon the solidity of its past. An act committed today may be the consequence of a process begun a decade, even a century, ago; in its turn, it becomes another influence on the party's character development. Few decisions will be made which radically alter character, but none will be taken which violate it.

The selection of Barry Goldwater would not have been possible had it been outside the framework of Republican character. The Goldwater choice was not inevitable; other possibilities were available within that framework. But to assert, as have some, that the Goldwater nomination transgressed the boundaries of Republicanism is sorely inaccurate. Goldwater's candidacy was a choice toward which the Republican party had been moving throughout its history. There is nothing surprising about the fact that it was made. If Goldwater's views were politically unconventional, it suggests only that the Republican party no longer speaks in a language that the majority of the electorate understands. But Barry Goldwater, the politician, is no less the realization of the character of the Republican party.

In 1968, the Republican party chose Richard Nixon, a quite different candidate. He was not the Republican ideologue that Goldwater was. He was much closer to the pragmatic wing of the party. His strength, as a contender for the nomination, lay not in any personal magnetism but in his capacity to bridge the chasm between the party's two segments, with the added virtue of his holding an attraction for the Whig delegates from the South. Nixon was, so to speak, the lowest common denominator among Republicans, but he was not necessarily the most appealing nominee to the national electorate. He had lost his two previous election contests, for President in 1960 and for Governor of California in 1962. Widely regarded as a failure, he had formally said goodbye to politics. Though nominated overwhelmingly at the Republican national convention, he was certainly not regarded as a sure winner, even though 1968 had been widely predicted to be a Republican year. Any of a half-dozen candidates, it was agreed, would probably have been stronger. But the choice of any of them would have meant that the party's first consideration was victory—and it was not. The party's first consideration was the nomination of a candidate who truly embodied the Republican nature. Even the tantalizing prospect of power could not keep the Republican party from being faithful to itself. It would lose, rather than betray its Republican character.

It is the purpose of this book to explore that Republican character. The character of the Republican party, however, reposes not in documents or campaign buttons or statistics but in people, and people are often unpredictable in their behavior.

Some people, in fact, are so inconsiderate that they will violate any generalization, no matter how hard an author has labored to bring it forth. So there are, for example, Senator Jacob K. Javits of New York, who joined the Republican party, and Senator Wayne Morse of Oregon, who abandoned it. For reasons very personal to them, they were exceptions to the rules. This book does not presume to account for the idiosyncrasies of individuals. Since it is not a work of mathematics, every figure will not fall neatly into a pattern. In explanation rather than in apology, it can be said that this is a work of political interpretation and, therefore, will show some ragged edges. This book is presented as an effort to understand the Republican party, the people it represents, and, in some measure, the American nation. The Republican character merits attention because it is an essential element in the dynamics of American life.

FALL
FROM
GRACE

The Republican Party
and
The Puritan Ethic

CHAPTER 1

The Yankee and His Faith

IN 1844, a band of Yankees migrating from New England founded the town of Ripon in Wisconsin. Puritans by conviction, they had little time for frivolity. They worked hard, governed well, and they prospered. Within a few years, they had even established a college. In this frontier community, these Yankees, impassioned over the slavery issue, organized a political instrument to speak for them. It was called the Republican party.

The strong-willed Yankees who settled Ripon were part of a wave that poured relentlessly forth from New England to colonize the American Northwest. Yankees moved first into the counties of upstate New York and down into Pennsylvania, then through the Ohio Valley and across the Great Plains, finally over the mountains and on to the Coast. Over the course of a century that began with the War of Independence, hundreds of thousands of Yankees, perhaps even more, left their homes to establish new communities in the West. It was this great migration from New England that, more than any other, rolled back the Northwestern frontier. These Yankees, said the historians Morison and Commager, became "the most persistent ingredient in the American mixture." These descendants of the early New England colonists set the pattern for the civilization of the North.

The Yankee pioneers spread across the West in the manner in

which they had settled the interior of New England itself. Typically, they detached themselves in compact groups from older communities, not as bands of adventurers but as responsible burghers, carrying with them their women and children and their household belongings. Though they were not strangers to harsh circumstances, they migrated not as an escape. They were tormented at home neither by tyranny nor famine. The hardship they faced was surely greater than that which they chose to leave behind. The Yankees migrated to extend their own society into lands of new opportunity. Theirs was, in many ways, a mass missionary movement. In their baggage they conveyed not humility about their origins but inordinate pride in the culture they had fashioned. As they traveled onward, the Yankee pioneers were satisfied to make the North into a vast province of the culture of New England.

The Yankees were largely townspeople. Even the farmers among them oriented their lives to the rhythm of the towns. Their experience provided them with the skills to master the complexities of urban social organization. The Yankees understood the techniques of self-government and went methodically about the processes of forming themselves into bodies politic. Adroit in the practices of commerce, they established markets for the exchange of commodities, and they built mills to grind their grain and saw their logs. They founded churches, schools, and newspapers, modeled on those that remained behind them in the East. To be sure, they had to adapt to new conditions by modifying many of their practices. But to guard against decline in their standards, they maintained their ties to the lands from which they had come. They corresponded with the kin who had stayed behind and read the magazines, journals, and books that arrived from them. If they could, they sent their children to school in New England or, as a second choice, in Ohio; then they welcomed these children back as teachers, ministers, and editors. Guided by their Puritan codes, these Yankees had no sympathy for the disorder that characterized other segments of the frontier. Self-possessed and sure of themselves, they knew how to apply law to the conduct of a community and invariably they did.

But the Yankees, of course, were not alone in settling the Northwest. Perhaps they were never even a majority. From the

South, the outcasts of an aristocratic plantation culture drifted past Kentucky and Tennessee into the path of the Yankee migration. From the Middle States came the Scotch-Irish in search of lands of their own to till. In subsequent waves arrived foreign immigrants, most of them of peasant origin, from the semi-feudal societies of Europe. The Yankees had no choice but to share with these others the stubborn rewards of the frontier. Better prepared to master the frontier, however, they had little difficulty in imposing their own standards on the civilization that emerged. Whatever resentments they may have provoked, the Yankees tended to stamp their own ideas and practices on whoever chanced to live among them, not by force but by example, organization, and will. In 1899, a Yankee historian of Wisconsin wrote: "Though few in numbers, the New England men have been a potent factor in shaping this commonwealth, and however the foreign blood may predominate, theirs is the pattern that has been set and must be followed. . . . Wisconsin institutions have been dominated by Americans of the Puritan seed from the beginning." By absorbing some of their rivals and dominating others, the Yankees succeeded in establishing their own social and economic hegemony wherever they made their homes.

Ultimately, the Yankee migration all but depopulated New England of the men and women whose forebears, as religious dissidents, had settled these lands from England. Gradually, the Yankees who remained behind were overwhelmed by new Americans coming from abroad. Towns like Marietta in Ohio, Northfield in Minnesota, and Portland in Oregon had become, by the start of the current century, more purely Yankee than Hartford, Pawtucket, and Manchester. Dr. Dooley, Finley Peter Dunne's perceptive Irish-American critic of the nation's folkways, observed that the "dayscindints" of the New England fathers "mostly live in Kansas now." Not New England but the Midwest became the heartland of America's Puritan culture.

But the Puritans, in quest of a much greater prize, seemed barely to mourn New England. As a Yankee pastor at a Fourth of July celebration in 1876 declared: "Who cares for the growth of New England? Who cares, so long as she can give principles and institutions and men to the Nation?" In churches, in schools, in newspapers, in politics, the men of New England—and the women, too—exercised a proportion of influence that far exceeded their numbers. Frederick Jackson Turner, the great romanticizer of the American frontier, has noted with obvious satisfaction that "the continuous advance of this pioneer stock from New England has preserved for us the older type of the pioneer of frontier New England." With considerable accuracy, James H. Baker, former president of the University of Colorado, wrote in his massive history of Colorado: "Puritan standards have become the public standards of America, and you will find more of New England in Colorado Springs, Boulder, or Greeley than in most towns of Massachusetts. This is not a partisan claim, but recognition of a fact."

The pioneers of the West, the civilizers of the frontier, the founders of the Republican party, these Yankees traced their descent directly from the Puritan culture established in New England early in the seventeenth century. It was a culture that emerged directly out of the Reformation, in defiance of Rome and of the feudal society to which Roman standards seemed intrinsic. The Puritans rebelled against the limitations imposed on them by a corporate social organization. They arrived in America as heralds of a new age, in which men were not hobbled by traditional obligations, politics stifled by a fixed hierarchy, or economics circumscribed by medieval proscriptions. The doctrines they possessed fitted them peculiarly for triumphing over the rigors of the new continent. The Puritans, abandoning feudalism to their European past, planted in the New England colonies the seed of the modern middle-class mind. From this ancestral seat, they transmitted it through successive generations across three thousand miles of territory. It enabled the Yankees to shape the destiny of the nation.

John Greenleaf Whittier, a century ago, drew a graphic picture of the Puritans he knew. They were, he wrote:

Church-goers, fearful of the unseen powers
But grumbling over pulpit tax and pew-rent,
Saving, as shrewd economists, their souls

And winter pork with the least possible outlay
Of salt and sanctity.

Samuel Eliot Morison, the celebrated Yankee historian, called his people: "A tough but nervous, tenacious but restless race; materially ambitious, yet prone to introspection, and subject to waves of religious emotion." The Yankees, he wrote, are "a race whose typical member is eternally torn between a passion for righteousness and a desire to get on in the world."

However well Morison understood the characteristics of his Yankees, he created a false impression in maintaining that they are typically torn between "a passion for righteousness" on the one hand and "a desire to get on in the world" on the other. For it is the triumph of the Puritan faith that it has succeeded, perhaps more than any other religious doctrine man has devised, in eliminating the inherent conflict between material ambitions and spiritual injunctions. Puritanism's remarkable capacity to reconcile two fundamentally antithetical forces—greed and abnegation—is, in fact, at the base of the Yankee conquest of the North. It has been the Yankee's strength—and perhaps his weakness, as well—that he has been able to forge a society dedicated to the satisfaction of man's avarice while sincerely believing it to be the expression of his own virtue. As he moved westward, the Yankee built and dedicated to the glory of God a stunningly materialistic civilization.

John Calvin, the stern patron of reformed Christianity, devised the complex and subtle doctrines that shaped the Yankee spirit. His was no mean intellectual achievement. Calvin did not concede any weakening of piety in commanding his followers to pursue their worldly ends. On the contrary, Calvinism was a rejection of Roman theology, which it took as lax and indulgent, while Calvinist dogma was meant to be rigid and constantly demanding. Out of the conviction that they worshiped God in uncorrupted fashion, the Calvinists of England came upon the name of Puritans. In settling New England, the Puritans professed to establish a commonwealth devoted to the practice of rectitude. As they moved westward, they gloried in the conviction that they were extending God's dominion. The culture the Yankees brought to the North took shape from their transformation of Calvinist theology into a consistent pattern of secular action.

The first principle of Puritan theology was that man stood face-to-face and alone before God. The Puritan rejected the authority of the established clergy to intercede between him and the Deity. He repudiated the Roman concepts of church supremacy and the required submission to ecclesiastical rule. His own church was a simple device through which he maintained his personal relationship with God. Like his ritual, his church was spare, unadorned with frills, almost superfluous to his needs. The Puritan faith made its demands on men directly. The Puritan saw himself as an individual struggling to make his way in the world, responsible for his own conduct and accountable only to God.

The Puritan believed with equal fervor that God had, in somewhat arbitrary fashion, consigned all but a few souls to eternal damnation. In contrast to the tolerant God of the Romanists, theirs was a forbidding God, an object of trepidation rather than of affection. They were convinced that God's decision was immutable, once He had selected the few whom He would save. Neither good works nor prayer, they believed, could change the predestination of souls, some to heaven and others to hell.

But though preoccupied with the afterlife, the Puritan faith was actively concerned with the here-and-now. Worldly conduct, in fact, played an important role in Puritan theology. Guided by Calvin, the Puritans reasoned that God, though unmoved by earthly behavior to reconsider the status of any soul, nonetheless communicated to individuals the choice He had made by the conduct He inspired. Though each man was, of course, the product of his own free will, he whose behavior conformed most closely to the Puritan ethic was recognized, by himself and others, to be among the chosen of God. The Puritan, then, was enjoined to perform his secular duties according to the highest religious standards, even though he was theologically convinced that his behavior would not change his standing with God. The Puritan was prevailed upon to follow God's commandments, not to earn

God's favor—which was impossible—but to persuade himself and others that God had already selected him for eternal life.

The Puritan thus dedicated his life on earth, transitory as it was, to demonstrating his worthiness for eternal salvation. He did this by devoting himself furiously to his secular calling, his worldly work. "God doth call every man and woman," wrote an early Puritan philosopher, ". . . to serve Him in some peculiar employment in this world." As the Puritan understood it, work was man's fundamental expression of his submission to God. Industriousness was a sign of God's favor.

George Norris relates in his memoirs how, as a young man growing up on the frontier, his mother expressed her Puritan faith. He recalls that one day he said:

> "Why do you work so hard, Mother? We now have more fruit than we can possibly use. You will be dead long before this tree comes into bearing."
> The little farm was well stocked with fruit. It had its apples, its peaches, and its sour cherries.
> Her answer was slow to come, apparently while she measured her words.
> "I may never see this tree in bearing, Willie," she said, "but somebody will."

One of the favorite Biblical quotations of the Puritans was: "Seest thou a man diligent in his business? He shall stand before kings." By keeping himself busily at labor, the Puritan saw himself as an obedient servant of God. He had no obligation to perform *good works,* in the Romanist sense, but only *hard work.* "Man will be at a great loss," wrote an early Puritan philosopher, "if he does not keep his own vineyard and mind his own business." In minding his own business, the believer was to keep pure his relationship with God, unencumbered by extraneous obligations to man. Frivolity was forbidden to the Puritan because it diverted his energy from God's service. To the Puritan, therefore, the slothful man was twice condemned, once for failing God and again for disclosing the evidence of his damnation. Work, for the

Puritan, was not a worldly departure from spirituality but an act of religious devotion itself.

In the Puritan reasoning process, it was the next logical step to conclude that the most favored of God received the greatest tangible reward. If industriousness was a favorable hint about the fate of a man's soul, then surely success was a sign of certainty that a man had been selected for salvation. It was in this way that the Puritan came to look on wealth as the measure of God's approval. "We ought not to prevent people from being diligent and frugal," wrote one of the seminal Puritan thinkers, challenging traditional feudal concepts. "We must exhort all Christians to gain all they can; and to save all they can; this is, in effect, to grow rich." Still, the Puritan did not countenance self-indulgence. On the contrary, he made a distinction between acquiring wealth and enjoying it. "You labor to be rich for God, though not for the flesh and sin," wrote a Puritan divine. Puritanism thus sanctioned the pursuit of riches, then commanded the rich to resist the temptations of their reward. It was, as one analyst has put it, a "worldly asceticism." Whatever the spiritual consistency of the doctrine, ultimately it proved a secular paradox, more than the Puritan ethic could viably absorb. Nonetheless, it is accurate to assert that the Puritan, in equating wealth with virtue, quite literally came to believe that the rich were the chosen of God.

By sanctioning, as religious acts, hard work and the acquisition of wealth, the Puritan ethic generated what Max Weber has called the "spirit of capitalism." As many have observed, Calvinist thinking was fundamental to the growth of capitalism in the Western world. Calvin, in the eyes of many, was Christianity's prophet in dealing with the shift from medieval to modern economics. In New England, however, there was no shift. From the very beginning the colonies were organized along capitalist lines. As early as 1632, it was noted that the New England colonies—in contrast to the colonies of the South, which had been founded by commercial companies—had established an economy based on profit-seeking, although they had been founded as religious refuges. "The growth of New England," wrote Francis Parkman, a great historian, "was the result of the aggregate efforts of a busy multitude, each in his narrow circle toiling for himself, to gather competence or wealth." The distinction which Parkman suggests is that in New England everyone worked for gain, while society in the South was so stratified that only a few were expected to get rich. The Yankees were comfortable making money, for their church assured them that they were also being pious.

Purantism, the progenitor of the "spirit of capitalism," may not have been the only reason that America's industrial revolution began in New England. All the necessary components were there: capital, power, transportation, and an excellent climate for textile manufacturing. Perhaps most important was the plentiful supply of labor that was, being Puritan itself, dedicated to hard work and deferential to the profit system. But certainly without Puritanism as the unifying factor, New England's potential would have gone unexploited and the industrial revolution been indefinitely delayed.

To the factory towns of New England flocked uncounted Yankee maidens who, for two dollars a week, tended spindles in the textile mills. Absent was any sense of class resentment or disgruntlement over the burdens of labor. The Puritan lasses toiled to exhaustion and were grateful that their employers were proper New England gentlemen with concern for their morality and their character. "Dear Mamma," wrote one of the girls in a letter home in 1840:

> The Millowners are the kindest men imaginable. All of us employees are encouraged to read the Bible and the North American Review, which has some fine thoughts expressed in elegant language; and those few girls who are derelict in their attendance at Sabbath School are called upon gently and chided seriously by our Mill overseers, all good Christian men who are also our Teachers on the Sabbath.

The millowners and overseers, in teaching Christianity every Sunday to nubile Yankee maidens, were undoubtedly satisfied with themselves for doing their duty. That the girls sometimes went home with arms mangled or fingers lost in the textile machinery was no reason for a Yankee to feel distressed. A Puritan, after all, was not a humanist but a moralist. He was free to pursue gain in all varieties of endeavor, so long as these endeavors were not sins. A Yankee historian of Wisconsin, writing at the turn of the century, pointed out that Yankees were prominent in every important industry in the state but one, "which"—he noted with satisfaction—"was brewing." The faithful Puritan, sanctioned in a single-minded absorption with his own self-interest, was, by showing concern for the souls of young girls and potential inebriates, doing *more* than God commanded. It was not his duty to contemplate what was best for others, but only to do what was best for himself. "What the Puritans gave the world was not thought," said Wendell Phillips, the nineteenth-century reformer, "but action." The Yankee millowner and the Yankee overseer—determined to serve God by getting rich—turned the Yankee communities of New England, then of the West, into the business and industrial bastions of the nation.

To the Puritan, if the rich man demonstrated his exceptional virtue by his triumphs in the marketplace, then the poor man showed in his material degradation that he was a moral failure. The Puritan, persuaded that the rich were the saved, believed that the poor were the sinful and the damned. Quite appropriately, he looked on them not with pity but with contempt. "No man in this land," said the Reverend Henry Ward Beecher, the celebrated Yankee preacher, "suffers poverty unless it be more than his fault . . . unless it be his sin." Man, the Puritan believed, had no more right to be poor than to be sick. If a more primitive form of Christianity maintained that the rich would not enter the Kingdom of Heaven, the Puritan argued that poverty was the route to hell.

The Puritan was thus enjoined to be indifferent toward the poor. He was taught to reject the feudal conception that society was a corporate—even a familial—organism, in which all members had duties to one another, and the rich had the heaviest duties of all. Having liberated the individual from his place in the medieval hierarchy, Puritanism exalted a principle of social irresponsibility. It offered the believer the license to pursue his secular goals as he saw fit, with no more than a minimum of restraint imposed for the sake of public order. The Puritan ethic was not even sympathetic to the practice of charity, which it contended would only discourage the poor from working to improve themselves. "As for idle beggars," wrote a seventeenth-century Puritan, "happy for them if fewer people spent their foolish pity upon their bodies, and if more showed some wise compassion upon their souls." In some measure, the Puritan recognized a duty to social morality, an obligation to the domain of the soul. But in corporal matters, the Puritan was strict in believing that each man had to fend for himself. By serving God, the Puritan was excused from serving mankind. He was especially absolved of serving those who were sinners enough that they were poor.

Throughout history, it is true, the miserly of civilizations everywhere have sought means of justifying their stinginess. Puritanism, however, is probably the first body of religious thought that succeeded intellectually in turning stinginess from a sin into a virtue. With ecclesiastical sanction, the Puritan told himself that charity not only perpetuated suffering but defied God's will. Tight-fistedness, his God assured him, was the essence of piety itself.

But the Puritan's indifference to poverty did not mean that he was unmoved to crusade for good causes. On the contrary, the Puritan could be a zealot in behalf of God's good morality. Periodically, the Puritan turned reformer to restore what he regarded as the moral integrity of his community. Sometimes he acquired peculiar ideas about the morality that God commanded, but rarely did that interfere with the ardor of his crusade or his own belief in his righteousness.

Frederick Jackson Turner, the historian who idealized the Puritan pioneer, maintains that "if we follow back the line of march of the Puritan farmer, we shall see how responsive he has always been to *isms,* and how persistently he has resisted encroachment on his ideals of individual opportunity and democracy. . . . He is the Abolitionist, the Anti-Mason, the Millerite, the Woman Suffragist, the Spiritualist, the Mormon of Western New York."

He is also the advocate of Sunday observance and dress reform, of anti-prostitution and the establishment of foundling homes, of vegetarianism and the prevention of cruelty to animals. Throughout American history, he has been associated with the temperance movement, particularly when he has felt the soundness of his society threatened by foreigners and others who failed to share his stern standards of good conduct. "The Holy Spirit," said a temperance pamphlet in the post-colonial period, "will not visit, much less will He dwell with him who is under the polluting, debasing, effects of intoxicating drink." What the Puritan did not care about reforming was the class structure and the distribution of wealth in society. With these, he believed God was not concerned.

In devising political forms to correspond to the egalitarianism felt *within* the community, the Puritans made a direct contribution to the development of American democracy. James Russell Lowell, thinking of the political equality that existed inside the New England colonies, wrote that Puritanism laid the "egg of democracy" in the United States. But the Puritans, then and later, looked on democratic principles with considerable reserve. They saw small resemblance between the majority decisions reached in New England town meetings and the mass decisions, exercised through the device of universal suffrage, reached by a nation with a highly heterogeneous population. The Puritans, democratic as they were, were exceedingly chary of a system that extended the franchise indiscriminately to every citizen in the country, Puritan and non-Puritan alike.

It is true that to the Puritan, government was relatively inconsequential. What counted was the individual, who was the object of God's judgment. The Puritan believed that society, as such, scarcely existed in God's eyes. His rebellion against feudalism had been directed largely at the restraints imposed on the individual by the state, the agent of organized society. There was more than a touch of Puritanism in the colonists' fight against the English monarchy and in the limited government they enshrined in the Constitution. The Puritan asked of the government only that it leave him free to pursue his interests as he saw fit. He did not contemplate with pleasure the prospect that, through democracy, the control of the state could fall into the hands of those whose objectives were different from his own.

Thus, while building inside their own community a policy that was generally egalitarian, the Puritans adopted toward outsiders the aristocratic perspective that they had themselves sought to escape in their flight to the New World. Within the "egg" that Lowell extolls was contained an elitist belief, basic to Puritanism, which could have stopped dead in its tracks the evolution of American democracy. Hatched from the Puritans' "egg of democracy" was a bird that was later fed on Jeffersonian and Jacksonian doctrines to become the institution that it is today. The historical evidence suggests that had Puritan democracy grown to maturity free of this leveling influence, it would have become a republican process open to the small numbers of the saved, while piously shutting out the overwhelming masses of the damned.

The Puritan outlook generated tensions in American society not simply over the franchise but over the question of religious practice as well. With much accuracy, Artemus Ward, Charles Farrar Browne's fictional folk hero, declared: "The Puritans nobly fled from a land of despotism to a land of freedom, where they could not only enjoy their own religion but could prevent everyone else from enjoying his." One almost forgets that the early years of New England colonization were rife with conflict generated by the Puritans' claim to the unique possession of religious truth. It seemed reasonable to predict that the new land would face constant disorder, perhaps even the kind of religious warfare that had characterized Europe. Finally, out of the sectarian hostility of the colonial era, there was established the principle of religious tolerance, along with its concomitant, the separation of church and state. By judicious compromise, Puritan and non-Puritan averted constant religious strife.

Religious tolerance, however, included no recognition that one sect was as worthy of God's grace as another. Rather, it represented a truce, an expedient designed to promote political tranquility. Unquestionably, the early establishment of the principle of religious toleration was indispensable to the subsequent formation of the nation, diverse as its population was to become. But acquiescence in the principle did not mean the Puritans had shed the conviction that, in that nation, their faith had a special and privileged place.

Out of the Puritan faith, there also emerged a dedication to formal schooling unequaled by any other major group in the American mixture. This dedication was probably as important to the formation of the national character as any contribution the Puritans made. Writing about early New England, Lowell declared: "It was in making education not only common to all, but in some sense compulsory on all, that the destiny of the free republics of America was practically settled." If it was Puritan culture that civilized the Northwestern frontier, it was Puritan education that permitted the civilization to thrive and grow.

The Puritan acquired a belief in education because he was, in a real and important sense, a rationalist. To be sure, he subscribed to the doctrine of predestination, which put his ultimate fate in God's hands and rendered him powerless to modify it. But in contrast to the Romanists, he had eliminated magic as a means of salvation. He had done away with the priests, who claimed the power to forgive him his sins and invoke miracles in his behalf. The Puritan, though he relied on faith, had great respect for the intellect as the instrument for guiding him along the proper path.

Since right conduct was the province of each individual, the Puritan was advised to spare no effort to prepare himself for his responsibilities. Thus the Puritans founded schools, not out of any love for abstract learning but out of concern for their worldly duties. The McGuffey Reader, with its entreaties to good conduct, was the heart of Puritan elementary education. The Puritan, however, with his determination to succeed in his secular calling, did not confine his schooling to simple moralisms. Puritan education was rigorous and disciplined. It demonstrated an appreciation not only for practical ends but for basic intellectual development. It trained more than a few excellent minds and many that were commendably equipped for the demands made upon them by Calvinist doctrine and American life.

Southern Calvinism, in contrast, took a markedly different turn. Predestination persuaded the Southerner to turn away from the exercise of the intellect. Belief in God made him a fundamentalist, not a rationalist. While the Yankee gave his attention to worldly triumph, the Southerner turned inward to individual repentance. For the Southern Calvinist, education consisted in rejecting all books but the Bible. His chief act of devotion to God was not hard work but an overt expression of intense religious emotion. The Southerner measured success not in the counting house but at the revival meeting. Schooling was a matter of no importance to him.

As the divergence grew between North and South, one cannot overlook that in the most primitive Yankee frontier town there was a school. Wherever Yankees settled in substantial numbers, a college was founded. While popular learning was dying on the Southern frontier, in the areas of Yankee dominance it flourished. Literacy followed the Yankee advance as surely as Puritan culture itself. The Puritan school, purveying Puritan attitudes and Puritan values, was perhaps the most powerful agent of all in the Yankee conquest of the North. It also prepared the Yankee for the role of leadership he was to play in the affairs of the nation.

It was probably inevitable that those who subscribed to the Puritan faith should have acquired the conviction that they somehow belonged to a secular elite. God Himself, after all, had established the principle of castes by dividing mankind irrevocably into the Saved and the Damned. Puritans, commanded to conduct themselves as if they were saved, tended naturally to believe that they were. Whatever shred of uncertainty remained with them served as a kind of bond that reinforced the cohesion of the group. The Puritan faith generated a sentiment of camaraderie among the members of the community. There was, to be sure, a rigorous social ranking among Puritans, based on the tangible measures of success. But Puritans, faced with common risks and the prospect of a common triumph, tended to look on one another as equal contenders for the favor of God.

Contemptuous of non-Puritan behavior and the inference it

conveyed of God's displeasure, Puritans were led to close ranks against outsiders. The Puritan faith generated an attitude of condescension, a propensity for exclusion, a feeling of indifference toward those who did not belong to the group. To characterize the sentiment as snobbery is inadequate. To call it racist is, perhaps, to frame it in unduly contemporary terms. Nonetheless, the net effect was to create within a framework of national diversity a powerful community which thought of itself as both socially and racially privileged. The Puritans, from the beginning, have taken pride in being members of God's elite, and have been reluctant to admit others into it.

By coincidence or not, God's injunctions to the Puritan fitted him astonishingly well to meet the harsh demands of the New World. In the isolation of his frontier community, he was comforted by his personal relationship with God and the confidence that he was serving His will. In the face of the monumental challenge of creating a City of God in the desolate wilderness, he was braced by his enthusiasm for hard work. The Puritan's indifference to the amenities of life enabled him to see his objective in its long-term perspective. His rejection of frivolity permitted him to direct all his energies to tangible achievement. The Puritan, to survive and prosper in the New World, had to be unsparing with his labors, cautious with his capital, and utterly self-reliant. He arrived in America with a set of ideas that equipped him to meet these demands. In New England, the onerous conditions he found toughened his spirit and prepared him for the conquest of the West. As he pressed back the frontier, his very success persuaded him that the doctrines with which God had outfitted him were, indeed, immortal truth.

In their relentless migration westward, the Yankees behaved as if they were a driven people. The land, pure and undefiled, appealed to their Puritan souls. This was a New World, sinless and uncorrupted. The Yankees seemed to be compelled, almost obsessed, to move onward. "If hell lay in the West," it used to be said irreverently of them, "they would cross heaven to reach it." The Yankee, merciless not only on himself but on his wife and children, pressed ever forward. His mission was to domesticate the

West, to make it into a Puritan commonwealth, worthy of the favor of God.

It was natural that these Yankees, proud as they were of their values and proficient as they were at organization, should think of establishing a political party to represent them in the nation. Such a party would stand as a safeguard of their culture. It could serve as a vehicle for the radiation of their ideas. Most important, it could become the means of expressing the Yankee preeminence in American society. In brief, it would be the Yankees' agent for running the country. Thus, from the beginning of the Republic, the Yankees were a people in search of a political party of their own. What they needed was a deeply felt passion to make it into a reality. In Ripon in 1854, they found their passion and undertook their crusade.

CHAPTER 2

Ancestors and Origins

THE Republican party's genealogy reveals a disturbing trait. All of the party's ancestors, since the first days of the Republic, have died young. Some, while flashing briefly, contributed much to American political life. Others, fulfilling a temporary need, made no lasting impact. But each, in its way, had some genetic influence on the Republican party. Significantly, not one possessed the characteristic of longevity.

The explanation, in brief, is that the Yankee created the Republican party's ancestors—as he did the Republican party itself—in his own image. Since he has never been a majority in the nation, the Yankee has had great difficulty keeping his party alive.

The Yankee, of course, might have joined one or another group in a political coalition to form a permanent majority. But only in rare instances has he been willing to share power. For the Yankee, it has been important to maintain the purity of his party. To compromise its character would be to sacrifice his objective. The Yankee, time after time, has shown a willingness to risk his party's existence rather than modify its Puritan goals.

Despite his lack of success with them, the typical Yankee has been faithful to his political parties. Because of his own worship of material achievement, he has regularly let his parties fall under the control of the rich, who have used them for their own purposes. But he has nonetheless stayed with them. Out of devotion to his clan, he has, consciously or not, been cavalier with his pocketbook. To be sure, he has sometimes strayed to the right, to reform the morality of a sinning society. When extremely pressed, he has on occasion strayed to the left, to reform the abuses of a sinful economy. Mostly, however, he has been content to vote for the Yankee party, as if self-interest commanded a gesture of community solidarity. The Yankee has remained a cohesive political body—with a higher regard for this cohesion than for the thin gruel of coalition rule. He has preferred losing elections to winning them on others' terms.

The task that the Yankees of successive generations have set before themselves, thus, is the transformation of a minority force into a majority party, without making concessions on principles, precepts, or ruling-class prerogatives. The task has not been easy. During the period of exhilaration that followed the War of Independence and the adoption of the Constitution, the Federalists possessed the confidence of the country. During an era of political flux, the Whigs brilliantly exploited electoral tactics to win a few elections. During the long decades from 1860 to 1930, the Republicans dominated American politics and had, by outward appearances, succeeded in establishing themselves as a permanent ruling elite. But as events in each case demonstrated, the Yankees never solved their dilemma. Republicans today, like Federalists and Whigs of another age, face the frustrations of turning themselves into a majority without compromising the purity of their character or the integrity of their beliefs.

It may be an impossible challenge.

The Federalists, the first of the Yankee parties, could count on retaining their popularity as long as George Washington remained their symbol and the glories of a victorious war remained ripe memories. The party itself began as an alliance of the commercial rich of the North, particularly those of the New England port cities, and the plantation aristocracy of the South. In the formative days of the nation, the interests of the Federalists coincided with those of a broad constituency, cutting across all classes.

It was in their role as Founding Fathers that the Federalists commanded widespread support.

But the Federalists never thought of themselves as a party in the conventional terms of organization, campaigns, and response to an electorate. The Federalists conceived of their role as that of a ruling aristocracy, entitled to govern by their eminence and virtue, and because, for the most part, they met Hamilton's qualifications of being "rich and well-born." They regarded the first duty of government to be the maintenance of order and the protection of property. They were frightened of democracy, for if all men voted, as John Adams of Massachusetts wrote:

> Perhaps at first prejudice, habit, shame or fear, principle or religion would restrain the poor from attacking the rich, and the idle from usurping the industrious; but the time would come and pretexts be invented by degrees to countenance the majority in dividing all the property among them, or at least in sharing it equally with its present possessors. Debts would be abolished first; taxes laid heavily on the rich, and not at all on the others; and at last a downright equal division of everything be demanded and voted. What would be the consequences of this? The idle, the vicious, the intemperate would rush into the utmost extravagance of debauchery, sell and spend all their share, and then demand a new division of those who purchased from them.

As Adams's words suggest, the Federalists turned their Puritan predilections into a rationalization for preserving their own wealth. In his apprehension, Adams undoubtedly underestimated the compelling quality of the Puritan ethic on the American electorate generally. Even at their most impetuous, American voters have never been revolutionary. But step by step, the Federalist leaders of the North became so single-minded in their dedication to preserving their commercial advantages that they alienated not only the deprived but even their patrician allies to the South.

Only in New England was the appeal of the Federalists unimpaired by economic conservatism. To be sure, Federalist programs were favorable to New England. If maritime subsidies enriched the shipowners, they also stimulated the employment of seamen and shipyard workers. If tariff rates assisted the growth of industry, they gave jobs, at the same time, to workingmen in the Yankee towns. The Federalists pleased the Yankee farmer with the temptation of Western land, the better with which to broaden their own markets. But even among the Yankee voters who had nothing to gain from Federalist programs, there remained a remarkable loyalty to the party.

It has been asserted that whenever the democratic heresy showed signs of making extensive conversions in New England, the substantial citizens of each community—merchants, teachers, ministers, editors—mounted a campaign in behalf of Puritan orthodoxy. "I am persuaded," wrote Lyman Beecher, the celebrated Yankee minister, as he watched the Federalists disintegrate, "that the time has come when it becomes every friend of this state to wake up and exert his whole influence to save it from innovation and democracy." The unity of the New England electorate confirms the observation of one historian that "New England Federalism was not so much a body of political doctrine as a state of mind." Long after their national alliance had fallen to pieces, the Federalists could count on New England for unwavering support.

In an effort to salvage their dwindling power, the Federalists resorted to desperate measures. It never occurred to them that the surest access to office might lie in a willingness to share the rewards of office with some other interest group. Their chief tactic was an attempt to evoke a feeling of patriotic obligation by relentless identification of themselves with the War and the Constitution. In leaning heavily on the Society of Cincinnati, an organization of the officers of the Continental army, they foreshadowed Puritan practices of another era—and suffered the accusation of seeking to create a military nobility. They stirred up hostility, as the circumstances presented themselves, against the British, the Spanish, and the French. For a few years, the Federalists probably survived on the investment they had made in American glory, but in a country in which nationalism did not yet run deep their margin grew steadily thinner.

By the closing years of the eighteenth century, the Federalists no longer possessed the capacity to stop the disintegration. Instead of providing an alternative to their opponents, they tried harassment, by passing laws first to silence political criticism, then to disfranchise recent immigrants. In 1800, they lost their first Presidential election and began groping wildly for some expedient by which to recoup. They thought they had found it in 1812 by siding against the United States in the war with Britain. As a body they tried to undo the Constitution they had themselves created and a few even proposed that New England secede from the Union. In the War of 1812, the Federalists forfeited their claims to be the party of patriotism and American nationalism, and thereby lost all appeal. Under the stigma of disloyalty, the first of the Yankee parties vanished, leaving its faithful to search for some new instrument for their political designs.

Scarcely had the Federalists planted the Yankee emblem in American politics than Thomas Jefferson founded a rival party, which was to become the bearer of a totally different tradition in the governing system. To the Yankee, Jefferson stood for two ideas that were anathema—deism and democracy. The Yankee saw both as the product of the licentious French Revolution, which he regarded as a threat to social order everywhere. He considered democracy to be political heresy, an open door to the debasement of public authority. He saw deism as something even worse. Jefferson boasted of his religious radicalism and avowed his inability to accept the tenets of revealed religion. In the eyes of the Puritan, he was a man who invited both impiety and immorality. He was a scoffer, who lacked all sense of divine guidance. To the Yankee, Jefferson and his party would not only despoil the state but would undo the very bonds that held organized society intact.

As matters turned out, the Jeffersonians did not differ fundamentally from the Puritans in the exercise of power. They favored free enterprise, the advancement of education, and the practice of individual rights. They proved remarkably conservative in their treatment of private property. But the coincidence of means could not conceal the basic differences between Jefferson and the Puritans on ultimate ends.

Jefferson understood life as a quest for happiness; the Puritans took life as an ascetic experience designed to please a stern and arbitrary God.

Jefferson conceived of government as an instrument for advancing the material and intellectual well-being of the masses of men; for the Puritans, government was a device to clear away the obstacles to the individual's pursuit of his own self-interest.

Jefferson abhorred the unequal distribution of property, characterized the earth as "common stock for man to labor and live on," and affirmed society's obligations to render justice to the poor; the Puritan extolled man's drive to surpass his neighbor in property, and acknowledged neither pity nor duty to those who fell behind in the competition.

Jefferson was reconciled to the imperfection of human institutions and believed that intelligence could improve them; the Puritan was convinced that imperfect institutions were the consequence of man's sin and that morality would set them aright.

As a political philosopher, Jefferson has frequently been cited as an opponent of any strong central authority. To be sure, Jefferson feared abuses of power. But, while the Puritan saw the state as nothing better than an obstruction to individual ambitions, Jefferson objected not to the state itself but to the abuses to which it might be put. The distinction has been elusive to many, even among Jefferson's followers. By conservatives, it has been deliberately distorted to keep the state from acting as an instrument of social change. Jefferson's criterion was human happiness. Within the framework of his time, his advocacy of small government was understandable. But if he had seen that happiness would be best served by a powerful state, he would certainly have favored its creation.

Jefferson's party, the despair of the Puritans, began simply enough as an indiscriminate coalition of anti-Federalists. Its leadership and objectives were as diverse as those of the Federalists were unitary. With Jefferson as broker, the South's plantation aristocracy, unhappy in its alliance with the North's commercial plutocracy, joined with the spokesmen of the farmers on the frontier and the wage earners in the cities to seek an end to Federalist domination of the nation. Within Jefferson's diverse coalition, the interests were at best complementary. Often they were in outright conflict. Still, each of the members could look forward to reward from whatever power was acquired by the group. Jefferson's experiment demonstrated that a multitude of interests could form a viable coalition. If it was less cohesive than the Yankee party, it could at least be more successful.

Jefferson's ideas passed into the possession of the party he founded. Their very disorder, their nondoctrinaire quality, their openness to interpretation and reinterpretation, lent themselves conveniently to a coalition characterized by the commotion of diversity. As the party evolved—Republican by name to begin with, then Democratic-Republican, and finally Democratic—Jefferson's ideas by no means fixed its nature. On the contrary, they served as a reservoir from which each member of the coalition would draw what he chose to suit his own purpose. But there forever remained within the party—to distinguish it from the Yankee party—Jefferson's fundamental dedication to the worldly well-being of the common man. Repeatedly, after periods of eclipse, this dedication would emerge to give the party new vitality.

If, by the second decade of the nineteenth century, the Federalists were no longer able to withstand the assaults of Jefferson's party, it was because they had already become, in a very real sense, an anachronism. By now the Federalists had ceased to speak for the Yankee community. They were inbred, exclusive, even effete. More significant, they represented the New England coastal interests, while the new Yankee leadership belonged to the frontier. The new Yankees were lusty. Their society was nouveau riche, without either the refinement of the East or its rigid stratification. The Yankees of the West had supported the War of 1812 with enthusiasm and were prepared to capitalize on the fresh wave of self-confidence that swept the nation when it was over. Their hero was Henry Clay, proponent of the "American System," a program to build canals and roads to stimulate internal commerce and to erect tariff barriers to protect native industry. The new generation shed no tears for the Federalists, who had deliberately chosen to narrow the constituency they represented until they could not make meaningful claim even on Yankee power.

But for the twenty-four years that followed Jefferson's election to the Presidency in 1800, the Yankees made no real effort to forge a new political instrument. Jefferson welcomed to his coalition whoever chose to join, and even the surviving Federalists, having nowhere else to go, accepted his hospitality. As for the Western Yankees, content to give their energies to building a new civilization, they were willing to work within the Jeffersonian party as long as it did not interfere with their getting rich. The Jeffersonian coalition, as it turned out, was no great threat to the objectives of the Puritans. With all its egalitarianism, it had within it so many conflicting forces that neither Jefferson nor his immediate successors tried to overturn the established economic and social order. In New England and among the Yankees of the West, the party was profoundly conservative. The period was unique in American history. By the time it culminated in President Monroe's "era of good feelings," the country had begun to think of one-party politics as the natural state of the system.

But the first serious depression revealed the cracks in the party structure. As the banking interests foreclosed on the farmer, as wages dropped and unemployment grew, as the planters watched their cotton stand unsold, old class animosities reappeared. The power blocs within Jefferson's coalition began shifting for advantage. In 1824, four candidates stood for the Presidency. All carried the banner of Jefferson's Republican party, but the rival interest groups that each represented were angry and determined.

The Yankee vote was divided between East and West. John Quincy Adams, son of the second President, stood as the heir to the Federalist tradition and won every county in New England, as well as the Yankee counties of New York and Ohio. Henry Clay, candidate of the commercial Northwest, polled heavily in the Yankee towns and cities of the frontier. Carrying Virginia and much of the South was William Crawford of Georgia, favorite of the planters. But the most votes of all—though substantially fewer than a majority—went to General Andrew Jackson, idol of the laboring man, hero of the struggling farmer, symbol of the fight against privilege. With no candidate strong enough to take the Presidency in the electoral college, the contest was transferred to the House of Representatives, where Clay shifted his support to give the victory to Adams. Politically, the move was justifiable enough, but Jackson was outraged and vowed revenge. So much bitterness did the election engender that it ended the one-party system in the United States forever.

For the Yankees, the election of 1824 served as a watershed. Out of Clay's deal with Adams came the reunion of the Eastern and Western wings of the Puritan community. The resultant Yankee party adopted the nationalist objectives of Clay's "American System" and called itself the *National* Republicans. In 1828 and 1832, it ran creditably, but it obviously lacked the widespread backing to defeat Jackson's popular *Democratic* Republicans. In the final years of Jackson's Presidency, however, the National Republicans seized an important opportunity. Jackson had so alienated the Southern aristocracy that it became willing to switch its party allegiance. The Yankees welcomed the Southerners, and to accommodate the Southern aversion to national over states' rights, they obligingly changed the name of their party to "Whigs." Thus the Yankee and the plantation aristocrats reestablished the intersectional liaison that had enabled the Federalists to govern during the first years of the Republic. The alliance was no more comfortable than it had been before, but it was nationwide and had considerable potential for winning elections.

For a while, a curious movement among the Yankees stubbornly resisted fusion with the majority of the community. It was known as the Anti-Masonic movement and began in the Yankee counties of western New York as a reaction to the murder in 1826 of one William Morgan, purportedly by a Masonic conspiracy. The movement spread into New England, then south into Pennsylvania. Finally, it took on a political coloration and formed its own party. In New York, where it was strongest, politicians attempted to exploit the party to overthrow the state's Democratic administration. They were unsuccessful, however, and the Anti-Masons assumed the mission of challenging both of the existing parties.

The Anti-Masons were rigid in their Puritanism, both in its religious and its secular manifestations, but to this day the movement's appeal remains somewhat mystifying. It consisted largely of the Yankee poor, whose obvious interest lay in following Jackson. But clearly, these Puritans were ill at ease among the Jacksonians. According to the most persuasive explanation, the Anti-Masons were an expression of the Puritan resentment against political domination by the former Federalists, among whom Masonry was very popular. The Anti-Masonic party was, apparently, the impoverished Puritan's way of registering his opposition to the economic practice of the rich, without in any way abandoning his faith.

In 1832, the Anti-Masons nominated William Wirt for President. He received 255,000 votes, which was not substantially less than the total for Clay, the National Republican candidate. By diverting to himself a sizable segment of the Yankee support, Wirt contributed to the margin of Jackson's victory, but that was not his intention. Normally, the Anti-Masons cooperated closely with the National Republicans and directed most of their political energy to thwarting the aims of the Democrats. In 1832, the Anti-Masonic party also won two governorships and appeared well established in the Yankee community. But the appearance was deceptive. By the mid-1830's, the fierce emotions evoked earlier by the Masons had significantly cooled and the party quickly disintegrated, its remnants merging painlessly into the Whigs.

The Whigs were essentially a rich men's coalition. The Yankee businessman dominated the party, though he shared some of the power with the planter aristocrat. Neither, however, was very respectful of the other. Each looked upon the other's society with thorough disdain. What planter and businessman possessed in common was a conservative approach to property, whether landed or commercial. Their common objective was to forge winning combinations within the electorate, so as to install governments favorably disposed to their property interests.

The Yankee voter, whether rich or poor, was the single most reliable supporter that the Whig coalition had. But obviously, the typical Yankee stood behind the Whigs not simply to attain conventional political goals. Unless he was rich, he had little to gain from Whig programs. To the Yankee, the Whig party was a focus of comradeship. It was, in his communities, a semi-exclusive club which set its members apart from their non-Yankee neighbors. A Whig vote was a Yankee vote. Wherever there were Yankees, in New England or in the West, there were solid Whig majorities.

In the South, the Whigs could count on the votes of substantial numbers of poor men, clients of the planters and deferential to their whims.

From the working quarters of the seaboard cities came an even more important source of support. There, the workingmen of native stock were engaged in a struggle for status and jobs with the growing community of Irish immigrants. Since the days of the Federalist harassment in the 1790's, the immigrants had gravitated into Jefferson's party. In it, they felt secure against the condescension of the Yankee. The native artisans might have joined them, out of class interest, and voted Democratic. Instead, they chose to identify with the propertied rich and voted Whig. This division of the working class into natives and immigrants had a profound influence on the development of the party structure. For the Whigs, the immediate impact was the acquisition of a bloc of supporters who voted more for their self-esteem than for their pocketbooks.

Though the Whigs possessed the loyalty of important constituencies, they were still by no means assured of national majorities. As the party of the propertied interests, they had particular difficulty making an appeal for widespread popular support. Furthermore, their coalition was so volatile that any of the major issues of the day—the tariff, the National Bank, states' rights, access to Western lands, internal improvements—had the potential for tearing the party apart. It was not easy for the Whigs to devise an electoral strategy that would bring them victory.

It is to the Whigs' credit as politicians that they seized on the one strategy available to them and pursued it with relentless energy and genuine skill. The Whigs had no choice but to obscure issues, rather than to clarify them. Their strategy was one of obfuscation. The very name "Whig" was meant to imply that their opponents—because of Jackson's regal exercise of executive power—

were "Tories," however unfitted such an epithet was to the champion of the common people. Unlike the Federalists before them, the Whigs did not regard the rough-and-tumble of electoral politics as beneath their dignity. They willingly went out in search of votes. Determined to spare no effort to numb the reasoning process of the average voter, the Whigs added a new dimension to the American political process.

The Whigs' campaign of 1840, in which they elected General William Henry Harrison, was a classic in obfuscation. Harrison was a Western man, a hero of the Indian wars that had opened the first Northwestern territories to white settlers. His running mate was John Tyler, a Virginian whose appeal was to the Southern branch of the coalition. Fortunately for the Whigs, the West was suffering from a painful depression. The Democrats had renominated President Martin Van Buren, who was linked in the public mind with the very Eastern financiers the West held responsible for its troubles. In the face of his advantages, Harrison did not even bother to offer a platform. Instead, he sought to cast himself in the image of Jackson, man of the people and military hero. He leaned on slogans, claimed humble origins, and, of course, referred to his battlefield record. He traveled widely and spent heavily. At campaign rallies in the country, he provided music for dancing and whiskey for drinking. In the cities, he sponsored torchlight parades and promised the workingman "two dollars a day and roast beef." His "log cabin and hard cider" campaign was a startling success and it gave the Whigs their first Presidential victory.

But luck was ungallant to the Whigs. Harrison died shortly after his inauguration and Tyler, the Southerner, proved an uninspired successor. By vetoing Clay's bills to enact the "American system" into law, he exposed the raw edge of the economic and geographical conflicts within the coalition. In 1844, Clay himself got the nomination, but his candidacy required a complete shift in electoral strategy. Clay, famed as the spokesman of the Western businessman, was totally incapable of blurring the issues as Harrison had done. His defeat, though it was by a very small margin, persuaded the Whigs to turn back to a war hero in the next election.

General Zachary Taylor campaigned in Harrison's style in 1848 and won impressively, but, like Harrison, he died soon after he took office. His successor was Millard Fillmore of New York, who in conjunction with Clay and Daniel Webster, the stately Massachusetts Whig, diverted the threat of Southern secession by skillfully negotiating the Compromise of 1850. Despite Fillmore's achievement, the Whigs abandoned him in the conviction that they needed a soldier to win. Their candidate in 1852, General Winfield Scott, proved so inept that he squandered an election that the Whigs, for the first time, had the right to claim on the basis of accomplishment. The party might have survived Scott's landslide defeat, but it came increasingly under the disintegrating pressure of the slavery issue, which its volatile constitution was unable to withstand.

In winning two Presidential elections in four major tries, the Whigs compiled a respectable record, but neither victory could be construed as a mandate for a set of policies. Both contests were won by generals who relied on their heroic image and took pains to befuddle the electorate on issues. Both elections were won during economic depressions, against unpopular rivals. On the one occasion that the Whigs submitted their unvarnished conservatism to the electorate, they were beaten. To be sure, the Whigs surpassed the Federalists by far as electoral tacticians. They learned to offer an attractive alternative to voters tired of the party in office. But they failed to turn the Yankee party into the dominant political force in the nation.

That the Whigs kept together an intersectional coalition while slavery was working to tear it apart was in itself a remarkable feat. Rather unjustly, the Whigs are accused of having been barren of ideas. Their problem was not so much a deficiency of ideas as an incapacity to enact into law any ideas that would not disrupt the coalition. The candidacy of generals, by obfuscating issues, proved not only the best tactic for getting votes but the best compromise for papering over fundamental differences within the party.

Recognizing that their coalition was viable only so long as the slavery issue remained dormant, the Whigs labored valiantly to suppress intersectional strife. When slavery finally superseded all other questions in the public mind, the Northern and Southern wings could no longer find common ground. In the nation's determination to settle the slavery question, the Whig party fell to pieces. The planters returned to the Democrats, leaving the Yankees once again alone. With the Northern Whigs as their nucleus, the Yankees set out once more in search of a party.

But even as the Whigs thrived, there was dissension in the Yankee ranks. Out of New England in the 1830's came the abolitionist movement, more faithfully Puritan than the Whigs. A recent study has shown that its leaders were the children of old Federalists, discontent with a society that no longer observed the codes of their fathers. Its chief spokesman was William Lloyd Garrison, who published the *Liberator* in Boston to affirm the sins of the South. Garrison's indignation touched the Puritan conscience. Soon abolitionist societies had been organized throughout the North and by 1840 had grown to an estimated 150,000 members. Though abolitionism was politically weak, it intensified the instability of the Whig coalition and called attention to the distinctiveness of the Yankee community.

Not until abolitionism began attacking slavery on economic and social grounds did it become a significant political force. In the depression of 1840, a group of middle-class Yankee farmers, merchants, and manufacturers formed the Liberty party in the conviction that the Southern aristocracy was responsible for the slump. "Slavery," the party declared, "must be destroyed or the agricultural, mechanical, manufacturing, and commercial interests of the country must perish." The Liberty party argued that slavery had insensitized the planters to moral issues. The moral failure that most disturbed the party was the nonpayment of debts. It did not even consider the morality of human enslavement. The Liberty party's objection to slavery was not the condition of the slave but an attitude of economic irresponsibility which it alleged to be endemic to the system.

At the first party convention, delegates from throughout the North, but chiefly from New England, issued appeals for support directed at the pocketbooks of businessmen and laborers in the free states. In 1844, the Liberty party nominated a candidate for President who won 62,000 votes, just enough of them in New York to swing the state's electoral votes and the election itself to the South's candidate, the Democrat James Knox Polk. But prosperity, by discrediting the argument that the slave system meant depression, soon took its toll. The Liberty party lost its identity, while its objectives and its adherents passed on to a more broadly based successor.

The Free-Soil party, the next in the line of antislavery parties, began modestly enough in 1848 by uniting the remnants of the Liberty party and a body of dissident Democrats. It became a major force when a segment of the Whigs, disenchanted by the party's continued alliance with slave power, took the name of "Conscience" Whigs and joined the coalition. The Free-Soil party held its first convention in Buffalo, in the heartland of Yankee territory. Represented were seventeen Northern states and a cross-section of social classes. What inspired the delegates was, again, not the abolition of slavery but its exclusion as an institution from the Western territories. "Let the soil of our extensive domains," they said in their platform, "be kept free for the hardy pioneers of our own land and the oppressed and banished of other lands, seeking homes of comfort and enterprise in the new world." The Free-Soilers were even less troubled than the Liberty party had been about the condition of the slaves in the South. Their interest was to bar slavery from the lands they themselves wanted to settle. "Free soil, free speech, free labor, and free men" became their motto and former President Van Buren, a New York Democrat, their first Presidential candidate. The impressive vote that the party polled throughout the entire area of Yankee culture suggested strongly that a dynamic, new regional force was coming into existence.

But suddenly, another force burst into the political arena, a force that threatened to upset party alignments as profoundly as slavery and, perhaps, in even uglier fashion. The force was nativism, an emotion that had been smouldering in the body politic since the waves of Irish Catholics began arriving at the turn of the century. For two decades, the Whigs had derived political advantage from nativism, but without seeking to indulge it. As employers, they were satisfied to receive worker support, but they had no interest in stirring up worker unrest. The Whigs, anxious to enlarge the pool of labor, had no intention of supporting a program to limit immigration. Native workingmen, then, found little practical solace in the Whig party.

In the years preceding mid-century, a sharp rise in the rate of immigration intensified nativist hatreds. The annual arrival of hundreds of thousands of Irish generated bitter resentment, particularly among the native workers in the seaboard cities—New York, Boston, Baltimore, and New Orleans. The fresh feeling of desperation could not be channeled into the conventional political process. The outraged native workingman seemed to have no choice but to go outside the familiar structures to satisfy his grievances.

In 1841, the Native American party was formed in New Orleans. It spread quickly to New York, where in 1844 it elected a mayor and six congressmen. For a few years nativism receded, but it revived savagely in 1848 with the arrival of a torrent of economic refugees from the Irish potato famine and of political refugees from a series of European uprisings. In New York, center of the revival, a secret society known as the Supreme Order of the Star-Spangled Banner was founded. Because its members were instructed to profess complete ignorance about its purposes, they became known as the "Know-Nothings." During the peak of nativist hysteria at mid-century, Know-Nothing gangs roamed the streets of northern cities, administering beatings to Catholics and destroying their property. But though the violent phase soon exhausted itself, Know-Nothing sentiment endured and was to have an important impact on subsequent political events.

The Know-Nothing party began to grow spectacularly during the temporary lull in antislavery agitation that followed the Compromise of 1850. After their humiliating defeat in 1852, the Whigs attempted to recapture some of their lost prestige by blaming foreign-born voters. But instead of support returning to the Whigs, Whig supporters defected in increasing numbers to the Know-

Nothings. In the North, the Know-Nothings thus took on the appearance of a hyper-aggressive, proletarianized reincarnation of the Whig party, while in the South, where few foreigners ever settled, the Know-Nothings became an instrument for those anxious to cut off the North's manpower supply. In a sense, the old Whig coalition was functioning again, though the end objectives of the two wings were more incompatible than ever. But because the Know-Nothings were national, not sectional, many men of good will supported them in order to strengthen the Union. In the madness of the moment, the immigrant became a rather helpless political pawn, while the Know-Nothings pressed their claim to being the party of the future.

But, with equal abruptness, the climate shifted once again, to restore slavery to chief prominence in political debate. Senator Stephen A. Douglas, the Illinois Democrat, submitted to Congress a devastating new bill designed to undo the painfully contrived compromise that had for so long averted a direct confrontation between North and South. In the Kansas-Nebraska bill, Douglas proposed to open the remainder of the West to settlement under the principle of "popular sovereignty." To the North, this meant that none of the new territories would be assured immunity from slavery, not even those from which slavery had been explicitly banned by the Missouri Compromise of 1820. The embers of Free-Soil sentiment burst suddenly into flame. By the time Congress passed the Kansas-Nebraska bill in the spring of 1854, the slavery issue had become an unquenchable fire.

In Yankee communities from Massachusetts to Oregon, the Kansas-Nebraska bill all but spontaneously stirred men to action. The bill threatened to halt the Yankee movement into the vast expanses of the West that were still unsettled. It raised the possibility that the West would become one vast slavocracy. It bid fair to frustrate forever the Yankees' ambition to create a haven for their values, to bestow their culture on a great empire, to rule the United States. The unrest required no leader, no nationwide direction, no centrally planned mobilization. Throughout the North, Yankees responded to the threat by forming political groups to carry their protests. Through invisible but powerful channels, the word was passed within the Yankee community that the time had come to act.

Thus it happened that in Ripon, Wisconsin—even before the Kansas-Nebraska bill was enacted into law—a group of antislavery enthusiasts met and reached a decision to conduct a state convention to nominate a full slate of candidates for the fall election. The Ripon meeting, in February, 1854, is regarded as the founding of the Republican party.

But before the Wisconsin delegates summoned by the Ripon organizers had assembled for their convention, a group of Michigan partisans rallied in the town of Jackson. "The state of Michigan," wrote an esteemed Republican historian in the 1920's, "then was peopled by inhabitants of old American stock, far above the average in education and intelligence, and we can see this section of the American people at its best." At Jackson, these partisans adopted a resolution that is justly regarded as the Republican party's charter. "Resolved," it declared, "that in view of the necessity of battling for the first principles of Republican government, and against the schemes of an aristocracy, the most revolting and oppressive with which the earth was ever cursed, or man debased, we will cooperate and be known as Republicans until the contest be terminated." To the Yankee settlers in the Nebraska territories battling to hold the line against the influx of slaveholders and Southern sympathizers, the Jackson convention declared: "Be of good cheer, persevere in the right, remember the Republican motto, 'The North will defend you.' "

The name "Republican," like the cause itself, never seemed to be in doubt in the new party. The name immediately established an identity with Jefferson, the most revered figure in the nation's political past, who had called his own party Republican. It was Jefferson who was said to be the author of the law that banished slavery forever north of the Ohio River. He was also the sworn enemy of aristocracy, which was the target not only of the Jackson Republicans but, centuries before, of the Puritan revolution itself. In the fight against slavery, the name Republican had a noble ring, as noble as the goal to which it was attached.

Though the Republicans were in the field, the Know-Nothings remained the strongest opponents the Democrats faced in the fall election of 1854. But in these muddled days neither opposition party was highly organized, and antislavery candidates, whether Republican or Know-Nothing, usually carried only the designation "Anti-Nebraska." When the returns were in, the Anti-Nebraskans had won 117 seats in the House of Representatives, against 79 for the Democrats. It was a remarkable victory and the Know-Nothings, convinced of their momentum, looked forward to taking the Presidency in 1856.

But like the Whigs before them, the Know-Nothing coalition foundered on the rocks of the slavery question. Nativism had once again receded as a unifying force. At the national convention of the Know-Nothings in 1855, Northern and Southern wings faced each other coldly. When the Southerners provoked a showdown on a series of pro-slavery resolutions, much of the Northern wing, largely composed of old Conscience Whigs, walked out. The residue of the party nominated Millard Fillmore, the former Whig President, whose vain hope was to avert dissolution of the Union. The Northern Know-Nothings floated unattached, ready to fight on over the slavery question. As a party, the Know-Nothings were now finished, with neither a national constituency nor a relevant issue.

In the spring of 1856, the Republicans met in Philadelphia to name their Presidential candidate. Though it was new to politics, the party had experienced leaders in former Whigs and Know-Nothings, as well as a few former Democrats. Like any party anxious to win, it sought a candidate unlikely to stir undue antagonisms. Its selection was John C. Frémont, the romantic "Pathfinder of the Rockies," who offended no one and whose name attached itself as if by magic to the old Free-Soil slogan: "Free soil, free speech, free labor, and free men." To do battle against slavery, the Republicans left Philadelphia enthusiastic in their determination to take control of the national government.

Who were these pioneer Republicans who met in Philadelphia in 1856, and whom did they represent?

One might begin by establishing who they were not. The

Republican founders were not the very rich. They were not the wealthy merchants and certainly not the wealthy planters who, a decade before, had controlled the Whig party. When the Whigs collapsed, the men of great property calculated, more carefully than most, where their money was likely to get the best political return. The Republicans threatened to divide the nation, separating producers from their markets and debtors from their creditors. The Democrats, in contrast, held out the prospect of preserving the Union and, with it, the money that Northern investors had put into the South. Thus the very rich gravitated to the most conservative party, the Democrats, who promised to safeguard the status quo.

The early Republican party was, most of all, the embodiment of the Yankee middle-class. Its chief partisans were those struggling for fortune and status in business, whether in shops, on farms, or in mills. They were white, Calvinist, and overwhelmingly Anglo-Saxon. Most were descendants of the colonial settlers. Politically, the Republican party represented a loose amalgamation of the old Free-Soilers, Conscience Whigs, Know-Nothings, and a few independent Democrats. Culturally, its strength came, above all, from those regions of Yankee civilization which had been the backbone of the Federalists and the Whigs.

The first Republicans saw great promise for the radiation of Yankee society onto the prairies of the West. They were, by their own proclamation, religious missionaries of a material culture. Solid and substantial citizens, they were anxious to get rich. They imagined a busy commonwealth of Yankee towns serving abundant Yankee farmlands through networks, run by Yankees, of rails, canals, and national pikes. Southern society, with its self-indulgent aristocracy and its slave labor, was an object no less of their fear than their contempt. On one issue, more firmly than any other, they all agreed: that slave culture would not be established on lands they regarded as their own and on which they envisaged their own glowing future. The early Republicans were intensely ambitious and firmly determined that the South must not frustrate their designs.

Deep within the early Republican party there also ran a strong belief in an intrinsic Yankee superiority. The feeling was part racial, part cultural, part the conviction that descent from the first settlers bestowed title on the entire land. A major segment of the party had actually been Know-Nothing, openly hostile to foreigners. But the nativism of the Know-Nothings and the welcome they found among the Republicans simply reflected Yankee attitudes. The Yankees bristled at whoever threatened the integrity of their civilization. Slaveholders were a threat to their society. So were Irish-Catholics. Germans and Scandinavians, as Protestants and opponents of slavery, were accepted within the party, but with considerable and obvious reserve. The Republican party's coolness to outsiders was a permanent facet of its aggressive determination to extend the society of Yankee America.

The early Republican party, then, was dynamic, not conservative. The Republican founders thought in terms not of preservation but of risk—risk as inherent in capitalism itself. They believed they had little to save by acquiescing in the status quo and much to gain by challenging it. If anything, they were radicals, willing to disrupt the political order and profit unrepentantly from the disruption. So radical were the early Republicans that though they risked even war, they marched boldly in pursuit of their ends.

If, in retrospect, it seems peculiar that the early Republicans were radicals, it must be remembered that their forebears were not only Federalists and Whigs but Anti-Masons, Free-Soilers, and Know-Nothings, to say nothing of abolitionists, prohibitionists, and vegetarians. Each of these Puritan splinter groups was radical in rebelling, in the name of a higher ethic, against threats to status and property. By directing Yankee indignation toward slaveholders, foreigners, or Masons, they had diverted energy from any campaign against the rich. While Jackson inveighed against privilege, the Yankees decried immorality. Each of the splinter groups, brief though its claim on national attention may have been, foreshadowed a source of Republican strength. Each, however transitory, represented a radical response to a threat, real or imagined, to the integrity of the Yankee community. The Republican party itself was just such a response.

But lest there be confusion—in view of the current mythology—let it be reaffirmed that the Republican party, however radical, was in no sense sympathetic to the condition of the slave. From its Puritan perspective, it unquestionably saw slavery as a sin, but though it saw a need to chastise the sinner, it recognized no obligation to the sinned against. In the tradition of the Liberty and Free-Soil parties, it opposed the slavocracy chiefly as an economic and social system, incompatible with its own free society of the North. At no point in its antislavery campaign was there any sign that the Republican party was moved by any compassion for the black man.

On the contrary, the Yankee was motivated by an aversion to the black man. Whether farmer or townsman, the Yankee knew that he did not want the Negro as his neighbor or competitor. In the Republican constitution of Kansas, adopted by the Yankee in the heat of the antislavery campaign, free Negroes were forbidden even to enter the state. In Illinois, a popular referendum ratified, by a 2 to 1 margin, a ban on all Negro immigration. Throughout the entire Yankee territory from Ohio to California, Negroes were specifically excluded from voting. The Republican press in the Northwest proudly supported the politics of what it called, with much precision, "the white man's party." If the Republicans declared that they were antislavery, they meant only that they wanted to confine the slaves to the South, rather than be disconcerted by their presence in the North.

But by its crusade against slavery, the Republican party redeemed the Yankee in the search he had conducted since the beginning of the Republic. It was the ideal instrument for the Yankee—not hierarchical like the Federalists or expedient like the Whigs, not limited in conception like the Anti-Masons, the Free-Soilers, and the Know-Nothings. It was dead set against sin, and it promised to be a massive political weapon for waging the Lord's battle to spread virtue. It thus became the political incarnation of the Puritan spirit. The Republican party held out the prospect not only of preserving the Yankee's hegemony in the North but of extending it to less fortunate segments of the nation from the Great Lakes to the Gulf of Mexico.

In their first attempt at winning national power, the Republicans did remarkably well. Frémont polled 42 percent of the total vote and won all but four of the Northern states. He carried every district in the zone of Yankee culture, from New England to the frontier. But he carried scarcely anything else. The Democrats won solidly in the South, in the border areas that were largely populated with Southerners, and in the immigrant quarters of the great cities. James Buchanan, the Democratic candidate, became President. But the election returns showed beyond equivocation that the Yankees had forged a powerful instrument for contesting Southern ambitions.

The passions of the slavery question thus provided the Yankees with the impulse to re-form their ranks. It offered the kind of cause—at once material and moral—that exalted the Yankee spirit. It promised a crusade that would serve both God and Yankee power. In the heady days of the mid-1850's, the Republican party's goal was clear. Barely a soul stopped to question what might ensue if the Yankees actually won control of the country.

CHAPTER 3

Metamorphosis by War

AFTER the campaign of 1856, Abraham Lincoln officially became a Republican. No Yankee himself, Lincoln had not rushed to enlist in the antislavery crusade. A Southerner by birth, Lincoln was raised in humble circumstances in downstate Illinois, where to this day Yankee and Southern cultures meet and clash. Ambitious for social and political advancement, he had calculated carefully where his best interest might lie. He chose finally to align himself with the Whigs, the "better people" of the community, rather than the Democrats, the party of the Southern poor. Lincoln had none of the Puritan's passion for moral causes. That he resolved, finally, to become a Republican, meant not that he had decided to do battle against slavery but that he had recognized the solidity of the new party. Lincoln chose the Republican party as the most appropriate vehicle for his political aspirations.

Abraham Lincoln was far more a Jeffersonian than a Puritan, but he had no sympathy for the Democratic party of his day, which was stodgy in leadership and principle. As a Jeffersonian, he could be enthusiastic in championing the liberal capitalism that was fundamental to the emerging Republican party. Lincoln was all for freedom and individualism in enterprise. He was an ardent advocate of opening the West to the small farmers and businessmen he knew as neighbors. Lincoln shared the Republicans' contempt for slavery and the plantation system. If he also possessed a Jeffersonian dedication to human equality, benevolent government, and man's right to the pursuit of happiness, he had no occasion, in the turbulence of the day, to come into conflict with the party's Puritan temperament. Conflict would come later; for the moment, Lincoln's outlook captured the essence of middle-class Republicanism.

Lincoln's philosophy of the fluid society summed up the early Republicans' economic program:

I don't believe in a law to prevent a man from getting rich. It would do more harm than good. So while we do not propose to war upon capital, we do wish to allow the humblest man an equal chance to get rich with everybody else. When one starts poor, as most do, in the race of life, free society is such that he knows he can better his condition; he knows there is no fixed condition of labor for his whole life.

In an attack on the Kansas-Nebraska Act during his debates with Douglas in the senatorial campaign of 1858, Lincoln expounded to the farmer his views on the Western territories:

The whole nation is interested that the best use shall be made of these territories. We want them for homes of free white people. This, they cannot be, to any considerable extent, if slavery shall be planted within them. Slave states are places for poor white people to remove from, not to remove to. New free states are the places for poor people to go to, and better their condition. For this use the nation needs these territories.

The following year, Lincoln gave an almost classic expression of liberal capitalistic ideology to an audience of workingmen:

There is no permanent class of hired laborers among us. Twenty-five years ago, I was a hired laborer. The hired laborer of yesterday labors on his own account today, and will hire others to labor for him tomorrow. Advancement— improvement in condition—is the order of things in a society of equals.

On the slavery issue, Lincoln's relationship to the body of Republican doctrine was much more equivocal. In a letter to a friend, he once described himself as "one who abhors the oppression of Negroes," but as a candidate for public office in a section of diverse sentiment, he found it expedient to take a more evasive position. Normally, he straddled the issue, and at one point during his debates with Douglas in 1858, he said: "Let us discard all this quibbling about this man and the other man—this race and that race and the other race being inferior . . . and unite as one people throughout this land, until we shall once more stand up declaring that all men are created equal." But when Douglas responded with the charge that he was simply trying to disguise his abolitionist sentiments, Lincoln answered coarsely:

> I am not, nor ever have been in favor of bringing about the social and political equality of the white and black races— that I am not, nor ever have been, in favor of making voters or jurors of negroes, nor of qualifying them to hold office, nor to intermarry with white people; and I will say in addition to this that there is a physical difference between the white and black races which I believe will for ever forbid the two races living together on terms of social and political equality.

Lincoln's public statements indicate, at best, a major disparity between his private feelings and the requirements he believed that politics imposed on him. It is probable that he was at least a step ahead of the Republican party generally in his sympathy for the Negro as a human being. But on one point he was in firm accord with the Republican position. Lincoln would by no means risk war to free the slaves.

By the late 1850's, the rancor provoked by the Kansas-Nebraska Act had somewhat subsided and the Republicans—like the Whigs and Know-Nothings before them—moved toward a position aimed at neutralizing the political impact of the slavery question. By now, it had become clear that the Republicans' chief objectives were economic. After the election of 1858, in which the Republican party won the House of Representatives, the new majority made no assault on slavery but passed a program consisting of a protective tariff, an internal improvements bill, and a homestead measure. As the Presidential election of 1860 approached, some Republicans even talked of dropping the slavery issue to woo Unionist Democrats into a potent coalition. The fusion movement seemed to be making progress when, suddenly, John Brown's raid on Harper's Ferry fanned the flames of sectionalism to such a heat that it became impossible to restore tranquility. The North demanded a determined antislavery spokesman, and to the Republicans naturally fell the task.

When the Republicans met for their national convention in May, 1860, their prospects for victory in the Presidential election seemed almost certain. Though they were themselves no stronger than before, the Democrats had been sundered by the slavery question and neither of its two factions appeared powerful enough to win a majority. The Republicans had only to choose a candidate who would not estrange any substantial bloc of Northern support. The Republican leadership pondered carefully. One contender was rejected for fear his earlier pursuit of the immigrant vote would drive away the Know-Nothings; another because he had been so friendly to the Know-Nothings that he would surely alienate the Germans and the Scandinavians. One faction called for a candidate who would conciliate the South, another for a candidate whose antislavery credentials were unblemished. In effect, all the best known Republicans had disqualified themselves by their earlier positions. The party had to seek out a reasonably obscure candidate, one who had not had the opportunity to make many enemies.

Abraham Lincoln of Illinois met every qualification, though he had never had much experience in public office and had been defeated for the Senate only two years before. Lincoln was known as an antislavery Republican, but he was not an extremist. His Southern origins gave assurance to those who wanted no irremediable break with the slave states, but he had made his way in politics as a Conscience Whig. He was far from a Know-Nothing, but his humane declarations had won him the confidence of native labor. He had long cultivated the Germans and was popular among them. By discreet travels around the country, he had made himself well-known to important people, without eroding popular strength by excessive exposure or indecorous public comment. The American Anti-Slavery Society asserted disapprovingly that Lincoln was "a sort of bland, respectable middle-man, between a very modest Right and the most arrogant and exacting Wrong; a convenient hook whereon to hang appeals at once to a moderate anti-slavery feeling and to a timid conservatism." But this was what the Republican party wanted. On the second ballot, the national convention nominated Lincoln unanimously.

Perhaps the temper of the Republican convention can be best established by noting that the delegates baldly rejected a proposal to endorse from the Declaration of Independence the statement that "all men are created equal." Later they thought better of the action and reversed themselves, but only after a bitter fight on the convention floor.

The cautious turn the party had taken was evident in the platform. While denouncing Democratic initiatives in behalf of the Southern aristocracy, it remained equivocal over its own stand on slavery. Without equivocation, however, it espoused protective tariffs, free homesteads, river and harbor improvements, and legislation "which secures to the workingmen liberal wages, to agriculture remunerative prices, to mechanics and manufacturers an adequate reward for their skill, labor and enterprise, and to the nation commercial prosperity and independence." It was not the platform of men complacent about their property; it was an expression of men anxious to enhance their material well-being. The platform abundantly demonstrated that the Republican party had safely made the shift from a coalition held together by a fear of slavery to one united by a common vision of material gain.

From the beginning of the campaign, Lincoln was the heavy favorite. His opposition was fragmented into three parts. Douglas ran for the Northern Democrats, John C. Breckinridge for the Southern Democrats, and John Bell for an odd alliance of Southern Whigs and Northern Know-Nothings who called themselves the Constitutional Union party and whose sole objective was the Union's preservation. Though not one of the candidates advocated division of the nation, it was tacitly understood by all that if the victory went to Lincoln, candidate of the only avowed antislavery party, the South would secede.

In winning, Lincoln carried every state in the North except New Jersey, where the Democrats had run on a united ticket. As might have been expected, he won every county in New England. He received 180 electoral votes to a total of 123 for his opponents, though in popular votes he polled far less than a majority. By acquiring control of both House and Senate, the Democrats demonstrated that they were still the most powerful national party. Having taken less than 3 percent of the vote in the South, the Republicans showed that they were decisively sectional. Despite their victory, the Republicans obviously remained a minority party. It seemed possible that once the Democrats healed their divisions, they would once again render the Republicans politically impotent. The Republicans' only hope, in the long run, was to seize some dramatic issue that would nullify the Democrats' advantage.

Meanwhile, the Republican party stood by in dismay as the Southern states proceeded to withdraw from the Union. Nowhere in the Republican program was there provision for reacting to such a contingency. Nothing in the Republican mandate gave any instruction on an appropriate response. Lincoln himself, while waiting for his inauguration, would take no step to commit the party, nor would he offer any guidance on his own feelings. If he had a plan, he was communicating it to no one, and while he procrastinated, the South's dismantling of the Union became more and more irrevocable.

Under the stress of Southern secession, the Republican party began suddenly to dissolve into disarray. Republicans dependent on trade with the South pleaded for concessions that would restore the Union. Most of those who looked westward for the nation's future seemed almost indifferent to the South's departure. The antislavery ex-Democrats distrusted the former Whigs, while both distrusted the outspoken abolitionists. Only in their determination to avert war did almost all Republicans agree. There appeared to be no significant sentiment for coercing the South by force of arms back into the Union. Otherwise, the triumphant Republicans agreed on nothing and presented a picture of a horde in disorder and confusion.

It was the South which made the decision that saved the Republican party. Though Lincoln had declared in his inaugural that the Union was "perpetual" and the right of secession nonexistent, he gave no indication that he would order an army to enforce his words. His most positive act was to dispatch a relief expedition by sea to Fort Sumter, a Federal installation in the harbor at Charleston. His order, though in defiance of South Carolina's warning, did not have to mean war. The choice was the South's. As the relief ship approached, Confederate batteries began the bombardment of the bastion. The shells which fell on Fort Sumter ended the equivocation. The South had given a new mission to the Republican party.

The Confederate attack left the Republican party no alternative to going to war for the preservation of the Union. Within the events that led to the war, there was contained a tantalizing irony, from which the Republican party was quick to profit. It transformed the politics of the nation.

The Republicans had been the party of a section, openly espousing the interests of the Yankee North. The Democrats were the party that, with constituencies North and South, had labored for decades to keep the nation intact.

The Republicans had never intended to make either compromises or sacrifices to maintain the integrity of a Union that included the South. To Republican objectives, the South was an obstacle. It was the Republicans' electoral victory that had split the country in two. Secession had meant, in effect, that the Republicans had achieved their objective of halting the spread of slavery. The Union, to them, was a matter of small concern.

Now, with Northern guns responding to the bombardment of Sumter, the Republican party had suddenly thrust upon it the defense of the nation's sanctity. The Democratic party, for having recognized a duty to the South as well as to the North, found itself stigmatized as the party of treason. It was irony that the Yankees and their party, having breached the Federal Union, now assumed the pose of its noble saviors.

Still, the Republicans were uncertain about how they were to acquit their responsibilities to the Union. At first, they appeared to agree that nothing more could be asked of them than to restore the Union as it was before secession. But as the months of bloodshed passed, Republicans began to see more meaning to the war—and to divide bitterly over what that meaning was.

Lincoln, leader of the Republican party and of the nation, viewed the war more as a Jeffersonian than as a Puritan. He regarded it as the American people's personal struggle to preserve the democratic system, which to him was the essence of the nation. In his first call for troops, Lincoln proclaimed that his aim was "to maintain the honor, the integrity and the existence of our National Union, and the *perpetuity of popular government.*" For Lincoln, the North, in seeking to suppress rebellion, fought to reaffirm the nation's devotion to the principles of the Declaration of Independence.

It was at Gettysburg in 1863 that he expressed most eloquently his conviction about the nature of the North's mission. The nation, he said, had been "conceived in liberty and dedicated to the proposition that all men are created equal." The war was the trial of "whether that nation, or any nation so conceived and so dedicated can long endure." He pledged that from the war "this nation, under God, shall have a new birth of freedom; and that government of the people, by the people and for the people shall not perish from the earth." Thus Lincoln endowed the Civil War with a purpose and a sublimity that had little relation to the Puritan framework within which most other Republicans understood it.

For gradually, there grew within the ranks of the party the recognition that the war was not merely the vehicle for preserving the Union but the opportunity to change the political and economic structure of the entire nation. The feeling was not unnatural. Hundreds of thousands of Northern men were shedding their blood on the battlefield. The North, justifiably enough, could not be asked to make such a sacrifice to no purpose. Besides, Northerners might have asked, what is civil war except a brutal instrument for achieving social and economic change? Many Republicans vowed that when the blood ceased to flow, the nation must no longer be subject to the whims of the old slaveholding aristocracy.

Among the Republicans, a small but influential group known as the Radicals were the most outspoken proponents of a policy to break Southern power. Radical they were, in their determination to transform the old system into something more congenial to Yankee objectives. The Radicals were the spearhead of the Puritan juggernaut. They would turn the South into a Yankee province to assure the conditions necessary to achieve Yankee ends. Said Thaddeus Stevens of Pennsylvania, the chief of the Radicals in the House:

> The whole fabric of southern society *must* be changed, and never can it be done if this opportunity is lost . . . . How can republican institutions, free schools, free churches, free social intercourse exist in a mingled community of nabobs and serfs . . . ? If the south is ever to be made a safe republic, let her lands be cultivated by the toil of the owners or the free labor of intelligent citizens. This must be done, even though it drive her nobility into exile.

To Stevens, the country would do well to be rid of the "proud, bloated, defiant rebels." Either the South must profoundly revise its way, said Stevens, "or all our blood and treasure have been spent in vain."

Meanwhile, the Republican Congress, unencumbered by the presence of Southern delegates, proceeded to enact into law a legislative program designed to bring about the society the Yankees envisaged. For years, the Southerners had obstructed any legislation that threatened to increase the preponderance of the North in population, industry, territory, or wealth. Now the Southerners were gone, and in short order Congress approved the Homestead Act to grant to settlers free farms in the West, a high protective tariff to give American industry a domestic market virtually free of foreign competition, and a series of railroad charters, accompanied by huge subsidies, to speed transcontinental rail construction. The Civil War Congress, in redeeming Republican party promises, laid the groundwork for transforming a simple agrarian commonwealth into a complex industrial nation.

At the same time as the Republicans were revolutionizing the economic structure, they were called upon to approve a program of military expenditures highly favorable to the heavy investors of commerce and industry. Their capitalist outlook made it easy for them to pass laws to step up the flow of money throughout the economy. Their Puritanism made it a matter of indifference who profited from them. Northern moneyed interests, angry with the Republicans for having disrupted their accustomed profit patterns, were suddenly presented with opportunities for gain that surpassed their wildest visions. Bankers, businessmen, and manufacturers, operating in a market of endless funds and constantly renewing demand, began to reap unparalleled returns. Under the pressure of war the Republican party created the conditions from which grew a new aristocracy of profiteers. Small wonder that the heavy investors quickly forgave the Republican party its egalitarian beginnings. In short order, the moneyed interests abandoned the Democrats and acknowledged that their future lay with the Yankee party.

The changes the Republicans generated in the nation's economy beginning in 1861 caused a decisive alteration in the structure of the party itself. The shift was accomplished almost imperceptibly. It produced no severe jolt in the party's operations. Marked by neither divisive argument nor bitter struggle, the transition was so natural that in retrospect it appears to have been almost foreordained. The new conditions transformed the Republican party from a loose association of free farmers, small businessmen, and native workingmen into an organization tightly dominated at the upper echelons by the leaders of financial and industrial capitalism. Out of the changes there emerged a total reorientation of the party, modifying its direction and altering its nature forever.

It was to the Radical wing of the party that the moneyed interests naturally gravitated. The Radicals did not, at least early in the war, consciously act in behalf of the flourishing new corps of millionaire capitalists. On the contrary, beneath the fury of the Radicals lay a streak of Puritan idealism, the end of which was a society in which national wealth was widely distributed among the conscientious, hard-working, and God-fearing people. But the Radicals and the plutocrats shared an interest in rapid and profound economic transformation. Gradually there developed an alliance of the Radicals' zeal and political position with the capitalists' abundant supply of cash. The alliance became a force of commanding power, both within the Republican party and in the country.

As the war rolled painfully onward, Lincoln viewed the achievements and aims of the Radicals with increased misgivings. The system the Radicals were creating, however inadvertently, was considerably harsher than the liberal capitalism that he had envisaged as a convert to the party. Lincoln approved of the Homestead Act and the railroad measures as encouragement to free men to settle the West. But he was too much a Jeffersonian to welcome the onrush of industrialism and the tremendous concentrations of capital. He had consented to the protective tariff on the grounds that it was a temporary revenue measure. He was deeply troubled by the deteriorating conditions of life of the burgeoning body of labor. In an early message to Congress, he declared that "labor is prior to and independent of capital. . . . Labor is the superior of capital and deserves much the higher consideration." It was a theme that in its suggestion of social consciousness appealed little either to the Puritanism of the Radicals or the self-interest of the plutocrats. But Lincoln was too preoccupied with conducting the war to take much interest in the Radicals' domestic program. His abdication of leadership in nonwar matters gave the Radicals and their allies a virtual free hand in shaping the nation's new economic structure.

The bitter differences between Lincoln and the Radicals erupted early over the question of emancipation of the slaves. The disagreement was far from humanitarian. Both sides recognized that the emancipation question could have considerable bearing on the duration of the war. Both sides also understood that, even more important, the fate of the Negro would have over the long term profound political and social implications for the nation. In the rancorous dispute about the Negro's future, there was summed up much of the divergence between Lincoln and the Radicals over the goals of the Republican party and of the war.

Lincoln's impatience to end the bloodshed was directed at binding the nation's wounds. He wanted to terminate the war "with malice toward none; with charity for all . . ." After years of fighting, he remained faithful to the view that the Negro was less a human being than a divisive factor between the sections. Leniency, he believed, would attentuate the South's determination to fight. Lincoln had no desire to envenom further the hatred between North and South by emancipating the slaves.

He also had immediate practical reasons for resisting the pressure for emancipation: fear of losing the loyalty of the border states, unwillingness to challenge the anti-abolitionists in both the Democratic party and his own, reluctance to offend conservatives who regarded slaves as inviolable property. Whatever Lincoln's real feelings about slavery may have been, he did not regard emancipation as important enough to justify prolongation of the war. In 1862, he wrote in explanation:

> My paramount object in this struggle is to save the Union, and it is not either to save or to destroy slavery. If I could save the Union without freeing any slave, I would do it; and if I could do it by freeing all the slaves, I would do it; and if I could save it by freeing some and leaving others alone, I would also do that. What I do about slavery, I do because I believe it helps to save the Union.

Lincoln's reasoning sounded remarkably like that of the Whigs of a generation before. Some, in fact, have speculated that Lincoln, drawing on his Whig heritage, envisaged the Republican party after the war as a resurrection of the old Whig coalition. If such speculation is correct, it would help explain Lincoln's generous impulses toward the South, his insistence on neutralizing the Negro question, and his willingness to leave white supremacy undisturbed. It would explain why Lincoln became so interested later in proposals to resettle the emancipated slave outside the United States and remained so indifferent to programs for his rehabilitation. Lincoln's attitude seemed, if anything, to have hardened over the course of the war. He spoke of black men as of a military commodity, of no more intrinsic importance than cavalry horses. If this attitude seemed totally at odds with his humane position toward the common white man, it was testimony to the popular unconcern over the future of the Negro and to his own determination to frustrate the designs of the Radicals.

The Radicals believed that to destroy the South's plantation system they had to make the black man their instrument. As they saw it, slavery was the chief pillar of the South's feudal economy. If this economy was to be replaced by a free economy on the Yankee model, slavery had to be abolished. The Radicals planned to use the Negro to undo the system that had so long oppressed him.

For the Radicals, the Negro had not only to be free but to have a vote. Negro suffrage, as they saw it, would keep themselves in office, with the power to conduct their revolution until it attained its objective. Before the war, the South received under the Constitution representation for three-fifths of its slaves. The Radicals feared that if the Negroes were freed without being enfranchised, the South might, with full representation for former slaves, return to the Union more powerful than ever. The Radicals assumed in Negro enfranchisement the establishment in the South of a great body of voters anxious to advance Republican aims. As the Radical Senator Charles Sumner of Massachusetts said to his colleagues:

> Only through him [the Negro] can you redress the balance of our political system and assure the safety of patriot citizens. Only through him can you save the national debt from the inevitable repudiation which awaits it when recent rebels in conjunction with Northern allies [Democrats] once more bear sway. He is our best guarantee. Use him.

The goal of the Radicals was to make the Southern states, under Negro governments, safe fiefdoms for their own wing of the Republican party.

Though neither Congress nor the country as a whole sympathized at the start of the rebellion with Radical objectives, the polarization of sentiment generated by the fighting gradually drew more and more of the party into the Radical camp. Step by step, the Radicals emerged as the real spokesmen of Congress in dealing with the President. In the congressional election of 1862, the Radicals gained significant strength, while Lincoln lost an important segment of his support. Within the Republican party, the pressure for emancipation steadily grew, and with it, a demand for punitive treatment of the South when the rebellion was finally crushed.

Lincoln sought to abate the fury of Congress by half-measures. He consented to compensated emancipation in the District of Columbia, the prohibition of slavery in the territories, and repeal of the Fugitive Slave Law. He agreed to free those Negroes who belonged to Confederate officers and those who served in the Union armies. At the end of 1862, he proposed to provide funds for gradual, compensated emancipation to last through the year 1900. At the same time, he suggested resettling the freed men in Africa, to spare "both races from sudden derangement." But the Radicals would have none of Lincoln's resettlement compromises, any more than the half-measures on emancipation. All of their designs, political and social, hinged on the continued presence of the Negroes in the South.

On January 1, 1863, Lincoln issued the famous Emancipation Proclamation, which by no means freed all slaves, but only those in the states that were still in rebellion. In doing so, he remained faithful to his pledge to act only in defense of the Union. The Proclamation was a bid for public sympathy in Europe, where several major governments were proposing to extend diplomatic recognition to the South. Lincoln successfully forestalled recognition, but he left in bondage all the hundreds of thousands of Negroes in the border states and in that part of the Confederacy which had already been occupied by Union armies. The Emancipation Proclamation was a strategic ploy, not the realization of a principle. The Radicals were unappeased by it. They had by now rejected the concept of gradual and compensated emancipation and had taken their stand on a Constitutional amendment to free all slaves immediately and unconditionally.

With the approach of the Presidential election of 1864, Lincoln and the Radicals were more than ever locked in discord. Northern armies had already taken control of enough of the Confederacy to give practical meaning to the differences between them over restoration of the rebellious states to the Union. Lincoln wanted the Southern states to recover their full prerogatives quickly and with a minimum of formality. The Radicals regarded such an objective as absurd. They rejected consideration of any plan, even if it might shorten the war, that would readmit the South prior to the realization of fundamental reforms. In mid-1864, Congress approved a readmission program of which a Radical senator told Lincoln: "The important point is the one prohibiting slavery." Coldly, Lincoln replied: "That is the point on which I doubt the authority of Congress to act." In vetoing the measure, Lincoln did not succeed in obtaining a more lenient alternative. On the contrary, he provided the opening for the Radicals to adopt programs that were increasingly severe in the conditions they imposed on the defeated rebels.

Had the Radicals been able, they would have blocked Lincoln's renomination for the Presidency. The Republicans, however, had entered into an alliance with those Democrats who favored a vigorous prosecution of the war, and the coalition— which was not meant to be permanent and, temporarily, was calling itself the "Union party"—believed that Lincoln was the most popular political figure in the country. Andrew Johnson, a Tennessee Democrat, rounded out the coalition ticket as the candidate for Vice-President. Throughout the summer, while the Union armies floundered on the battlefield, the Radicals demanded loudly that Lincoln withdraw in favor of a stronger contender. On August 12, they issued the Wade-Davis Manifesto, an extravagant denunciation of Lincoln's reconstruction policies. But on September 2, Sherman captured Atlanta, and in the elation of victory the Radicals' campaign against Lincoln collapsed.

With none of the rebellious Southern states participating, Lincoln's margin in the election of 1864 was 2,200,000 votes to 1,800,000. He polled 55 percent of the total cast, some 15 percent more than the same Northern states had given him in 1860. But the Union party label had undoubtedly attracted to Lincoln a sizeable body of Democrats. It was by no means clear that they were permanent converts to the Republican cause. Taking into account the voting potential of the white South, the Republicans still represented substantially less than a majority of the country. They probably did not represent a majority even in the North.

Republican politicians were not comforted by the message which the election returns conveyed. Having turned back the rebellion, they believed they had earned the right to direct the nation's destiny. But the Northern Democrats had proven themselves remarkably strong, and in the postwar South, the Democrats would undoubtedly be able to call forth almost unanimous support. By 1864, the Republicans knew they had no grounds for complacency. On the contrary, it was obvious that they would have to search aggressively for new support if they were to retain control of the government.

Joining the politicians in their anxiety were the Northern capitalists, who had gained so much from the Republican administration that they had established a clear stake in its perpetuation. For the most part, they remained in obscurity, willing to let the politicians conduct their own affairs. As long as the Republicans were in power, they considered their interests in safe hands. Secretary of State William H. Seward, who had made the trek from the Anti-Masons to the Whigs to Republican orthodoxy, had, after all, assured them of vigilance when he called the party "a joint stock association, in which those who contribute most direct the action and management of the concern." The Northern capitalists contributed plenty. As the war drew to a close, the commercial, financial, and industrial interests prepared to pay whatever it took to maintain the Republican party's dominance.

As for the small businessmen and the farmers of the Northwest, they had no complaint against the party. The Republicans had promised them the settlement of the West, free of the competition of slaves, and had delivered on their promise. Emancipation did not seem to worry them, since they regarded the black man, on his own, as no particular threat. In the Northern frontier states most dedicated to the party, the Republicans doubled their vote between 1860 and 1864. Kansas, admitted to the Union by the Republican Congress in 1861, voted for Lincoln's reelection by a margin of 5 to 1. The Northwestern voters, beneficiaries of Republican programs, looked like a large and loyal source of party support. The Republicans were confident of holding on to them.

At the same time as the Northwest was confirming its loyalty to the Republicans, the native workingman of the cities—third member of the early Republican coalition—was showing that his reliability was in doubt. Over the course of the war, his welfare came into direct conflict with the moneyed interests that had assumed control of the party. Though he was the object of Lincoln's solicitude, the urban workingman paid more dearly than anyone else for the North's participation in the fighting. He grew poor from inflation or he went into the army. He became outraged that the government paid the passage of immigrants to the United States to enlarge the labor force and depress his wages. Significantly, Lincoln polled fewer votes in the working-class quarters of the cities in 1864 than he had four years before. The native workingman, more Know-Nothing than Republican in habit of mind, would certainly have gone elsewhere had another party offered him some reward. The election of 1864 showed that native labor voted for the Republican party without really belonging to it. If the Republicans expected to buttress their strength in the North with the labor vote, it was clear that they would be in serious trouble.

The Republican coalition was thus far wealthier, but no more secure, than it had been eight years before when it first presented a candidate in a Presidential election. It had achieved its objectives of halting the spread of slavery and opening the West to white settlement. But it had been consumed by its own doctrine and come to worship the great men of wealth who would use it as long as it brought profit to them. By 1864, the Republican party had lost little of the loyalty of the mass from which it had emerged a decade before. But it was no longer this mass that the party chose to serve.

As long as Lincoln lived, he was a barrier to those who would make the Republican party into a brazen instrument of personal enrichment. The Jeffersonian in him softened the Puritan ethic and kept it a doctrine serviceable to the common man. What Lincoln would have done for the emancipated slave is impossible to say. Even Lincoln's humanity did not seem to extend beyond the white race. Certainly, he had no grand design with which to oppose the carefully calculated program of the Radicals. Had he survived the war, Lincoln would perhaps have been impotent to change the course set by the alliance of Radicals and plutocrats. But without him, the Republican party fell easily to those who would forge a society in which the common man, black and white, had small place.

Lincoln had many mourners when he was shot down in April, 1865, but he had few apostles. In his lifetime, he had made among Republicans few converts to his humane interpretation of Puritan goals. Lincoln left within the Republican party not a tradition but a mythology, exploited ruthlessly since his martyrdom to serve partisan ends. An object of Republican homage, he never became a source of Republican guidance. Progressively isolated from his party during his life, Lincoln had no followers to carry on after his death.

"Johnson," said Senator Ben Wade of Ohio, a Radical firebrand, to the new President, "we have faith in you. By the gods, there will be no trouble now in running the government."

Andrew Johnson, a Jacksonian Democrat and son of a poor Tennessee laborer, was, to be sure, no exponent of leniency in reconstructing the South. But the Radicals encountered in him a different and far more willful man than they had anticipated. Like the Radicals, Johnson yearned to overturn the social order in the South. But his goals were fundamentally different from theirs. The Radicals intended to make the South an adjunct of the industrial economy of the North. Johnson aimed to transfer power from the Southern planter to the disinherited white farmer and wage earner. The Radicals' revolution was to be Republican, Puritan, and commercial; Johnson's was to be Democratic, Jeffersonian, and agrarian. The two were incompatible.

On the emancipation issue, Johnson sided with the Radicals, "because in the emancipation of slaves we break down an odious and dangerous aristocracy. . . ." But on the question of Negro enfranchisement, he and the Radicals broke sharply. To the Radicals, the Negro was to be an agent of Northern control. To Johnson, the Negro was just another obstacle to the white man's democracy he wanted to establish in the South. Johnson had no intention of giving power to the black man. His policies thus threatened to snatch from the Radicals, at their apparent moment of triumph, the rewards for which they had so long persevered.

Johnson's white egalitarianism further alarmed the Radicals when he directed it at Northern business. Champion of the poor farmer and laborer, Johnson had the Jacksonian's distrust of banking and finance. When he proposed that only actual settlers be granted government lands, the railroad men, the contractors, and the speculators who had acquired vast Western tracts through Republican largesse suddenly recognized the threat Johnson posed. The Radicals and their moneyed allies concluded that they had to destroy Johnson or would risk being destroyed themselves.

As events ensued, both Johnson and the South played into Radical hands by their political ineptness. Johnson, an unstable man, turned more and more to discredited Democrats and defeated Southerners in his vexation at the Radicals. The South, meanwhile, squandered away much of the sympathy it possessed in the North by its defiant attitude during the months after surrender. Step by step, the Republicans who had been inclined to conciliation turned to the Radicals for leadership. The Radicals, playing skillfully on Johnson's weaknesses, thus reasserted with increasing firmness their dominance over the Republican coalition. As the struggle between the President and Congress reached its climax in the immediate postwar period, they emerged as the very embodiment of the Republican party.

In the Congressional elections of 1866, the Radicals worked adroitly to stigmatize Andrew Johnson as a rebel sympathizer. They talked little of their interest in high tariffs, sound money, and railroad subsidies, even less of Negro suffrage. They had, apparently, only to display their patriotism and their nationalist virtues to evoke a glow of appreciation from the electorate. The pathetic Johnson failed miserably to reverse his fortunes. In both House and Senate, the Republicans won enough seats to override any Presidential veto. In victory, the Radicals could for the first time claim an unequivocal mandate for their stringent policies of Reconstruction.

In the summer of 1867, the Radicals were a legislative juggernaut. They nullified the proclamations of Lincoln and Johnson under which state governments had been established throughout the South. They disfranchised all but a handful of Southern whites. They then gave the signal for the assumption of power by the black man, assisted by the carpetbagger and the scalawag, and protected by the Union army of occupation. In each of the states of the old Confederacy, new constitutions were written to end the domination of the wealthy planters. From the North, it looked as if the Radicals had written a revolution into law.

With the establishment of Radical reconstruction in the South, the Republican party's Puritan crusade appeared to be won. The war had enthroned the Puritan conception of morality on the ruins of the slave society. It freed the Yankee to extend his dominion not only to the Pacific but to the Gulf of Mexico. When the Confederacy collapsed, the carpetbaggers, ready to exploit misfortune, were not the only ones who hastened South. Countless Puritan teachers and ministers followed in the track of the conquering armies to proselytize their beliefs among both Negroes and whites. The objective was, at last, to rescue Southern society from sin. Whatever else it was, the Civil War was the vindication of Puritan morality. It sanctioned the Yankee to drive remorselessly forward to convert all of the nation to his ideas and practices. In the Civil War, the sons of New England made the Puritan ethic into the national church.

But the strategy of the Radicals for preserving political control over the South had a serious flaw. The Radicals' objective was to make the Negro into a tool, not into a productive, self-reliant human being. The freedman, at best, could have emerged as a real citizen only by acquiring some land to till. For a time, there was talk of confiscating major rebel estates for the distribution of parcels among the Negroes, but the Republicans were too devoted to the sanctity of private property. They had delivered forty million acres to the railroads and once had promised "forty acres and a mule," but in the end they gave the Negro nothing but the ballot, which he was dutifully to mark in the Republican column and return. The South, obviously, would tolerate this practice no longer than it had to. It took the Radicals no time to recognize that the Negroes could be useful only as long as the Union army remained in occupation in the South—but as long as the Union army was in occupation, they barely needed the Negroes. Because the Republican party cared nothing about the fate of the black man, the Radicals' expectation of redressing the political balance through his vote was destined to abandonment. Destined to abandonment with it was the Negro himself.

As another Presidential election approached, the Republicans once again resumed the search for a winning formula. The Radicals had largely discredited themselves in their shabby and unsuccessful impeachment proceedings against Johnson. A postwar reaction had set in and the electorate seemed indifferent to the major issues of the day. The yearning now seemed to be not for passion but serenity. The nomination of a candidate having a strong identification with Radical ideology was sure to provoke unfavorable consequences. And, whatever the electorate might prefer, the Republican party had lost its taste for a Lincoln.

Why not, the Republicans reasoned, try the old Whig trick of a generation before? So in 1868, the Republicans nominated Ulysses S. Grant, general of the victorious Union armies. The reception Grant received set them on a path that would keep them in power, with rare interruptions, for as long as memories of the Civil War remained alive.

CHAPTER 4

The Yankee's America

"IN the name of the loyal citizens, soldiers and sailors of this great republic of the United States," said General John A. Logan from the speakers' platform at the Republican national convention of 1868, "in the name of loyalty, of liberty, of humanity, of justice; in the name of the National Union Republican party; I nominate as candidate for the chief magistracy of this nation, Ulysses S. Grant."

With lofty words such as these, the Republicans made their bid to the American people. During the war, patriotism had rushed over the land with a great consuming might. The Republicans were determined to ride with the momentum. Their intent was to present themselves as the embodiment of patriotic virtue. The practice permitted them to evade the issues that risked alienating substantial blocs of the electorate. Under the cloak of Americanism, Republicans could hide a multitude of unpopular goals. They could reap the ardor and avoid the turmoil sown in the passions of the war. In the years after victory, the habit of thinking of itself as the party of the American nation became permanently embedded in the Republican character.

In a major sense, the Republicans had a real foundation for their nationalist claims. The Civil War, after all, established the first principle of nationhood, the supremacy of the central government over the states. The war had made clear, in blood if not in law, that the states were not sovereign at all and therefore not free to go whatever way they chose. During the course of the conflict, the Federal government gradually extended its powers. It superseded the states in chartering banks and other corporations, in regulating business, in subsidizing means of transportation. It imposed the first income tax, which set the precedent for Federal supremacy in the field of taxation. It established a national banking system, primitive though it was, and, by a confiscatory tax, drove state bank notes out of existence. In short, the Civil War reduced the states to a condition of juridical inferiority, which was the very objective that the Federalists had had in Philadelphia three-quarters of a century before. Under Republican guidance, the Civil War *did* turn the United States into an integral nation.

But these solid achievements were not what the Republicans had in mind when they went in search of a candidate for 1868. They were not prepared to argue in behalf of a political record. They wanted only to transmit an image of what they were and were likely to be.

It made no difference to the Republicans what Ulysses S. Grant's political philosophy was, so long as it was innocuous. In 1868, the Republicans were not looking for a man of intellect and action, a politician who could present a meaningful and coherent program to the country. On the contrary, they wanted a non-politician, someone who could—in the manner of the successful Whig, General William Henry Harrison—obscure the meaning of programs, who disdained political action and ignored the intellect. Grant undeniably met these qualifications. Why burden the voters with responsibility for such problems as the tariff, monetary policy, and railroad financing when they asked nothing more than to have their emotional needs succored by their most victorious general? Grant ran not as a political man but as a symbol of Appomattox Courthouse and the Federal Union. From the party's point of view, the less he believed in the better.

With remarkable skill and admirable audacity, the Republicans wrapped up their economic objectives in the raiments of patriotism. Apprehensive of the Democratic promise to pay off in greenbacks the government bonds that rich Republicans had acquired during the war, the party retrospectively turned the Civil War into a crusade for sound money. The Republican platform piously intoned that "all forms of repudiation"—which included repayment in cheap money of even those bonds purchased in cheap money—were a "national crime." At the same time, the platform was silent about the tariff, one of the most disputed of Republican policies, and about railroad land grants, one of the most questionable. "For every dollar of the national debt," declared the chairman of the Republican convention, "the blood of a soldier is pledged. Every bond, in letter and spirit, must be sacred as a soldier's grave."

Most Republicans probably believed that the party embodied patriotic virtue. After four years of intense commitment to war, they probably believed also that the Democrats were the party of disloyalty. But whether they believed it or not, they exploited the distinction relentlessly. Their chief tactic was called "waving the bloody shirt." A speech by Governor Oliver Morton of Indiana in 1866 illustrates the technique in its still primitive form:

> Every unregenerate rebel . . . calls himself a Democrat. Every bounty jumper, every deserter, every sneak who ran away from the draft . . . Every man . . . who murdered Union prisoners . . . who contrived hellish schemes to introduce into Northern cities the wasting pestilence of yellow fever, calls himself a Democrat . . . . Every wolf in sheep's clothing . . . every one who shoots down Negroes in the streets, burns Negro school-houses and meeting-houses, and murders women and children by the light of their flaming dwellings, calls himself a Democrat . . . . In short, the Democratic party may be described as a common sewer and loathsome receptacle, into which is emptied every element of treason North and South, and every element of inhumanity and barbarism which has dishonored the age.

A decade later, the bloody shirt still dripped profusely. In 1876, a prominent Republican declared in words that bore a curious resemblance to Morton's:

Every State that seceded from the Union was a Democratic State. Every ordinance of secession that was drawn was drawn by a Democrat. Every man that endeavored to tear the old flag from the heaven it enriches was a Democrat. . . . Every man that shot down Union soldiers was a Democrat. . . . Every man that raised bloodhounds to pursue human beings was a Democrat . . . . Every man that tried to spread smallpox and yellow fever in the North was a Democrat . . . . Soldiers, every scar you have on your heroic bodies was given you by a Democrat. Every scar, every arm that is missing, every limb that is gone, is a souvenir of a Democrat.

As late as 1890, Republican orators were proclaiming the same message. Both content and style had refined over the twenty-five years since the Confederacy fell, but the formula remained fundamentally the same. Senator George F. Hoar of Massachusetts might have been an echo of an earlier age, but it was an age that Republicans worked furiously to prolong. Hoar declared:

The men who do the work of piety and charity in our churches, the men who administer our school systems, the men who own and till their own farms, the men who perform the skilled labor in the shops, the soldiers, the men who went to war and stayed all through, the men who paid the debt and kept the currency sound and saved the nation's honor, the men who saved the country in war and have made it worth living in peace, commonly and as a rule, by the natural order of their being, find their places in the Republican party; while the old slave owner and slave driver, the saloon keeper, the ballot box stuffer, the Ku Klux Klan, the criminal class of the great cities, the men who cannot read or write, commonly and as a rule, by the natural order of their being, find their congenial place in the Democratic party.

Quite apart from the Puritan contempt for the lower classes contained in Hoar's words, there was considerable truth in what he said. The Republican party, as he suggests, was a repository of respectability and responsible conduct. It was the party of the men who had built the libraries, the schools, and the courthouses across the great Northwest, to say nothing of the factories, the stores, and the banks. It was remembered for having brought the railroad and the telegraph and a thousand other innovations of a modern material civilization. It was the party of the men who had not only succeeded in saving the Union but in changing two thousand miles of wilderness into a rich panorama of American culture. By the time the century drew to a close, two generations of Westerners had grown up in the Republican party and genuinely thought of it as synonymous with the nation. Naturally, the Republicans made every effort to nourish this conception.

Among their efforts was to run for the Presidency, from 1868 to 1890, only former officers in the Union army, most of them retired generals. What was more natural than for the people's leaders in war to become their leaders in peace? Yankees felt comfortable with their former generals and thought of their hold over the Presidency as normal succession, almost like an American version of monarchy. To be sure, the generals were not guides for the future but reminders of the past. But sufficient reminder of the glories of the past, to the Republicans, was the real hope for the future of the party.

No voters were solicited by the Republicans as vigorously as the Union veterans, and no bloc was more faithful. The Grand Army of the Republic, which rose to some 400,000 members at its peak, was probably the most powerful soldiers' lobby of all time. Each Republican victory, to which G. A. R. support was indispensable, was followed by an increase in pensions. In 1888, General Benjamin Harrison owed his narrow margin of victory to G. A. R. protests of President Cleveland's order to return all Confederate battle flags, though his campaign was financed by the forces that opposed Cleveland's low tariff views. After the campaign, Harrison, grandson of the old Whig President and a celebrated trial lawyer, declared solemnly that "it was no time to be weighing the claims of old soldiers with apothecary's scales" and proceeded to put on the pension rolls, in the words of the G. A. R. itself, "all of the survivors of the war whose conditions of health are not practically perfect."

Of the Presidents from the Civil War to the World War, only

Cleveland, the single Democrat, resisted the Treasury raids of the G. A. R. By 1904, all Union veterans were pensioners. For the generosity of the Republicans with the public monies, the G. A. R. reciprocated by serving virtually as a party auxiliary. The G. A. R.'s identification with the Republicans—like that of the Society of Cincinnati with the Federalists, for the same reasons— was all but complete. It was useful to the Republicans in that it conveyed unmistakably to the public the notion that this party alone stood for loyal Americanism.

Throughout most of the period, the Democrats were manifestly unsuccessful in dispelling the taint of disloyalty that the Republicans attached to them. At times, in fact, they seemed to go out of their way to affirm it. During Lincoln's administration, they made a bad start in that the Peace Democrats, abandoned by their colleagues who favored vigorous prosecution of the war, became custodians of the party. The Peace Democrats' slogan was "The Constitution as it is, the Union as it was," which was not overtly different from Lincoln's position, but in reality it was simply a euphemism for calling off the war at any time. The Peace Democrats did not favor the Confederates; rather, they did not consider the Union important enough to fight and die for. Their stand made it easy for the Republicans to impugn their patriotism, even to class them as traitors, though the Peace Democrats' most grievous sin, like Lincoln's, was probably rejection of the Radical Republican design for the future.

The Peace Democrats were, on the whole, old Jacksonians who were deeply suspicious of the Republicans' dedication to capitalism and integral nationhood. They preferred a loose, states' rights conception of the Union. They had no sympathy for emancipation, economic expansion, or centralization. The Peace Democrats came largely from among the farmers of the Lower Ohio Valley, who traded more easily down the Mississippi than over the Appalachians. They also represented the immigrants of the cities, who feared the competition of black labor. In large measure, the Peace Democrats continued to look at politics, even during the Civil War, in terms of class, rather than of sectional rivalry.

"The great dividing line," said Clement L. Vallandigham of Ohio, the most notorious of the antiwar Democrats, "was always between capital and labor—between the few who had money and wanted to use the government to increase and 'protect' it, as the phrase goes, and the many who had little but wanted to keep it and only asked the government to let them alone." Vallandigham was so outspoken in his opposition to the war that he was arrested and convicted of sedition by a military court. When Ohio Democrats in 1863 nominated him for governor anyway, it seemed a sure indication that the party had been taken over unashamedly by Southern sympathizers. Whatever their real intentions, the Peace Democrats conveyed to many the impression that they were willing to sell out the Union cause.

The Democrats' campaign for the Presidency in 1864 demonstrated the difficulty of their finding an equilibrium point, leaning too far neither to peace nor to war. They nominated General George B. McClellan, who seemed disposed to continuing the fight. They vowed in their platform "unswerving fidelity to the Union under the Constitution. . . ." But, at the same time, they called for an end to the fighting. "After four years of failure to restore the Union by the experiment of war," they declared, ". . . [we] demand that immediate efforts be made for a cessation of hostilities, with a view of an ultimate convention of the States, or other peaceable means, to the end that, at the earliest practicable moment, peace may be restored on the basis of the Federal Union of the States."

It was the Democrats' bad luck—just as it was the good luck of Lincoln—that barely had the campaign begun than Sherman captured Atlanta. A few months later, peace was achieved—but in the form of the South's unconditional surrender, not the North-South compromise that the Democrats had envisaged. The Union was preserved, on the Republican party's terms. Victory had not merely stigmatized the Democrats as unpatriotic; it had also proven them wrong.

After Appomattox, the Democrats searched desperately for a direction by which they could most quickly regain the confidence of the American electorate. But they had been severely shaken by their wartime failures, and, deeply divided, they floundered about in confusion. The Republicans, by maintaining tight control over the electoral machinery in the South, the Democratic stronghold, nullified much of their potential following. The Democrats remained the nation's only intersectional party, but they seemed to have lost their capacity for offering a program that an intersectional majority could support.

As early as 1866, the prospects of a Democratic revival appeared promising. Moderates in both parties had become impatient with the Radicals. The Union party coalition was breaking up. A bipartisan convention was called to rally support for President Johnson and unload the stigma of sectionalism on the Radicals, where indeed it now belonged. But Vallandigham was at the convention, along with other Democrats of questionable loyalty to the Unionist cause. Those who emerged as congressional candidates against the Radicals were almost all former Peace Democrats. Johnson himself waged a clumsy campaign of vituperation. The result was that the Democrats played into the waiting hands of the Radicals and suffered a grievous electoral defeat.

By 1868, conditions had developed for challenging the Republicans on economic issues. Recession had imposed severe hardships on both farmers and labor. Class divisions, suppressed for two decades by sectional strife, had reappeared with fervor. There was a made-to-order Jacksonian campaign to wage in behalf of repaying government bonds in greenbacks. But out of their uncertainty, the Democrats nominated not a figure attractive to the debtor masses but an Eastern financier named Horatio Seymour, who was far more the symbol of wealth than any candidate the Republicans would have dared nominate. Seymour's Vice-Presidential nominee was former General Francis P. Blair, Jr., of the border state of Missouri. The Democrats thus went into the arena against Grant with an economic conservative and an apostate Republican. The ticket seemed almost calculated to emphasize Democratic weakness and Republican strength. But even in losing, the Democrats seemed to learn nothing about how to win elections in the postwar era.

For the three decades that followed the Civil War, the Democrats could do no better than to emulate the Republicans. They seemed to have abandoned for good the Jeffersonian doctrines that had once served them so well. They behaved in almost perverse fashion by competing for votes they could not get, rather than by contending for the votes that might, had they only been willing to shift direction, readily have been theirs. They left behind them the mass of the dispossessed, who, lacking a real alternative, may or may not have voted at all but certainly found no political satisfaction anywhere. It is understandable that Lord Bryce, the English observer of American affairs, explained in 1888 that the European "is always asking what the difference between a Republican and a Democrat is because he never gets an answer."

The disarray of the Democrats is reflected with much accuracy in the taunts of a prominent Republican delivered during the campaign of 1884. He said:

It is one of the peculiarities of modern Democracy [the Democratic Party] that the principles it avowed yesterday it repudiates today. The cause it espouses today it will abandon tomorrow. Indeed it may well be questioned whether as a party it has any fixed and abiding conditions. Its history for the last twenty-five years is a history of vacillation, insincerity, and folly.

In 1872, it demanded a speedy return to special repayments; in 1876, it denounced the resumption act and demanded its repeal.

In 1868, it demanded the payment of the interest-bearing obligations of the government in irredeemable paper; in 1872, it denounced repudiation in every form and guise.

In 1868, it demanded the abolition of all instrumentalities designed to secure Negro supremacy; in 1872, it recognized the equality of all men before the law, of whatever race or color.

From 1860 to 1865, it wielded its party power to obstruct the successful prosecution of the war for the Union; in 1882, it proclaimed itself the chief instrument in accomplishing its successful results.

In 1868, it publicly thanked Andrew Johnson for exercising the veto power to resist the aggressions of Congress; in 1880, it declared that the use of the veto power insults the people and imperils its institutions.

In 1860, it drove labor to the shambles and sold it at public auction; in 1880, it declared itself the friend of the laboring man.

In 1868, it was for a Democrat for President; in 1872, it enlisted under the banner of a Republican.

In war, it followed the leadership of a peace general; in peace, it supported a general who was for war.

One of your own number, the distinguished gentleman from Texas, Mr. Upson, has fitly characterized the course of the Democratic party as follows: "It can succeed," he says, "if the Democratic party will be true to its time-honored principles, true to itself, shake off its spell of vacillation and lethargy, cease its cowardly trimming at every doubting whisper, quit dodging at every flitting shadow, stop tweedling every political crank, and drag itself from the meshes of that dragnet policy thrown out to catch the followers of every new-fangled ism and popular whim."

And so, the Democratic party, for a quarter of a century, without chart or compass, has been cruising in every sea, intent upon and anxious to avail itself of any breeze from any quarter that might fill its sails and carry it into political power. I thank God that I belong to a party that in storm and sunshine has kept steadily on its course.

Certainly, any observer had reason to maintain that the Democrats were "without chart or compass" when, in 1868 and 1876, they picked their candidates from among the new millionaires whom even the Republicans kept out of sight; in 1872, they named no candidate of their own but supported the choice of a band of apostate Republicans; in 1880, they tried the Republican device of naming an ex-general of the Union army; in the succeeding three elections, they nominated Grover Cleveland, a stubborn and honest reformer but a dogged conservative and manservant to the capitalist class. By comparison, there was much justification to the contention that the Republican party had "kept steadily on its course."

The course was that of relentless service to the tycoons of big business. As events transpired, the Republicans had to transform their orientation drastically to perform this service. After some five years or more of energetic government—the kind that conservatives had favored since the days of the Federalists—the Republicans suddenly, after the war, made a shift to laissez-faire. The importance of the shift cannot be overestimated. Through most of a century, conservatives had called on government for positive assistance in the acquisition of gain. The Federalists had devised a constitution to make such assistance possible. The Whigs promoted the advantages of their "American system." Now big money interests asked of government only that it safeguard their markets with a tariff, their labor supply with an open door to immigration, and their property with an army. Their willingness to forego more positive programs is compelling evidence that American capitalism had come into its own, that it was now prepared to take the initiative itself and scarcely needed the government any longer. It was indeed disillusioning for the party that had inherited the tradition of a strong central government and had crushed states' rights with national power to be called on to perform a meekly passive role. But Republicans, under pressure from their patrons, proved themselves equal to the challenge. The government simply let the plutocracy take over.

Congressman James G. Blaine of Maine, a Republican with an astute mind that was frequently put to dubious purposes, signaled the party's versatility in adapting its means to its ends. Having enthusiastically endorsed generous land grants to the railroads, Blaine needed desperately to justify his opposition to railroad regulation. He would hear nothing of the government's right to impose conditions in return for its subsidies. In attacking the threat of regulation, Blaine managed to find profound Constitutional principles. His statement sounds mock-Jacksonian in its exquisite concern about the abuse of power. Blaine declared:

> If we have anything to boast of in this country, it is that we have limited the powers of the government . . . . Ah, there is not one law for a contract to which individuals are parties, and another law for contracts where the government is a party . . . . This is a government of granted powers. It derives all the powers it possesses from the people through the Constitution. It has no power to impair the obligation of a contract . . . nor to reserve such powers of altering contracts.

The Republican party was rarely so scrupulous about the limitations on government when it was writing tariff legislation or when labor struck capital for higher wages. On the whole, the party was content to sit back and leave the initiative to the big investors. It accepted its stipends and went about its own quest for gain.

In their own quest for gain, the Republicans reflected a new concept of the functions of the political party. After the war, a fresh generation of politicians grew up, envious of the private profiteer. They looked upon the political party as their own vehicle for the acquisition of wealth. Both Republicans and Democrats subscribed to the concept of the party as a form of private enterprise. The Republicans normally conducted this enterprise at the Federal and state levels, the Democrats at the municipal level. Patronage was the principal source of gain for both, although both showed considerable talent at common graft as well. With few ethical reservations, politicians turned to these gainful activities just as financiers turned to banks or manufacturing. They made the years after the Civil War the most venal in American political history.

It was during this period that Lord Bryce wrote his grim assessment of American politics. In *The American Commonwealth*, which appeared in 1888, he reported:

> Neither party has as a party any clean-cut principles, any distinctive tenets. Both have traditions. Both claim to have tendencies. Both have certainly war cries, organization, interests, enlisted in their support. But those interests are in the main the interests of getting or keeping the patronage of the government. Tenets or policies . . . have all but vanished . . . .
> All has been lost except office, or the hope of getting it.

Bryce acknowledged but underestimated the importance of the "traditions" and the "tendencies" that separated the two parties. Beneath the surface of each, there remained important currents of attitude and thought, flowing in quite different directions. Ultimately they would emerge, to create two entities with conflicting social aims. But he was certainly right in that, as a system, the parties had reached a lowest common denominator. In sheer rascality, they were indistinguishable.

Some Republicans, of course, were disgusted by the general pattern of corruption that pervaded party politics. But much of the opposition focused on the belief that the "stalwarts," heirs to the Radicals as caretakers of the party, were no longer sufficiently attentive to the interests of the party's backers. Some of the backers had begun to feel that the party rulers had become so profligate that they had achieved autonomy, which conflicted with the conception of the party as a *responsible* agent of the capitalist class. Some became alarmed because dishonesty had become so rampant that it threatened the operation of the government itself. The feeling began to grow that the Republicans, as a whole, were overdoing a good thing.

A few Republicans, at least, reminded themselves that the plutocrats did not profess loyalty to the party out of personal conviction. When Democrats served their interests better—as they did on the eve of the Civil War—the big money turned Democratic. "I was a Republican in Republican districts," said Jay Gould, the railroad financier, with mischievous candor, "and a Democrat in Democratic districts. But everywhere I was for Erie." On the national level, however, the Democrats scarcely had the assets to compete for the Goulds. The Republicans had the power and, what is more, were doctrinally more reliable. Obviously, the big capitalists would take what steps they could to prevent the Republican party from forfeiting its responsibilities.

Reformers appeared within Republican ranks as soon as the profligate character of the Grant regime became apparent. If probity in government, as Max Weber has postulated, is a means of assuring the protection of property rights against administrative disarray, then the reformers scarcely qualified as either altruists or democrats. Evidence suggests, in fact, that demands for civil service reform, with the aim of restricting the traffic in patronage, had at their source a general anxiety about the government's capacity for keeping order. In the cities, at least, reformers were almost invariably property-conscious conservatives. Within the

Republican party, an opposition faction held steadily to the position that corruption should be kept within manageable bounds.

Whatever their motives, in 1872 a band of rebels who called themselves "Liberal" Republicans—with no relation to those who have adopted the name in the current era—nominated their own candidate for the Presidency. Though they were joined by the Democrats, they were defeated overwhelmingly. In victory, Grant declared: "Throughout the war, and from my candidacy for my present office in 1868 to the close of the last Presidential campaign, I have been the subject of abuse and slander never equaled in political history, which today I feel that I can afford to disregard in view of your verdict, which I gratefully accept as my vindication." The repudiation of the Liberal Republican movement was thus taken by the party regulars as a popular mandate for dishonesty, which henceforth was practiced with greater enthusiasm than before. It was not until the end of the century that a trustworthy and plodding form of conservatism had stepped in to replace rapacious greed as the driving force of the Republican party. It saved the alliance between the party and big capitalism. Each returned to the performance of its pristine function, from which both were the natural beneficiaries.

Many voters, to be sure, took no offense at the public alliance established between the politicians and the financiers, even if they had no occasion themselves to share in the material rewards. The Yankee, after all, was taught not to covet what eluded him but to labor tirelessly for what he could acquire. Inequities of wealth had never bothered him as much as inequities of opportunity, and the Republican party, whatever its internal flaws, promised ever-expanding opportunity.

If the Yankee was disturbed that the Republican party squandered public land and gave away public money, he was nonetheless filled with pride at the result: at the conquest of the prairies, the raising of a thousand smokestacks, and the making of homes, schools, and jobs for millions of people. The country, it was clear to all, was endlessly abundant. This was an era when exploitation, not conservation, was regarded as the great public objective.

It made sense for a party that personified a strong and growing young giant of a nation to press America forward, even in disregard of some of the niceties of political conduct, to greater size, wealth, and power. Yankees were pleased with themselves for thinking in grandiose terms. They were not Democrats, hobbled to the Jeffersonian tradition of loyalty to the modest craftsman and yeoman, the little people satisfied with a meager life. Republicans stood for a thrilling new land, spreading bounty and profit from coast to coast. The Yankee regarded the price he paid as well worth the product.

In 1887, an anonymous bard, writing in the *Kansas City Journal*, composed an ode to the new civilization, which reflected the Yankee's satisfaction with himself and his creation. Rhetorically, he asked:

> But whence this wealth that makes all this possible? Did the birds of the air carry it to them? Did the winds from the prairies waft it to them? Did the waters of the Smoky Hill, with its source in what used to be called the great American desert, bear it to their feet? No. They have never been enriched by any phenomenal act of nature.
>
> Then whence these farms in Dickinson County, worth $10,000,000, and wealth in stock, factories, business blocks, homes, railroads, salt wells, gypsum beds, etc., to the amount of $15,000,000—nearly $1,000 for every man, woman and child in the county?
>
> The answer is easy and sufficient. They have industriously tilled this great garden of nature, containing 851 square miles—more than half a million acres—and its enormous product has been most wisely disposed of by a progressive people.

If the Yankee's paeans began to reflect the sin of pride, it may very well be that in his race to accumulate he had lost sight of the God he pretended to serve. After all, the civilization's new heroes were the industrialist and the financier, those who had built the land to become rich. The Yankee had no reason to doubt that their recognition had been justly won. He seemed, however, to forget Calvin's lesson that the end of wealth was not self-indulgence but service to God.

In the years after the Civil War, the Puritan ethic—as Republican orthodoxy interpreted it—became the driving force behind the unprecedented industrial and commercial expansion that took place throughout the North. It liberated incredible economic energy. It sanctioned a daring new class in its commitment to economic adventurism. The Puritan ethic, of course, did not condone lying, cheating, and stealing, on the part either of politicians or businessmen. But neither did it condemn shrewd dealing, sharp practices, and the exploitation of the full potential of the marketplace. What man, under such circumstances, was so fastidious that he could unerringly make the distinctions in conduct between right and wrong? J. P. Morgan, the financier, stoutly argued that success in business was the product of a man's good character, while the railroad magnate, William H. Vanderbilt, declared in the conviction that he spoke God's will, "The public be damned." With dazzling speed, the Yankee buccaneer, spurred on by his Puritan beliefs, had changed the face of the North. Feeding on its own triumphs, the Puritan ethic became the behavioral guide of America's lusty, defiant industrial civilization, while it served, in the form that the barons of capitalism professed it, as the political handbook of the Republican party.

But not long after the Civil War, the Puritan ethic began to show signs that however well it had facilitated adaptation to the frontier, its consequences in the industrial age were manifestly antisocial. Hundreds of thousands of little Yankees—the farmers, tradesmen, and craftsmen who made the Republican party—were becoming perplexed at what they had created. Even the most vigorous defenders of the system could not conceal that it was producing a permanently depressed proletariat. The Yankees of the 1850's had gone out to fight for free enterprise, liberal capitalism, and a decent chance to win the glory and display the blessing of material achievement. But their own success had, in large measure, destroyed them. They were no longer threatened, to be sure, by the shackles of the slavocracy, but they were, instead, fettered to finance and monopoly capitalism. The great, free markets of which they had dreamed had become controlled markets. The railroads they had yearned for were threatening to strangle them. The land on which they had sought to get wealthy had turned out, in many instances, to impoverish them. Something, it appeared, had gone wrong.

But as doubts were intensifying, a new and powerful cosmology suddenly entered to reinforce the Puritan ethic. The cosmology was "Social Darwinism," Darwin's theory of evolution transplanted to the domain of human relationships. It contended that man in civilized society is subject to the same "natural" laws as plant and animal life in a state of savagery. In such a state, only the fittest survive. The rest drop by the wayside to die, preferably without progeny. Thus, in the collective misfortune of individuals, the race as a whole climbs upward, shedding its weaker members, being left only with the strong and fit. Social Darwinism offered to the Puritan the opportunity to modernize his beliefs without fundamentally changing them.

In the cold, unsentimental terms that he appreciated, Social Darwinism told the Puritan that there was more purpose to his social indifference than he had hitherto suspected. To his religious conviction that individual failure deserves no reward, the new cosmology added the scientific claim that individual success possesses a transcendent social value. It reaffirmed, with the stark appeal to reason that the scientific age demanded, the old Puritan conception of the elect and the nonelect. "We accept and welcome," wrote Andrew Carnegie, the great steel magnate, in 1899, "as conditions to which we must accommodate ourselves, great inequality of environment, the concentration of business, industrial and commercial, in the hands of a few, and the law of competition between these, as being not only beneficial, but essential for the future progress of the race." Social Darwinism went beyond the Puritan ethic, in extolling the acquisition of power and the accumulation of wealth as steps to a higher order.

Not surprisingly, Social Darwinism made a greater impact on Puritanized and industrialized America than on any other country. The capitalists loved it when Herbert Spencer, England's celebrated popularizer of Darwin, denounced poor laws, public education, governmental supervision of housing, sanitation, and medical practice, and virtually every other restraint on the use of private property. Spencer's rival for popularity was his disciple, William Graham Sumner of Yale, who wrote that "millionaires are the product of natural selection, acting on the whole body of men to pick out those who can meet the requirements of certain work to be done . . . . They get high wages and live in luxury, but the bargain is a good one for society." The Puritan, though he might have been distressed at Sumner's sanction of luxury, was inclined to agree. At a time when Europe's industrial masses were learning of Marxist inevitabilities, their counterparts in America were being confronted by the inevitabilities claimed by Social Darwinism.

The impact of Social Darwinism on the Republican party was enormous. It thrust responsibility back on the individual at a moment when the gravest social ills had begun to elude his every power to prevail. For the Republicans, it was a fresh invitation to laissez-faire. Blandly, President Rutherford B. Hayes, in the midst of a depression, could announce that "in the condition of things . . . I suggest whether it is not the highest wisdom to let well enough alone; not now to disturb legislation—not now to tinker." Social Darwinism imparted to the Republican party's predisposition to inaction the aura of a grand social design. The new cosmology, of course, was felt within the Democratic party, too, but Darwinism and Jacksonianism were scarcely compatible. It was within the Republican party, where Puritanism had prepared its reception, that Social Darwinism exercised a lasting influence.

John R. Commons, a noted economist and social theorist, writes enlighteningly in his autobiography of the close relationship between Social Darwinism and the Republican party in the Middle West. Writing of his father in the decades after the Civil War, Commons describes what must have been a typical setting. Commons said:

> He and his cronies talked politics and science. Every one of them in that Eastern section of Indiana was a Repub-

lican, living on the battle cries of the Civil War, and every one was a follower of Herbert Spencer, who was then the shining light of evolution and individualism . . . I was brought up on Hoosierism, Republicanism, Presbyterianism and Spencerism.

George F. Babbitt, who is Sinclair Lewis's stereotype of the Midwestern Yankee, disclosed with eloquence how little the Puritan-Social Darwinian ethic had changed after more than a half-century of wear. With his usual pungency, Lewis recounts Babbitt's angry lecture to his ne'er-do-well children.

"Now you look here! The first thing you got to understand is that all this uplift and flipflop and settlement work and recreation is nothing in God's world but the entering wedge for socialism. The sooner a man learns he isn't going to be coddled, and he needn't expect a lot of free grub and, uh, all these free classes and flipflop and doodads for his kids unless he earns 'em, why, the sooner he'll get on the job and produce—produce—produce! That's what this country needs, and not all this fancy stuff that just enfeebles the will-power of the working man and gives his kids a lot of notions above their class. And you—if you'd tend to business instead of fooling and fussing—all the time! When I was a young man I made up my mind what I wanted to do, and stuck to it through thick and thin, and that's why I'm where I am today . . . ."

Social Darwinism, to this day, joins with the Puritan ethic in a war against the Jeffersonian conception of society. Sixty years after Spencer's personal vogue, a businessman of Middletown told the Lynds: "You can't make the world all planned and soft. The strongest and best survive—that's the law of nature after all— always has been and always will be." Spencer himself could scarcely have summed up the Social Darwinist doctrine with greater precision. Just as the Puritan ethic had begun to generate uncertainty, Social Darwinism came to the rescue. The new cosmology reinforced the determination of the Republican party to remain faithful to its old ways.

Social Darwinism also tended to buttress the Republican party in its periodic excursions into imperialism. Since the Civil War, Republicans had flirted with overseas expansion. It was the counterpart to their impatient drive westward. It was an understandable attitude for those hungry for markets, sources of raw materials, and exploitable domains. It was a facet of the missionary quality in their religious beliefs. Perhaps most important, it was an expression of their conviction that America was a great and powerful nation, called upon to influence the course of world events. Though not all Republicans were imperialists, nor were all imperialists Republicans, the concept of "manifest destiny" was fundamentally a Republican one, based on a commitment to a dynamic nationalism. After the Civil War, Republican governments annexed Alaska and toyed with plans to absorb Canada, Santo Domingo, and various Caribbean islands. The imperialist argument in Social Darwinism, then, did not fall on barren soil.

Beginning with Social Darwinist premises, the reasoning to an imperial conclusion is not difficult to follow. Josiah Strong, a noted Puritan reformer of his day, talked of the "final competition of races, for which the Anglo-Saxon is being schooled." He declared: "If I read not amiss, this powerful race will move down upon Mexico, down upon Central and South America, out upon the islands of the sea, over upon Africa and beyond. And can anyone doubt that the results of this competition of races will be 'the survival of the fittest'?" The words of Strong were more than an invitation. They made it virtually a duty that the United States, as a good Darwinian competitor, test its capacity in a bigger arena.

Among the Presidents in the decades after the Civil War, only Grover Cleveland, the lone Democrat, resisted the temptations of American imperialism. It was McKinley, reversing Cleveland, who consented to the annexation of the Hawaiian Islands and conducted against Spain a war which brought the Philippines, Guam, and Puerto Rico under the American flag. While Democrats, for the most part, inveighed against imperialism as a threat to democracy, the Republicans won from a reluctant world recognition for the United States as a significant power. For the most part, the imperialist policies were popular at home and enhanced the image of the Republicans as the champions of American nationalism.

Thus the Republican party went on for decades as master of the nation's political fortunes. Venality or reform, prosperity or recession, imperialism or restraint, nothing seemed to make much difference. Throughout the Northern tier of states, the Republican party remained imbedded in the civilization, like the English language and free public schools. Obviously, the Republicans in the post-Civil War years were a professional organization, no longer the spontaneous embodiment of the Yankee spirit or the keenly sensitive expression of its will. But the party leaders understood what slogans were necessary to indulge their constituency. However estranged its policies from popular needs, the Republican party never strayed so far as to alienate itself from its Yankee base.

Still, the party was not nearly as dominant as the string of its victories appeared to suggest. Relying on a minority faction as their base of support, the Republicans never quite managed to find a majority that was consistent and reliable. In 1868 and 1872, Grant won respectively by 300,000 and 750,000 votes, but in both elections virtually all of the white voters of the South were disfranchised. In 1876 and 1888, the Republican candidate actually polled fewer popular votes than the Democrat, while achieving victory in the electoral college. In 1880, the Republican received more votes than the Democrat but, as the result of a third-party candidacy, had less than a popular majority. In 1884 and 1892, the Democratic candidate was elected President. Thus, of the seven elections from 1868 to 1892, the Republicans won five, but in only one—Benjamin Harrison's narrow victory in 1888—could they claim a nationwide majority. During this same period, the Republicans had control of both Houses of Congress less than half the time, although they had a majority in at least one of the Houses in all but four of the years. Considering the disorder of the Democratic party, it is fair to conclude that the Republican party's dominion over the government was actually rather tenuous, nor could its perpetuation, in either the long term or the short, be considered a foregone conclusion.

Throughout these Republican years, the principal swing states in the Presidential elections were New York and the Ohio Valley threesome of Illinois, Indiana, and Ohio, in each of which Yankee culture was significantly challenged by outsiders. The Democrats normally based their strategy on New York by naming New Yorkers as their candidates. The Republicans turned to the Ohio Valley. It is significant that every Republican from Lincoln to Eisenhower who ever won a Presidential election—except for the two who succeeded from the Vice-Presidency and were then nominated on their own—came from the Middle West, and all but Hoover and Eisenhower himself came from Ohio, Indiana, or Illinois. Only in those instances when some local interest was severely threatened was there significant abandonment by the Yankee states of the Republican party. These instances were rare enough to keep the Republicans in command.

That the Republicans were able to maintain the loyalty of this great region was tribute to their own ability to evoke the Yankee's feeling of camaraderie. The region was deeply diverse. East resented West; farmer was hostile to capital; commerce was suspicious of industry; labor was indignant at employer. It is not as if master strategists showed some degree of solicitude for each of the various members of the Yankee coalition. On the contrary, the party persistently served the interests only of business. It ignored the masses without wealth to assist the few who were rich. In many ways, it was remarkable that the Republicans were able to hold their body of support so successfully in line.

The Yankee coalition retained its unity, in the words of one historian, through "the powerful solvent of patriotism." It was the one factor that the Republicans could exploit to the maximum without being divisive. It was sufficient to draw in enough peripheral votes to keep the party a consistent victor. Even after the "bloody shirt" had lost its appeal, the Republicans were not discouraged. They had established themselves in the image they had sought, having husbanded their emotional capital so astutely that their resources seemed unlimited.

Only a pious Republican, comfortable with party symbolism and convinced of its truth, would have dared speak the words with which William McKinley, the quintessence of turn-of-the-century Republicanism, defended the party platform at the national convention of 1892. He declared:

> We stand for a protective tariff because it represents the American home, the American fireside, the American family, the American girl and the American boy, and the highest possibility of American citizenship. We propose to raise our money to pay public expenses by taxing the products of other nations, rather than by taxing the products of our own.

If McKinley was hoodwinked by his own rhetoric, it is difficult to believe that the Republican electorate was, too. The Yankees were, after all, the best educated segment of the population. By reputation, they were shrewd and calculating. As farmers, laborers, or small businessmen, they may or may not have become wealthy —but it is unlikely that many thought of themselves as beneficiaries of a protective tariff. The Yankee accepted the symbolism of the Republican party because he was, like McKinley himself, comfortable with it. There was pride and status and even love in a Republican vote. He voted Republican not to advance his own, narrowly conceived, economic interests, but to support a set of values he considered superior, to gratify a psychological need, to enhance his own subjective feeling of well-being.

The semi-mystical quality of Republicanism emerges from the words of Brand Whitlock, who served as mayor of Toledo and American ambassador to Belgium during World War I. Whitlock wrote:

> The Republican party was not a faction, not a group, not a wing, it was an institution like those Emerson speaks of in his essay on politics, rooted like oak trees in the center around which men group themselves as best they can. It was a fundamental and self-evident thing, like life and liberty, and the pursuit of happiness, or like the flag or the federal judiciary. It was elemental like gravity, the sun, the stars, the ocean. It was merely a synonym for patriotism, another name for the nation. One became in Urbana and in Ohio, for many years, a Republican just as the Eskimo dons fur

clothes. It was inconceivable that any self-respecting man should be a Democrat.

George Norris, who in his later years was to abandon the Republican party in bitter protest at its callousness, notes in his memoirs that while he was growing to manhood, working to make money and studying to be a lawyer:

> Something else was taking place.
> Unconsciously I was being confirmed in an unflinching, devoted Republican party faith. My mother was a Republican. Most of the farmers of the region were Republicans; most of Ohio adhered to Republicanism.
> In those early days I was as intense a partisan as could be found.
> Rutherford B. Hayes, later President, lived in Fremont, very close to Clyde, my home.
> When Hayes was nominated, I, a boy, caught up in the enthusiasm that swept over his homeland and carried away by the red lights, the marching bands, stole my stepfather's old mare to ride to Fremont to hear Hayes make his acceptance speech.
> Along with all the others I thought he was a great Republican.

It was from this semi-mystical, emotional quality that the name "Grand Old Party" emerged in the decade after the Civil War. Throughout the literature of the period, the party is often called, only half-facetiously, the "church." Norris himself talks, with utmost seriousness, about his "Republican faith." To the Yankee of that day, the Republican party had a meaning that far surpassed a political organization. It was a social institution, sacred and venerable, rendered homage each Fourth of July. The Yankee had no need to make an intellectual decision to join the Republican party. It required no affirmative act. He simply gravitated to it, as he did to God and country.

How natural, everyday, humdrum, the Republican party became in the vast belt of its strength from the Atlantic to the prairies, and even beyond! Though its presence may scarcely have been noticed, its absence would have meant the crumbling of a pillar of Yankee civilization. The G.O.P., at its pinnacle, represented the values that millions of Americans took satisfaction in embracing.

As Sinclair Lewis said of Babbitt in 1922: "A sensational event was changing from the brown suit to the gray the contents of his pockets. He was earnest about these objects. They were of eternal importance, like baseball or the Republican Party."

Millions of Yankees have continued to feel precisely the same way.

CHAPTER 5

The Lost Constituencies

IN THE years after the Civil War, the Republican party, though it had become the party of business, enjoyed the support of three important constituencies which by no means shared the economic interests of the business community.

These constituencies were the Negroes, the Northern farmers, and the native wage earners.

It was on the Southern Negro that most Republicans, in the early days at least, believed the future of the party depended. It was from the farms that came the battalions of voters who made the West a Republican domain. It was the native working-men who voted with the commercial classes to establish the Republican party's dominance in the industrial East.

Since the business community was by itself outnumbered, it became vital to the Republican party to retain the support of these independent constituencies. Otherwise, the Republicans might easily suffer the same tragic fate as befell the Federalists and the Whigs.

But with an indifference rooted in the conviction that profit-seeking was the most moral of man's pursuits, the Republican party managed to magnify rather than reduce the areas of incompatibility with its supporting constituencies. The Yankees who were not in business found themselves ignored. In what appeared to be painstaking fashion, the Republican party alienated rather than attracted support.

It was the party's good fortune that over the years the Democrats were too uncertain of their own course to capitalize on Republican vulnerabilities. The absence of an abiding Democratic faith strengthened the Republican cause.

The Republicans might, perhaps, have recognized that they could not forever rule on the basis of Democratic weakness. If the Democratic party ever found a course, they would be in serious trouble. The Republicans, however, were unwilling to contemplate such an eventuality. Paralyzed by their Puritan outlook, they pressed ever forward, pausing to look neither right nor left for fresh ideas for the management of a dynamic society. As the decades rolled on, the Republicans appeared supremely confident that they would dominate the country forever.

THE NEGROES

"The way we can best take care of ourselves," a Negro leader once told Lincoln, "is to have land, and . . . till it by our own labor."

By possessing his own farm, the Negro might have made the transition from slave to responsible citizen. The land was there, much of it still untilled. The Negro, who for centuries had worked it without recompense, had a claim on it. With the promise of "forty acres and a mule," the Republicans had tantalized him, and some Radicals, like Thaddeus Stevens of Pennsylvania, undoubtedly hoped to turn the emancipated slaves into a class of free farmers. The Radicals, anxious to break up the plantations, might have written the legislation to buy up Southern land, even confiscate it from former rebels, to distribute to the Negro without cost, or even to sell to him on favorable terms. But the Puritan in the Yankee soul rebelled. *The Nation,* spokesman of the Yankee ruling class, said:

Now we totally deny the assumption that the distribution of other people's land to the Negroes is necessary to complete the work of emancipation. . . . If [the Negro] has inherited it from an honest father, as most of our farmers have, or has bought it with the proceeds of honest industry, it is pretty sure to prove a blessing. If he has got it by gambling, swindling, or plunder it will prove a curse. . . . A large fortune acquired by cheating, gambling, or robbery is almost sure . . . to kill the soul of him who makes it—to render all labor irksome to him, all gains slowly acquired seem not worth having, and patience and scrupulousness seem marks of imbecility. . . . A division of rich men's lands amongst the landless . . . would give a shock to our whole social and economic system from which it would hardly recover without the loss of liberty. . . . [A proposal] in which provision is made for the violation of a greater number of the principles of good government and for the opening of a deeper sink of corruption has never been submitted to a legislative body.

Though Stevens, who understood his Puritan ethic well, did not equate land redistribution with "gambling, swindling, or plunder," the average Yankee apparently did. The Republicans made not a square foot of land available to the freedman. Inevitably, the Negro became a tenant and a sharecropper, forever at the edge of starvation and at the mercy of a white master.

To transform the Negroes into a propertied class, the Radicals would have had to defy popular sentiment in the Yankee North, to say nothing of the South. The Yankee felt he had made good on his obligation to wipe away sin when he ended slavery. Even William Lloyd Garrison, the fiery abolitionist of the Antebellum era, maintained that emancipation had ended his crusade. From the end of the war until the ratification of the Fifteenth Amendment in 1870, Yankee majorities in Connecticut, Wisconsin, Minnesota, Kansas, and the Colorado Territory defeated referendums for Negro enfranchisement. It took, in fact, the Reconstruction governments of the South, controlled by the Radicals, to provide the margin for the Fifteenth Amendment's ratification. To transform the freedman into a responsible citizen, the Yankees might have facilitated his acquisition of homesteads in the North-west. But on the contrary, they discouraged his leaving the South to move into the Yankee domain. The Negroes, faced with a hostile society with which they were ill-prepared to deal, inevitably slipped back into serfdom and political impotence.

But if the Yankee victors were insensitive in dealing with the Negroes, Radical Reconstruction policies nonetheless made it almost inevitable that the white South would unite against the Republican party. Republican symbolism was too strong for any self-respecting white Southerner to accept. Whether there was ever a chance for the Republicans to recapture the old Whig vote in the South is most questionable. Certainly, Radical Reconstruction drove the entire white South into the Democratic fold. In the South, the Democrats became more than ever a party not of class or of status, but of race. As long as race has some-how figured as a threat to white society, white supremacy has remained the dominating force in Southern politics and the chief concern of the Democratic party.

Only for a few years did the Radicals realize their dream of ruling the South through the black vote. With the whites disfranchised, Radical Republicans—black, carpetbag, or scalawag—were elected to office and spoke for the South in Congress and in the state governments. Through a facade of Negro delegations, Radicals drew up new state constitutions. For the most part, they were competently written, with provisions for civil rights, compulsory education, and administrative reform. But fundamentally they were conservative documents, not vehicles of social upheaval. They made no serious attempt to redress the inequalities that had been fortified by centuries. The constitutions enabled the Negroes to serve the Radical cause, but without their receiving payment in return.

Gradually, the flaw in the Radical program became obvious. Given nothing but the ballot, which he was dutifully to mark in the Republican column and return, the freedman was powerless against the pressure for the restoration of white supremacy. In 1870 and 1871, the Union army scattered the Ku Klux Klan and the other bands of whites who had turned to violence to intimidate the Negro. But it soon became clear that the North had no desire to continue hostilities against Southern whites. In 1872, Congress extended an amnesty to all but a thousand former Confederates. As the white electorate was restored to full strength, the Negro electorate—subjected to constant terror—steadily diminished. By 1876, all but three of the Radical state governments had been overthrown by white supremacist Democrats. A year later, the Republican party withdrew the remaining Federal troops in return for Democratic acquiescence in the dubious election of Rutherford B. Hayes. With the departure of the Union army, on which Radical designs and Negro hopes had come to depend, the white man's authority was restored throughout the South. Because the Yankee cared nothing about the fate of the black man, the Radicals' expectation of redressing the political balance through his vote had finally to be abandoned.

The Union army's return home marked the end of a distinctive era in the history of the Republican party. In three consecutive elections, Southern votes had provided the margin for Republican victories. But now there was no one to deliver the vote. Why did the Republican leaders sacrifice a major political advantage? Certainly much of the reason lies in the growing sentiment, North and South, for a sectional rapprochment. But public opinion notwithstanding, there had to be a better explanation for the party's willingness to risk the possibility of permanent political inferiority.

Evidence suggests strongly that it was not Republican politicians at all who wanted to put an end to Reconstruction, but the moneyed interests which dominated the party. The politicians, though recognizing that military rule could not be perpetuated indefinitely, were convinced that they could still count on it for several more elections. The capitalists, however, wanted stability. They wanted the Southern market restored, along with conditions favorable to its exploitation. Radical rule of the South, though pro-business, meant turbulence and disorder. As early as 1870, New York newspapers were clamoring for troop withdrawal. *The Nation* reported that "businessmen of the highest character" were discouraged by prospects in the South. Business had no interest in social revolution, the Negro, or chastisement of the rebels. It wanted profit, which could be attained only by renouncing the Radicals' program of reconstruction.

But the moneyed interests did not drop their support of Radical Reconstruction until they had ascertained that the old plantation aristocracy no longer ruled the South. What had emerged from the debris of the Confederacy was a ruling class that was new to the South, a commercial plutocracy—quickly dubbed "Bourbons"—very much like the Northern capitalists themselves. *Harper's Weekly,* once a zealous proponent of harsh Reconstruction, suddenly found that the Democratic party in the South was "wonderfully like the best Northern Republicanism." *The New York Times* noted with some condescension that "the consistency and decency of the Democratic Party in Congress are chiefly with the Southern members thereof." What had happened in the years since the war began was that Northern commercial ethics had penetrated the South more profoundly than had Sherman's armies. The South, on a smaller scale but not unlike the North, was economically transformed. "Southern acceptance of northern values and ways of life, the adoption of Yankee business practices, and the growing economic interrelationships between the once hostile sections," which one historian of the South observed, represented what was probably the most far-reaching aspect of the Puritan victory in the Civil War. The rulers of the South, though they wore a Democratic label, endeared themselves to the Northern business community because they behaved like Republicans. It was during the post-Reconstruction era that Northern Republicans and Southern Democrats first joined hands to form the conservative coalition that exists in American politics to this day.

Still, the Republican politicians were not completely happy with the arrangement. The party was their vehicle for success, financial as well as political. No matter how contented the capitalists were, the politicians achieved no satisfaction unless their party won elections. For years after the Union army withdrew, the politicians clung to vestiges of the restraint that the North exercised over the South. The Republican professionals, who for each election dutifully carried the "bloody shirts" to the barricades, hung on tenaciously in the hope that they might yet salvage some political benefit out of the defeated Confederacy.

Rutherford B. Hayes, who reached the Presidency on the compromise that brought the Union army home, made half a try to resurrect the Whig coalition by capturing the vote of the Bourbons, the new class of Southern entrepreneurs. To a Louisiana Republican, he wrote: "We cannot hope for permanent success in New Orleans until we secure conservative support among white men, property holders, who are opposed to repudiation and willing to give the colored people their rights." Hayes distributed Federal patronage liberally among rich Southerners, hoping to detach them from their Democratic affiliation. He undertook a program of internal improvements in the South, which bestowed on the old Confederacy its first funds from the Federal treasury since 1860. At the same time, Hayes sought to retain the allegiance of the diminishing Negro bloc by giving appointments to former slaves. But his program was not productive. In the elections of 1878, the Republican party could not find enough candidates in most states even to fill a complete slate. From the entire South, only three Republican congressmen were elected and the Whig experiment was quietly dropped.

A few years later, President Chester Arthur tried the opposite approach, aimed paradoxically at capturing the anti-Bourbon vote. Having failed to win over the rich whites, the party chose to go after the poor ones. But it met no success whatever in dividing the white South. The plan, unlike that of Hayes, did not even have the logic of a conservative alliance. The Republican party was scarcely the instrument for satisfying the grievances of the Southern poor whites. In the election of 1882, Arthur's experiment collapsed even more ignominiously than had Hayes' four years before.

In 1890, with a bill to establish Federal supervision of Southern elections, the Republican party made its last significant effort to retain a body of strength in the South. Its objective was to guarantee the voting rights of Negroes. Its chief protagonist was Representative Henry Cabot Lodge of Massachusetts, an unsullied Puritan who sneered at business Republicanism. Its opponents dubbed it the "force bill," but when President Benjamin Harrison put his prestige behind it, House Republicans passed it in a straight party vote. In the Senate, however, Southern Democrats filibustered. Finally, a compromise was arranged by which Republicans agreed to abandon the Force Bill in return for Southern acceptance of a higher protective tariff. The incident conveyed the unmistakable lesson that business interests still ruled the party. The surrender on the Force Bill was the signal that the Republican party had given up all hope for Negro suffrage and would not fight if the South chose to renew its campaign for Negro disfranchisement.

Interestingly, in the years after the Civil War that the freedman exercised the right to vote, neither rich nor poor in the South could resist the temptation to appeal to him for support. Most sympathetic of all to Negro suffrage was the dying planter aristocracy. General Wade Hampton, who came ultimately to symbolize the Old South, maintained that "no harm would be done the South by Negro suffrage. The owners would cast the votes of their people almost as absolutely and securely as their own . . . . Heretofore such men had served their masters only in the fields; now they would do no less faithful service at the polls." But between all the whites of the South, there remained the tacit understanding that while the Negro might be an auxiliary to some white faction he must never be allowed to become a power on his own. As long as Negroes voted, whites were willing to compete for their votes, but they agreed unanimously that they had a prior interest in keeping the Negroes from becoming an autonomous political force.

The Force Bill crystalized white apprehensions. It came at the pinnacle of the Populist campaign to mobilize poor farmers against the entrenched interests of capitalism. In parallel movements, poor Negro and white farmers organized to win economic reforms. Self-interest seemed to require that they unite for greater power. But the Bourbons astutely stepped in to divert attention from economic grievances to the preservation of white supremacy. They proposed that the whites declare a truce in their struggle and join forces to complete the work of Negro disfranchisement. The poor whites, more concerned about the Negro's threat to their status than the Bourbon's abuse of their resources, readily consented to the deal.

During the years from 1890 to 1908, the Southern Negro was, by a variety of disingenuous legal devices, deprived of all his political power. In some cases, literacy tests were invented. In others, tax or property qualifications were set. From state to state, the practices differed, but the result in all cases was that only a handful of Negroes in the South survived on the voting rolls. In Louisiana, one of the few states where reliable records were kept, 130,344 Negroes were registered for the 1896 election. Four years later, only 5,320 Negro voters remained and in 1904, there were but 1,342. Meanwhile, the last of the Negro congressmen from the South was retired, leaving the Negro almost extinct as a factor in national politics.

For the reaffirmation of his racial supremacy, the Southern poor white paid heavily. The clever schemes of Negro disfranchisement also succeeded in taking away the vote of a substantial number of poor whites. It was a brilliant maneuver for the Bourbons. Having diverted Populist animosities into a campaign for white reconciliation, they emerged more powerful than ever. Negro disfranchisement removed a major threat to the Bourbons and strengthened conservative political forces throughout the nation. The coalition of Southern Bourbons and Northern Republicans, along with the supremacy of business interests, was resoundingly reaffirmed.

The disfranchisement campaign reduced the Southern wing of the Republican party to a nullity. Though it retained some members—both white and Negro—it no longer had a constituency. Anomalously, however, it remained a force within the party itself. It distributed the patronage that came its way from Republican administrations in Washington. Even more important, the Southern state organizations retained large delegations to the Republican national conventions, though they made no contribution to the election of Republican Presidents. The explanation for the anomaly lies in the control that the regular party machinery exercised over these delegations and the use that was made of them to block potential insurgency. It was prophetic that Theodore Roosevelt, in 1901, complained that the Republican party in the South was composed of politicians "who make not the slightest effort to get any popular vote, and who are concerned purely in getting Federal offices and sending to the national convention delegates whose venality makes them a menace to the whole party." It was these delegates who stood firm for President Taft in 1912 and deprived Roosevelt, the insurgent, of renomination. Consistently, the party's leaders turned back all efforts to reform this system of "rotten boroughs." Not only did they serve the interests that were entrenched in the party but they also kept alive a weak vestige of Republicanism in the South.

Southern whites made no effort to stamp out this vestige because it had no impact on the power balance in the region. They even consented to keep a few Negroes on the voting rolls, as long as their influence was not more than symbolic. They allowed almost no Negroes to vote in local elections, where a small margin could make a difference. They were especially rigorous in keeping Negro voters from the Democratic primaries, where the important contests were decided. But in Presidential elections, where the outcome was never in doubt, Southerners were almost generous in the number of Negroes they permitted to vote. In noting that a Republican Presidential candidate once received 1,100 votes in his state, South Carolina's Senator Cole Blease said mockingly: "I do not know where he got them. I was astonished to know they were cast and shocked to know they were counted." Thus, by means of a few leaders enfranchised by white sufferance, the Negroes in the South retained their allegiance to the Republican party. At the same time, the handful of Negroes who had migrated to the North remained equally dutiful in their Republican loyalty. But at no time did this allegiance carry with it any influence or any reward for the Negro people.

Occasionally, some groups of white Southerners, heirs to Whig thinking, founded Republican organizations of their own, to challenge the local leadership. Theirs was called the "lily-white" movement, but apart from those few counties in the South with sentimental Republican attachments, "lily-white" Republicanism never succeeded in taking root. In most cases, the lily-white movement looked more like a challenge to the "black and tan" regulars over patronage than over doctrines or affiliation. It did little to establish the party in the South, and the national leadership, content with the status quo, did nothing to encourage it.

That the Republicans had written off the Southern white man as a source of electoral strength accounts for the steadfast devotion of the Negro voter to the party. Republicans laid claim to the mythology of Lincoln, emancipation, and the brief era of Negro rule, and with this the Democrats, the party of positive Negrophobia, could not even compete. To the Negro, the difference between the two parties was therefore substantial. To be sure, indifferent as the Republicans were, one could scarcely maintain that the Negroes had cause for gratitude. But it was easier for the Negro to cast a vote—in those rare instances when he could—for a distant Republican capitalist than for a local Democratic demagogue who preached race hatred whenever he mounted the stump. The Republicans were confident of Negro loyalty, though through the years they did nothing to warrant it.

THE NORTHERN FARMERS

At the close of the Civil War, no voting bloc was more committed to the Republican party than the Northern farmer. He had gone into battle knowing, perhaps better than anyone else, what his objectives were, and in abundant measure he had obtained them. The Republican party had opened the West and made its lands available almost for the asking. It had created the railroads to market his produce. It had even established a Department of Agriculture, which seemed to guarantee a continued concern for his well-being. So much, in fact, had the farmer obtained during the war that it seemed he had nothing more to ask. For serving farm interests so well, the Republican party won new recruits throughout the entire North.

But the war, in ways which both the farmer and the party

were in no position immediately to recognize, had transformed American agriculture in profound fashion. The national economy that emerged from the war was no longer agrarian, and the farm was now an appendage of the industrial system. No longer was the farm a self-contained economic unit, reserving for the market only a small fraction of what was produced upon it. No longer could the farmer dispose of his small surpluses by bartering with the local merchants for items he could not fashion himself. The Civil War propelled the farmer into the business of feeding all those who were now crowding into the cities and the factory towns. It is perhaps ironic that the opening of the West, which might have consummated Jefferson's dream of a nation of independent agrarians, actually made possible the system of urban industrialism, of which the agrarian became the servant. But whatever the irony, the war had made the farmer into a businessman, and farming became not simply a way of life but a commercial undertaking.

But the changes generated by the Civil War also hobbled the farmer in the marketplace. As long as the war raged, the produce which came out of the West and the Southwest was comfortably absorbed, but once the fighting stopped, the market contracted and the farmers were faced with an excess of land in cultivation. The Eastern farmers, nursing small yields out of tired soil, suffered first, but—less extended than the Westerners—retrenched more easily. In the West, there was a feeling of bewilderment over the sudden shift from prosperity to poverty. It was tempered in the beginning by the conviction that the setback was temporary, but optimism soon faded. American agriculture, having been trapped into the practices of maximum production, no longer had a market to absorb its yield. To this day, it has not resolved this basic dilemma.

Aggravating the farmer's difficulties were government policies that protected with high tariffs the markets in which he bought, but left unsheltered the markets in which he sold. He thus purchased his machinery, his fertilizer, his clothes, his building materials, at artificially high prices from manufacturers who could expand or contract their production at will. As the century wore on, furthermore, American industry tended to concentrate in fewer and fewer hands, so that those who sold in the marketplace actually controlled it. The farmer, meanwhile, put into the ground all he could at planting and took out all he could at the harvest. It was his misfortune that, competing against others who behaved just as he did, he was impoverished by low prices when his crops were most abundant and by insufficient crops when the prices were high. Throughout the decades after the Civil War, farm prices steadily fell while industrial prices consistently rose. The industrial and financial capitalist got richer; the agrarian capitalist became poorer and poorer.

But as if the farmer's natural handicaps were not enough, he had to face a host of manipulators who held him at their mercy. On both the railroads and the banks, he depended heavily, and both, run by strangers in the East, exploited him mercilessly. Without the railroads, he would never have settled the West or been able to sell his produce in the city markets. Without the banks, he had no source of money for machinery or seed. Both extorted outrageous prices in return for their services. Meanwhile, deflation made money progressively dearer and the farmer went deeper into debt.

The farmer may not have understood that he was the victim of a remorseless and impersonal marketplace, but he saw clearly that there were villains at hand with whom he could deal. The banker and the railroad man were his enemies. The protective tariff was against his interest. The East was hostile territory. Presumably the farmer was not unarmed against these hosts. He had, he assumed, only to look to his party for recourse.

The Republican party to which the farmer gave his allegiance, however, was not his party, reluctant as he was to accept that truth. Though it was the party of business, farming was not among the businesses about which it troubled itself. The banker and the railroad man, the farmer's foes, were the real powers of the Republican party. And the protective tariff was an article of Republican faith. Furthermore, it was in the East, lair of the enemy, that the party's decisions were made. In the higher councils of the Republican party, the farmer was an all but forgotten man.

It was easy enough for the Republican party, however unconscious the process, to justify its indifference to the Yankee farmer. The Puritan ethic was, after all, a middle-class, commercial doctrine, devised to challenge a feudal society that had forcibly tied its members to the soil. It was an assertion of the right to abandon the land, be a *bourgeois,* and make profit. In America, the yeoman farmer was a Jeffersonian, not a Calvinist, ideal. The Puritan hero was the city man, who kept his eyes on rows not of corn but of figures. Yankee business folk tended to think of Yankee farmers as brethren who had gone astray. It was natural for the Republican party, conscious of serving God's best people, to behave toward the farmer with the same insouciance it showed toward other unsuccessful citizens.

If the Western agrarian, then, was to achieve his ends by political means, he would have to fight for them. His problem was that he found it impossible to influence the Republican party and distasteful to become a Democrat. Within the Democratic party there remained a strong agrarian tradition, ready to be exploited to the farmer's advantage. The Democrats were vulnerable. But to the Yankee farmer, the Democrats still had about them the smell of treason, the quality of outsiders, the absence of respectability. Unwilling to fight within the Democratic party, unable to win within the Republican, the farmer had to turn elsewhere for his political weapons.

Out of the Western plains since the Civil War have come three major and countless minor challenges to the two principal parties in the political system. All have been radical, just as were the Republicans themselves in the mid-1850's. Radically, each has striven for a restoration—rather than a revolution—of the conditions of equal competition that were presumed to have existed in some pristine earlier era. All have been full of the crusading zeal of the Puritan reform movements, and, beneath the surface of each, there has been a strong hint of Know-Nothing intolerance. The agrarian third-party movements have fundamentally been Puritan rebellions against the rigidity of the established order. They have been expressions of Puritan wrath, largely directed against the Puritan ruling elite. Ironically, their impact has been greatest on the Democratic party, which stood much readier to absorb their lessons. Significantly, after each of these movements ran its course, Yankee farmers tended to return to the Republican party, though it remained virtually untouched. by them. Third-party protests were the Yankee farmer's way of seeking relief from his burdens without being disloyal to his heritage.

The Granger movement, in fact, began by insisting that it was not a party at all. It was founded in 1868 by Oliver H. Kelley, a Bostonian of an old Yankee family, and by 1875 it had 800,000 members organized in some 20,000 local Granges, most of them in the Midwest and the South. Its purposes, resoundingly Puritan, were: "To develop a better and higher manhood and womanhood among ourselves. To enhance the comforts and attractions of our homes, and strengthen our attachments to our pursuits. . . . To buy less and produce more, in order to make our farms self-sustaining. . . . To discountenance the credit system, the mortgage system, the fashion system and every other system tending to prodigality and bankruptcy." Throughout the Middle West, the Grangers succeeded in electing candidates to legislatures and judgeships, and they won enactment of a series of laws to curb the more outrageous abuses of the railroads and the banks. To the farmers' dismay, these "Granger laws" were ignored by the moneyed interests and ultimately nullified by the courts. But the lesson—that uniting for political action could bring results— was unmistakable. During the brief surge of prosperity in the late 1870's, the Granger movement disintegrated, but by the time the next depression arrived a few years later, the farmer had become a more astute political operator.

The Grangers gave way to the establishment of Farmers' Alliances, forthwith designated the Populist movement. By the late 1880's two Alliances—the Northwestern and the Southern—had emerged as dominant. The Northwestern Alliance took most of its strength from the Yankee states of Kansas, Nebraska, Iowa, Minnesota, and the Dakotas, where it challenged the regular Republican organization. The Southern Alliance, even larger, boasted over a million and a half members in the old Confederacy, where it aimed to upset the Bourbon hegemony entrenched within the

Democratic party. Potentially, the two alliances could have dominated the entire South and West, but they possessed fatal weaknesses. The Yankees could not bring themselves to help the
Southerners take over the Democratic party, while the Southerners
were indifferent to the Yankees' designs on the Republican party.
As a result, the two groups, whatever their community of interests, oriented themselves along different axes. The Southern Alliance, furthermore, fluctuated between class and race objectives.
After a brief flirtation with the counterpart Colored Farmers'
National Alliance, it turned to the defense of white supremacy,
which was precisely what the Bourbons wanted. But for a few
years, at least, the Populist movement put a genuine fright into
the country's economic and political leadership.

The Populist party, after an impressive series of victories in
state elections, organized nationally in 1890. From such inspired,
if eccentric, people as "Sockless Jerry" Simpson, Ignatius Donnelly, and Mary Ellen Lease in the West and "Pitchfork Ben"
Tillman and Tom Watson in the South, it received direction that
was earthy, dynamic, and evangelistic. In a camp-meeting atmosphere in Omaha on July 4, 1892, the Populists nominated James
B. Weaver, a veteran reformer, for President. In their platform,
they abandoned laissez-faire and showed that Puritans, albeit the
left wing of the community, could horrify the business interests
with demands for government intervention. The election, however,
was a severe disappointment. In the North, the overwhelming
majority of Yankee farmers rejected the Populists and deposited
their conventional Republican vote, just as in the South the
farmers remained loyal to the Democrats. Most of the strength
the Populists showed came from rural Democratic voters. In 1892,
Grover Cleveland became President but the real winner was
big business.

By the election of 1894, the country was suffering from a severe
depression, to which Cleveland had responded by smugly perse-
vering with laissez-faire and the gold standard. The Populists,
meanwhile, had reached the conclusion that prosperity could be
restored only by the unlimited coinage of silver, a position to
which they swung almost all of the Western wing of the Demo-

cratic party. When the Republicans, reaping the bitterness felt toward Cleveland, made dramatic gains in Congress, many reasoned that unless the Democrats took a radical stand on silver, the Populists would take over as the nation's second party.

By the time the Democrats met to nominate a Presidential candidate in 1896, the rebels of the West and the South had emerged as dominant over the Eastern, hard-money wing of the party. Free silver was their weapon and William Jennings Bryan, who refused to "crucify mankind upon a cross of gold," their hero. A few weeks later the Populists met and consented to fuse their campaign—but not their party organization—with that of the Democrats by nominating Bryan, too. With Bryan the Democratic-Populist choice and William McKinley running for the Republicans, political forces in the country repolarized. Cleveland Democrats gravitated toward McKinley; the silver Republicans of the Western mining states became partisans for Bryan. For the first time since 1860, the two parties clearly stood for different policies and conflicting philosophies of government. With Populism as the catalyst, a major political party had vowed to wrest control of the nation away from the moguls of big business.

Throughout the frenzied campaigning of August, it looked as if Bryan might actually win the election. But the odds against him were great. Yankee farmers remained reluctant to trust a Democrat. Eastern labor was suspicious of a Western farm candidate. Bryan was burdened by dissatisfaction with Democratic rule, though he was a far greater contrast to Cleveland than was McKinley. Perhaps most important of all, the Republicans—drawing heavily on their rich patrons—had an unprecedented amount of money and they spent prodigiously. But the killing blow came in the fall, when the farmer harvested a bumper crop which, because of peculiarities in the world market, brought excellent prices. It took the punch out of the agrarian protest. When the returns came in, McKinley had seven million votes to Bryan's six and a half, and had won in the electoral college by 271 to 176.

Bryan was defeated because he failed to make any dent in the Yankee strongholds in the East and in the Ohio Valley. For the first time since the Civil War, a Democrat failed to carry a single county in New England. Furthermore, he lost all of the ten largest cities in the nation, proof that he was unable to dispel the suspicion of the workingman. As expected, Bryan polled heavily in the Democratic South and in the silver states of the West. He did well in the restless farm region west of the Mississippi, though he lost Iowa. What his defeat indicated was that the Yankee voter, depression or no, was still overwhelmingly Republican and that his allies were sufficiently numerous to provide electoral victories.

But if voting patterns remained fundamentally unchanged, the Democratic party did not. Bryan, whatever his many shortcomings, had shattered the control of the Eastern moneyed interests over the party. With some justice, Bryan has been called an agrarian reactionary, a harbinger of racial and sectional prejudice, a man of limited understanding and intelligence. But he broke the deadly grip of orthodox conservatism in which the party had been locked since the years before the Civil War. Bryan had not put the conservatives to rout; the battle for control would ravage the party over the years. But even Henry George, the radical single-taxer, had to admit during the campaign that "the Democratic Party . . . is not the Old Democracy that has existed so long. It is really a new party. . . . Win or lose, the old party lines have been broken." Bryan, champion of the little man, had turned his back on the past. Following the lead of the Populists, he rejected laissez-faire and declared that "if you *legislate* to make the masses prosperous, their prosperity will find its way up through every class which rests upon them." Bryan brought the party's Jeffersonian tradition more closely into line with the demands of the new era and demonstrated that the two political parties need not be indistinguishably conservative.

As for the Populists, the election of 1896 proved to be the pinnacle of their influence. Their support dwindled with the return of prosperity. Confused by their subversion of the Democrats, they were uncertain where to turn. In 1898, they were reluctant to support Democratic candidates, and in 1900, they nominated a Presidential candidate of their own. But they fared dismally and their number in Congress steadily dwindled. Within a few years, the Populist movement had expired, some of its members going into the Democratic party, most reverting to the Republicans. Having absorbed Populism, the Democrats lost the Populists, but the American party system would never again be the same.

The last agrarian effort to form a third party came during the great agricultural depression of the 1920's, when farmers suffered from the same kind of economic contraction that had followed the Civil War. After both parties nominated conservative candidates in 1924, Senator Robert La Follette of Wisconsin, an insurgent Republican, pulled together an odd national coalition based chiefly on the discontented farmer of the West. He called it the Progressive party but it had virtually no party organization. Its platform differed only slightly from that of the Populists in 1890. Despite his handicaps, La Follette polled almost five million votes and in percentage surpassed the Populists in their most successful year. Though La Follette's flimsy coalition disintegrated almost immediately after the election, his performance was the most persuasive evidence since the Civil War that the Yankee farm vote was no longer a Republican monolith.

The figures of the 1924 election did no more than to confirm a trend, underway since Bryan's day, that the Yankee farmer of the West was loosening his ties to the Republican party. Obviously, he was not taking this decision frivolously. He was a Republican by instinct. But the Republican party, while abdicating its responsibility toward him, had become complacent about his loyalty. Under stress, the Yankee farmer's calculated self-interest could handily overcome his Republican instinct. The Republicans might have known better than to count forever on rewards for services performed during the Civil War. With the depression worsening, surely there was no excuse for their overlooking the unmistakable signs of the Western farmer's growing impatience.

NATIVE WAGE-EARNERS

In the days before the Republican party emerged as the spokesman of American business and the most powerful political force in the land, Abraham Lincoln had told a group of striking shoe-workers in New Haven, Connecticut:

> I am glad to see that a system of labor exists in New England under which laborers can *strike* when they want to, where they are not obliged to work under all circumstances, and are not tied down and obliged to work whether you pay them or not. I like a system that lets a man quit when he wants to, and wish it might prevail everywhere . . .

But within the Republican party this free and easy view of labor's prerogatives did not long survive. Lincoln spoke against a background of liberal capitalism, in which enterprise was small and the entrepreneur—ideally, at least—was just another working-man who had made good. Lincoln was expressing only the conventional idea of American society when he said: "The prudent penniless beginner in the world labors for wages a while, saves a surplus with which to buy land and tools for himself, then labors on his own account another while, and at length hires another new beginner to help him."

But Lincoln's was an era when the corporation, gigantic and impersonal, did not yet exist. Against the background of the nation's economic organization a few decades later, Lincoln's homilies seem curiously naïve, and Republicans, to say nothing of Democrats, were not to be heard lightly commending the worker to strike to better his condition. Gone from within Republicanism was the sentiment of comradeliness in which the worker was looked on as an incipient capitalist. Labor and capital were locked in a deadly struggle in which capital had the upper hand and depended on the Federal government to maintain it. More characteristic of reigning Puritan feeling as the century drew to a close was an editorial in the *New York World* which declared: "The American laborer must make up his mind henceforth not to be so much better off than the European laborer. Men must be contented to work for less wages. In this way, the workingman will be near to that station in life to which it has pleased God to call him."

In its preoccupation with the success of business, the Republican party shed the early concern derived from its Puritanism for the equal opportunity of all men. Instead, it became dominated by the other side of the Puritan coin, the feeling that the refulgent elite of commerce and industry had been selected by God for its virtue and that the coarse majority had no claim either upon the country's pity or its wealth. As financial power became concentrated in fewer and fewer hands, the dream of the fluid society which allowed, in Lincoln's words, "the humblest man an equal chance to get rich with everybody else" simply vanished. In its place the successful capitalist, still invoking the Puritan Diety, sought to substitute a kind of cruel paternalism, summed up most graphically in the pious vow of the railroad magnate, George F. Baer, who said: "The rights and interests of the laboring man will be protected and cared for, not by the labor agitators, but by the Christian men to whom God in His infinite wisdom, has given control of the property interests of this country."

It was Baer and men like him who controlled the Republican party. But it was George F. Babbitt and men like *him* who gave it a mandate each election day. Sinclair Lewis had to exaggerate precious little to make satire of Babbitt's labor philosophy. According to Babbitt:

> A good labor union is of value because it keeps out radical unions, which would destroy property. No one ought to be forced to join a union, however. All labor agitators who try to force men to join a union should be hanged. In fact, just between ourselves, there oughtn't be any unions allowed at all; and as it's the best way of fighting the unions, every business man ought to belong to an employers' association and to the Chamber of Commerce. In union there is strength. So any selfish hog who doesn't join the Chamber of Commerce ought to be forced to.

It was this team of Baer and Babbitt that set the tone throughout most of the Republican party's history for its relations with American labor.

Had the Democrats made a more positive effort, they might

have been more successful in winning over the bulk of the labor vote. In Jackson's day, they were known as the workingman's party. After President Benjamin Harrison broke up the Homestead strike with the National Guard in 1892, labor responded by voting overwhelmingly for the Democratic candidate, Grover Cleveland. But Cleveland, the essence of stodgy middle-class conservatism, proved as unsympathetic as the Republicans. His action in suppressing the Pullman strike demonstrated to labor that it had nowhere to turn within the two-party system. Neither Democrats nor Republicans seemed to care about labor's vote, and neither, in any serious fashion, cared to offer to labor any redress of its grievances.

In purely political terms, labor was itself largely to blame for this state of affairs, for it represented a classic case of a divided constituency. Native labor, since the early days of the century, had spent more of its energies in battle against immigrant labor than against employers. Immigrant labor, in turn, dedicated a large part of its strength to defeating the challenge of Negro labor. Status within the working class seemed to evoke greater concern than any general improvement of conditions, at least at the upper levels. A sense of class solidarity, which was growing among workers in Europe, never became rooted in the United States. With animosities so strong in labor's house, the political power of the American workingman was dissipated and rendered almost useless.

Considerations of status were fundamental to the American trade-union movement from the time that its seeds were sown in the 1830's. British workmen brought to the United States a long experience in craft unionism, for which they supplied much of the organizational leadership. Craft unions, small and elitist, appealed to the Yankee workman. It was not simply that he was reluctant to share his bargaining power with those who were less skilled. It was also that the hard labor, particularly the pick-and-shovel work, was performed largely by the Irish. There was thus, from the beginning, an overtone of racism to the craft-union movement. The Yankee craftsman, foundation of the Know-Nothing tradition, expected his union to bestow on him not only economic benefits but also social distinction.

The industrial union, rival to the craft union, never had much success in the United States. The Knights of Labor, founded shortly after the Civil War, presumed to speak for all the underprivileged and tended, almost inevitably, to look to utopian solutions as the only answer to the oppressions of American capitalism. The Knights had no affection for the craft unions, which its celebrated leader, Terrence V. Powderly, said "failed to recognize the rights of man, and looked only to the rights of the tradesman. . . ." Powderly's characterization was accurate, but while he was campaigning for the abolition of the wage system, the class of skilled workers sought what benefits it could get for itself. From its peak of 700,000 members in the 1880's, the Knights of Labor declined rapidly. Organized labor chose to make its bid within the existing system rather than overthrow it in favor of some utopia for all.

The American Federation of Labor had, by the turn of the century, emerged as the dominant voice of the American workingman. It did not pretend to speak for the oppressed but for the working-class elite. Its goals were pragmatic—shorter hours and higher wages for members—and not utopian. "At no time in my life," boasted Samuel Gompers, the A. F. of L. president for more than forty years, "have I worked out a definitely articulated economic theory." The A. F. of L. did have certain reformist objectives—free compulsory education, factory inspection, the abolition of child labor. But by firm policy, it abjured direct engagement in politics, especially partisan politics. If American capitalism had to face a union, it could scarcely have found a more innocuous one than the American Federation of Labor.

Of government, the A. F. of L. asked only neutrality in the struggle between capital and labor. As recently as 1923, Gompers lectured the A. F. of L. national convention against Federal regulation of industry, which "under the guise of reform, can but lead to greater confusion and more hopeless entanglements." Denouncing a proposal for compulsory unemployment insurance, Gompers declared that "it would open the door to the government agents and agencies who would spy and pry into the very innermost recesses of the home life." It is revealing indeed that labor, during the Republican era, was so suspicious of government that

Gompers could inveigh against unemployment insurance. But it was also symptomatic of the A.F. of L.'s indifference to the working class as a whole. The A.F. of L., confident of its power to satisfy its members, was quite willing to live with laissez-faire, as long as it was impartially applied to both capital and labor.

From one quarter and another during the period when the two political parties were extremely conservative, it was proposed that labor join with the farmer for positive political action. Both, presumably, were being exploited by the same capitalist interests. Both wanted nothing more than to redress the economic imbalance between big business and the common man. If the objective of the farmer and the workingman did not always coincide, it seemed equally true that they were rarely in conflict. The farmer and the worker, by most objective standards, seemed to be natural political allies. Yet the many efforts to create standing farmer-labor political coalitions invariably failed. Whatever the forces pressing for alliance, the divisive pressures seemed in every instance to prove stronger.

In practice, the workingman and the farmer never thought of themselves as natural allies. The farmer, after all, was an entrepreneur, while the workingman put in his time for a daily wage. The farmer looked down on the laborer as a hired hand, while the laborer mistrusted whoever was a real or potential employer. The farmer, furthermore, believed that the products he bought from the industrial East would be cheaper if wages were kept low, while the laborer was persuaded that his interest was to keep farm prices at their absolute minimum. The farmer believed in inflation and cheap money; the laboringman shared the preferences of his employers for price stability and even deflation. As for the Federal government, both conceded that it was unfriendly, but the farmer was outraged at the protective tariff, the most controversial of its policies, while the workingman tended to view protectionism as a safeguard of his job. Neither the farmer nor the wage earner ever seemed to consider seriously that the prosperity of one might in some measure contribute to the prosperity of the other, or that the impoverishment of one might mean the other's doom.

Beneath the practical considerations, there also ran a deep, irrational feeling of estrangement between the tiller of the soil and the laborer in the city. It was Bryan, in his Cross of Gold speech, who said: "Burn down *your* cities and leave *our* farms, and *your* cities will spring up again as if by magic; but destroy *our* farms and the grass will grow in the streets of every city in the country . . ." This, of course, was a public statement, in which Bryan was appealing for labor's vote. In less cautious moments, he undoubtedly expressed far less measured sentiments—the reflection of the prejudices of the American agrarian.

Closely tied to this feeling of rural-urban estrangement was the ever-present quality of racism. During the Populist era, Mary Ellen Lease, the dynamic organizer of the Western plains, openly preached Anglo-Saxon superiority, while Tom Watson of Georgia, once the Populist candidate for the Presidency, complained that "the scum of creation has been dumped on us. Some of our principal cities are more foreign than American. The most dangerous and corrupting hordes of the Old World have invaded us. . . ." For the immigrant workingman, if this was the meaning of a reform movement, he could do no worse by staying with his humdrum old party.

The first attempt at a farmer-labor coalition was made in 1878, when Powderly joined the Knights of Labor to remnants of the Granger movement to run candidates nationwide on a Greenback-Labor ticket. The outcome was startling. The coalition received more than a million votes and sent fourteen of its candidates to Congress. Its agitation resulted in the passage of the Chinese Exclusion Act, the first of the immigrant restriction laws. But the fortunes of the coalition declined rapidly with the return of prosperity, and by 1888, the Knights of Labor were back to supporting the Republican Presidential candidate.

Powderly attempted the coalition strategy once again after the Populists got underway, and he appealed to the A.F. of L., the railroad brotherhoods, and several independent unions to join him. Each, however, rebuffed him, Gompers offering a warning against entanglements with "employing farmers." The Populists did what they could to make labor feel welcome. In 1896, they proclaimed that "the union of the labor forces of the United States this day consummated shall be permanent and perpetual. . . ." But the workingman had no confidence in them. Despite Powderly's efforts, the Populist movement, as an attempt at coalition, was an utter failure.

Ostensibly, the election of 1896 was the optimum moment for labor to coalesce with the farmer. Before city laborers, Bryan assailed the Federal government's use of the armed forces to suppress strikes. He denounced government injunctions to suppress strikers. To the Eastern workingman, however, Bryan was a man of the sod, and free silver had the potential for making as much mischief as the "cross of gold." Not long before the election, Mark Hanna, the Republicans' organizational genius, received a report that "the labor organizations are against us almost to a man." The capitalists reacted by putting tremendous pressure on their workers to cast an orthodox vote. But it is probable that at least as many wage earners voted Republican on McKinley's assurance that "we want good prices and good wages, and when we have them we want them to be paid in good money . . . in dollars worth one hundred cents each." In the end, even much of immigrant labor abandoned the Democrats. The ten largest cities of the United States, with their massive laboring populations, all voted for McKinley, and a farmer-labor coalition was as distant a prospect as ever.

Soon after Populism collapsed, Eugene V. Debs, a brilliant and dedicated labor organizer, founded the American Socialist party as a workingman's reform movement. That the party grew spectacularly during the Progressive Era, when Democrats and Republicans competed for a humane image, testified to labor's sense of alienation from the normal political process. The Socialists were strong not only among New York Jews and Midwestern Germans but among old-stock natives throughout the North and West. Adamson in West Virginia, Berkeley in California, and Butte in Montana all contained substantial blocs of Socialist voters. Debs also was instrumental in founding the Industrial Workers of the World, a militant industrial union that challenged the craft movement and promoted socialism through direct action. On the

Socialist ticket in 1912, Debs polled almost a million votes, though he faced in Roosevelt and Wilson opponents campaigning as pro-labor progressives. Debs's pragmatic socialism seemed about to capture the overwhelming allegiance of American labor, but then World War I, which he bitterly opposed, directed attention away from social problems. The postwar Red Scare, with radicalism as its target, further damaged the Socialists. With its percentage of the vote diminishing, the party hung on until 1924, when it joined La Follette's alliance in a final attempt to overthrow the monopoly of the Democrats and Republicans.

La Follette's Progressives, though chiefly a vehicle of Western agrarian protest, was the only third party in which farmers and workingmen came together on anything like equal terms. Neither Calvin Coolidge, the Republican, nor John W. Davis, the Democrat, promised to give any relief to the hardships of the common man. Not only did the Socialists enlist in La Follette's cause but so did the railroad brotherhoods, the most stodgy of the unions, and the American Federation of Labor, departing for the first time from its policy of neutrality. The results, however, were disappointing; labor voters proved to be much less enthusiastic about La Follette than their leaders, and gave their overwhelming support to the candidates of the conventional parties. After La Follette's defeat, organized labor abandoned the third-party movement, while the Socialists disintegrated as a political force. The nation's workingmen showed that they still could not be persuaded to exercise their power in any positive and unified fashion.

Throughout the middle years of the 1920's, the workingman was moderately prosperous. The industrial system seemed to be functioning smoothly. Unrest was less than it had been a decade before. If there was any crossing at all of party lines, it was probably more often from Democratic to Republican. The workingman seemed to be the beneficiary, however indirect, of a system that exalted production. The Republican party found good reason to be confident that the system would go on and on generating new jobs for which the laboring classes would be grateful. It did not take seriously the periodic signs of discontent. If labor had

never before united against the Republican party to express its
wrath, there seemed to be good cause for believing that it
never would.

Thus the decades rolled on, one after another, and the
Republicans drew from their reign a sense of security. Cleveland's
two Presidencies were meaningless. Wilson's seemed almost
an accident. All the rest were "normal"; they were Republican.
The party had long since lost the habit of turning its mind to
holding on to the Negro vote, the farm vote, the labor vote. It
assumed it would hold on, and let matters go at that. When they
were not thinking of business the Republicans thought about
morality and eternal truths. The country seemed so loyally theirs
that it appeared unnecessary for them to think about challenge
and change or contemplate any threat to their hegemony.

CHAPTER 6

Yankee and Immigrant

FROM the beginning of the Republic, the Yankee set barriers around himself and his culture to keep away the outsider and the poor. The further the outsider departed from the Puritan norm or the starker the poor man's sign of want, the more inhospitable was the typical Yankee. When the immigrant arrived from abroad, he found the Puritan cold and unfriendly. The immigrant, after all, was both an outsider *and* poor. "The people who had come over in steerage," Big Tim Sullivan of Tammany Hall once said, ". . . knew in their hearts and lives the difference between being despised and being accepted and liked." Instinctively, the immigrant turned to the Democratic party and away from the Puritan party of the Yankees.

The Puritan spirit is, by its exclusionary nature, poorly fitted for politics in a diverse society. Before the days of the Republicans, neither the Federalists nor the Whigs made a serious effort to diversify the party's base of support. Both were particularly rigid in dealing with foreigners. When the Federalists saw their political dominance slipping away, they sought to disfranchise the foreign born and bar naturalized citizens from holding elective office. They were, as one historian said, "blind to the realities of pluralist politics to the last gasp." As for the Whigs, they tried for economic reasons to hold the line against virulent nativism, but under the pressure of the Know-Nothing movement they finally gave up. Thus its ancestors set the Republican party a poor example for achieving success among a heterogeneous electorate.

For decades, the Republicans were peculiarly complacent about the presence of the immigrant. They won elections, though they wrote off the immigrant quarters of the great seaboard cities as Democratic constituencies. They counted on native-stock working-men to neutralize immigrant strength. They seemed indifferent to Big Tim Sullivan's warning that "the America of the future would be made out of the people who had come over in steerage."

When the Civil War began, the population of the United States was estimated at some 31,000,000 people. In the course of the next forty years, 14,000,000 aliens arrived from abroad. In the decades after the turn of the century, some 18,000,000 more reached American shores. The migration was the greatest in all history. It altered the quality of American politics profoundly.

One might legitimately question why the Yankee ruling class consented to a migration that seemed clearly destined to overwhelm it. The answer is not simple. But it is surely founded on the confidence the Yankee drew from the Puritan ethic that he would remain preeminent over the outsider in American society. When he finally concluded otherwise, it was all but too late.

Throughout most of this period, American leadership actually took considerable pains to encourage immigration. In the underpopulated West and South, the states created official agencies to lure new settlers to farm the land. Representatives frequently went abroad to sell the virtues of this state over that, even to offer inducements to migrate. They worked hand in hand with the shipping companies, for whom the transportation of immigrants was a major business. Their joint efforts were in no small measure responsible for accelerating the transatlantic movement.

But still more important was the attitude of the capitalist class, which welcomed immigration as an eternal source of cheap labor. In a country that was constantly growing and eternally moving, the construction of buildings, canals, railroads, and factories created an insatiable demand for strong bodies. Throughout the nineteenth century, most Americans believed that immigration increased the national wealth. To the general public, the immigrant was a tangible economic asset. Near the end of the century, statisticians of the United States Treasury computed the worth of the average immigrant at $800. Andrew Carnegie, the steel baron, placed the figure at $1,500. Not surprisingly, the Republican party —even at the risk of exasperating some of its native supporters— stood loftily throughout the period for a policy of open immigration.

By the force of circumstances, the immigrant gravitated chiefly into the regions of the United States where the Yankees predominated. These were the lands of the greatest opportunity, where economic activity was most intense. For those who wanted to farm, the lands of the North were plentiful and fertile. For the others, there was plenty of work in the cities. Wherever he settled, the immigrant became neighbor to the Yankee. Here he first felt the condescending stare that he came to regard as characteristic of the Puritan American. Here, inside the strongholds of Republicanism, he helped to form fortresses of Democratic power.

At no point did the South attract more than a relative handful of foreigners. From the beginning, the immigrant was in no position to compete with the Negro. Before the Civil War, he was powerless in a market that offered up slaves. After the war, he could not bid for work as cheaply as the freedman. The South wanted white settlers, as a counter to the numbers of the black man, but it was foiled by its own social system. It watched the immigrant's emerging settlement pattern with dismay. When the immigrant began clearly to add to the strength of the North, the South became embittered. "The mistake with us," snorted an irate slaveholder, "has been that it was not made a felony to bring in an Irishman when it was made piracy to bring in an African." The South, where the proportion of foreigners was lowest, became the first region in the country to advocate seriously that immigration be restricted. Long before pressure began growing in the

North, the resentful South was advocating that America close its doors to newcomers.

Not all of the thirty million or more newcomers to the United States, of course, gravitated into rivalry with the Yankee ruling class. Although precise figures are not available, perhaps a fourth of those who settled from abroad during the era of the great migrations were English-speaking Protestants. England itself sent some five million immigrants, while Scotland, Northern Ireland, English Canada, and Wales sent several million more. The beliefs that these immigrants, as Protestants, brought with them were not in basic conflict and, in many respects, coincided with the Puritan ethic.

The migration of the Anglo-Saxons was less dramatic than that of other peoples because, physically and psychologically, it was less arduous. The Anglo-Saxons possessed more capital and greater occupational skills than the other immigrant groups. They had no language problem. They shared many of the Yankees' values and prejudices. They were not always pliant, of course. They tended, for instance, to be the most vigorous and talented union organizers, which made them an irritant to their Yankee employers. But, on the whole, the Yankees, always admirers of English culture, erected no barriers against them. The Anglo-Saxon immigrants thus fit rather painlessly into Yankee society. By the second generation they had, in almost all cases, lost their identity as foreigners. Slipping imperceptibly into the Yankee civilization, the Anglo-Saxon immigrant absorbed Puritan morality and, with his numbers, reinforced its authority. In an age when politics and society were becoming more fluid, his immigration weighed heavily, not in behalf of change but in behalf of the status quo.

The Germans and the Scandinavians, who came in numbers almost equal to the Anglo-Saxons, presented only a mild challenge to the Yankee hegemony. Teutonic peoples, they too were almost all Protestant. Though few were actually pioneers, most went west to settle, on land the Yankees had already broken. They tended to be much less individualistic, much more social than their Yankee neighbors. They gave themselves to pleasure with a spontaneity that was alien to Puritans. Occasionally they ran afoul of some Puritan crusade, particularly temperance. But the contrasts were neutralized by the values they held in common, and Yankees and Teutons lived side by side in relative cordiality.

The Germans and Scandinavians worked hard and were materially ambitious, although they were slower than the Yankee to equate success with salvation. They exulted in the freedom of private enterprise, not because they worshiped individualism but because they detested feudalism. If they were suspicious of government authority, it was not that they loved laissez-faire, like the Yankee, but that they had brought with them a resentment of official restraints. Though their reasons may have been different, Germans and Scandinavians rarely clashed with the Yankees over matters of policy.

The Germans and the Scandinavians were proud of their culture, but gradually it gave way before the powerful civilization of the Yankee. They tried valiantly to retain their Old World customs but they slowly yielded to Yankee ways. As determined foes of slavery, the Teutons joined the Yankee when he formed the Republican party. They, too, wanted to keep the West safe for the white man. Over the years, the Teuton was a Yankee ally, content, for the most part, to follow the Yankee's lead in the direction of the country.

The Irish were the first and for many decades the only substantial immigrant group in the United States that was not Protestant. They had begun migrating in the first days of the Republic and well before the Civil War were numerous enough to be a vexation to the Protestants in the cities. After the Civil War, they arrived at the rate of many hundreds of thousands each decade. By the time immigration was halted after World War I, an estimated ten million or more Irishmen had left their native land to settle in the United States. They have, throughout their entire history as Americans, never ceased to exasperate the Yankees, both inside politics and out.

The Irish turned against the Yankee ruling class as far back as the 1790's, when the Federalists sided with their archenemy, England, in its war with France. The Irish joined Jefferson's coalition, which was generally pro-French. The Federalists' retaliatory tactics only confirmed the Irish in their decision. In the Jeffersonian coalition, where all blocs were welcome, the Irish felt at home. In the Yankee party, it was obvious that there was no place for them.

Unlike the newcomers from Germany and Scandinavia, the Irish immigrant chose not to go farming in the West but to settle in the cities. To be sure, he was no less a peasant than the others when he arrived, but he brought with him poor memories of the land, which had yielded him famine and misery. He wanted no more of agriculture. The Irishman went out to make his living as a laborer. It was he who relieved the Yankee of the drudgery of digging the canals, the dams, and the foundations of the great new buildings going up everywhere. Instead of heading for the frontier, he remained in Boston, New York, and the other cities in which his ship docked or to which his first job might have taken him. At every port along the canals, at each successive railroad depot, Irish communities were established. The Irishman lived with his family in the shantytowns that soon became slums, in conditions of incredible filth, crowding, and discomfort. Unlike the Puritan, he rarely saved his money to get rich. He preferred to spend it on drink or on a steamship ticket to bring another member of his family to join him. The Irishman's temperament was not easily reconcilable to the demands of a Puritan society.

The Irish remained unwaveringly Democratic even during the antislavery crusade, though not out of sympathy for slavery as much as out of suspicion of the motives of the Yankee crusaders. "The only difference between the Negro slave of the South and the white slave of the North," said Congressman Mike Walsh of New York, one of the first Irish politicians to succeed on the national level, "is that one has a master without asking for him and the other has to beg for the privilege of becoming a slave. . . . The one is the slave of an individual; the other is the slave of an inexorable class." It was resentment such as Walsh expressed that kept the Irish linked in an unlikely alliance with the planter aristocracy, although on the eve of the war most followed the Democratic party's Northern faction willingly into battle. The Irish fought well for the Union, even if they were frightened of what the Emancipation Proclamation might do to the Northern job market and rioted in New York against discriminatory draft quotas. More than anything, they showed during the war that their own problems, not such abstractions as slavery and the Union, preoccupied them overwhelmingly. Despite the glory with which the Republicans emerged from the war, there is no sign that the Irish ever contemplated giving up their allegiance to the Democrats.

To the Yankee, their allegiance was costly. In the skills of democratic politics, the manipulation of people and power to achieve personal and social objectives, the Irishman was the Yankee's superior. Unlike the Puritan, he did not think of politics as something of a necessary evil. It was not, as it was for the Puritan, a quest for virtue or a compromise between the demands of body and soul. To the Irishman, politics was an instrument of collective action. Though it was the Puritan who rendered homage to the separation of Church and State, it was the Irishman for whom politics, as a practical matter, was exclusively Caesar's domain, entirely distinct from that of God. The Puritan never enjoyed the work of waging a harsh political struggle. The Irishman looked upon democratic politics as an exciting game, worthy of any man's full time and talent and one at which he proved himself remarkably adept.

The Irishman who took up politics, unlike his Yankee counterpart, made no claim to special righteousness. He did not pretend that he was making a sacrifice for public service. He did not deny that politics presented excellent prospects for a career, with substantial rewards in both money and status. The Irish politician made himself an institution in response to the needs of his community. He had a job to perform, and whatever his shortcomings in terms of conventional Puritan morality, as an institution he served the community's needs.

If the Irish politician did not invent the urban political machine, he brought it to a level of efficiency that has not been surpassed. The machine was the politician's instrument for acquiring and perpetuating power. But had it not served its constituency well, it would never have survived. The Puritan has traditionally loathed the machine. It is the antithesis of everything he regards as meritorious. It flourished, however, because it performed a useful social function, one in which the Puritan politician was himself unwilling to engage.

The urban political machine was built on a foundation of mutual service. The politician, in return for the loyalty of the voter, used his power to alleviate the austerity of slum life. The political leader controlled jobs, the patronage of unskilled labor which a bursting economy demanded. He could assign these jobs to those who needed them most or who best fitted his own purposes. If there were no jobs, in winter or during depression, or if a family, for reasons of illness or death, was without a wage earner, he could distribute food and coal and clothes and even money. The machine politician was the conduit to the public treasury, in the days before the government—local, state, or Federal—recognized an obligation to the unfortunate. What did the immigrant care if the political leader dipped into the municipal accounts to help himself, too? The immigrant expected it, in fact. It was looked on as the machine politician's rightful way of supporting himself. If the practice provoked the fury of the righteous Yankee, so much the better. More often than not, the immigrant took Yankee outrage as evidence of triumph for his own side.

When the Puritan reformer, well fed and elegantly dressed, called for honest and efficient administration to lower the costs of government, he was talking a language that the immigrant in the slums failed to understand. Honesty in politics was, after all, a Puritan virtue, not a practical consideration. It had nothing to do with the unemployed or the overworked, the hungry or the cold, the grim conditions of life in the ghetto. What did this constituency care if the machine's methods often included corruption and graft? Theodore Roosevelt, who was himself a municipal reformer in his early days in politics, complained in his autobiography:

The trouble is that the boss does understand human nature, and that he fills a place which the reformer cannot fill unless he likewise understands human nature . . . . There is often much good in this type of boss . . . . For some of his constituents he does proper favors, and for others wholly improper favors; but he preserves human relations with them all . . . . An appeal made to them for virtue in the abstract, an appeal made by good men who do not really understand their needs, will often pass quite unheeded, if on the other side stands the boss, the friend and benefactor . . . . They have a feeling of clan-loyalty to him . . .

The immigrant knew the Yankee as his exploiter, distant and pious and cold. The machine, whatever its faults, was his ally. As Mr. Dooley remarked pithily about Thanksgiving, " 'Twas founded by th' Puritans to give thanks f'r bein' presarved fr'm th' Indyans, an' . . . we keep it to give thanks we are presarved fr'm the Puritans." To the services that the machine rendered, the immigrant responded with his gratitude and with his votes.

Perhaps it is coincidence that the Tammany machine was despoiling the city of New York at the same time that the Republicans were plundering the Federal government. Both campaigns have been ascribed to a general, postbellum decline in morals, to which the public was remarkably indulgent. If the excesses committed under Grant can be blamed on the Puritan ethic run amuck, the excesses under New York's Boss Tweed and his successors might be regarded as machine morality in its rococo stage. Tweed, while attending to the needs of the slum constituents on whom his power depended, succeeded in robbing the city treasury of hundreds of millions of dollars. When he died in 1878, having spent most of his final years in jail, *The Nation*, then a conservative spokesman of the establishment, published the following word of caution:

Let us remember that he fell without loss of reputation among the bulk of his supporters. The bulk of the poorer voters of this city today revere his memory, and look on him as the victim of rich men's malice; as, in short, a friend of the needy who applied the public funds, with as little waste possible under the circumstances, to the purposes to which they ought to be applied—and that is the making of work for the working man. The odium heaped on him in the pulpits last Sunday does not exist in the lower stratum of New York society.

The Tweed scandals brought out the reformers in profusion. Most of them, recognizing the futility of functioning as Republicans in New York, worked within the framework of the Democratic party. For a time, millionaire businessmen wrestled with Irish politicians for control of Tammany's power. A Democrat, Samuel J. Tilden, finally broke the Tweed Ring's grip on New York and was selected governor of the state. "Samuel Tilden," wrote Matthew Josephson, "must be credited with having established the modern pattern of reform as fixing governmental economy—rather than any change in the social status—as its goal." Tilden and Grover Cleveland, both reformist governors, were the outstanding Democrats of the postwar era and both were Democratic Presidential nominees. As one of the small ironies of American history, they helped give the Democrats on the national level a reputation as the party of municipal integrity and administrative reform.

Though reformers had sporadic success in winning elections in New York, they never quite seemed to meet the requirement cited by Theodore Roosevelt of understanding human nature. During his own brief incumbency as mayor, Abram Hewitt, a millionaire iron magnate, could declare grandiloquently that "the people are determined to bring back that better era of the republic in which, when men consecrated themselves to public service, they utterly abnegated all selfish purposes . . . when to be summoned into the public service was a priceless honor and not an opportunity for private gain."

Such noble pronouncements failed to touch the immigrant voters. Until La Guardia in the 1930's, the New York electorate did not once give a reformist mayor a second term in office. The reformers, wrote William V. Shannon, "tried to repress the manifestations of social conditions without remedying the roots of the problem—the slum housing, low wages, unemployment and economic exploitation. . . . The majority of voters naturally disliked an administration that meddled in their public pleasures and left untouched their private burdens . . . . To most people, it seemed as if the business community liked 'reform' because it could go ahead and do for nothing what it at least had to pay Tammany for the privilege of doing."

Theodore Roosevelt, though he came finally to realize the understanding required of a successful reformer, displayed in a diary note of his own the ruling-class attitude that so infuriated the Irish voters of New York. After his election to the state legislature in 1881, he wrote that "the average Catholic Irishman of the first generation, as represented in this Assembly, is a low, venal, corrupt and unintelligent brute. The average Democrat here seems much below the average Republican. Among the professions represented in the two parties, the contrast is striking. There are six liquor sellers, two bricklayers, a butcher, a tobacconist, a pawn broker and a type setter in the house—all Democrats; but of the farmers and lawyers, the majority are Republicans . . ." What is clear is that Roosevelt, despite his upper-class contempt, would not have thought of himself as unfriendly toward the immigrant. He regarded his family as eminently generous to the needy. He spoke proudly of his father's compassionate interest in newsboys and "little Italians." He boasted of his own brief stint as a Sunday school teacher in a Protestant mission. It never occurred to him, at least in this stage of his life, that in his condescending sympathy there was no understanding at all of the immigrant's wants and hopes. It is no surprise that as a reformist candidate for mayor of New York in 1886, he ran a poor third in a three-way race. His attitude demonstrates the enormous gap between the ways of the ruling class and the culture of the immigrant.

Mr. Dooley, as usual, grasped exquisitely the essence of the immigrant's feelings. There is no mistaking in his deft phrases the Irishman's scorn for the political reformer.

A regular pollytician can't give away an alley without blushin', but a businessman who is in pollytics jus' to see that the civil service law gets thurly enfoorced, will give Lincoln Park an' th' public, libr'y to the beef thrust, charge an admission price to th' lake front an' make it a felony f'r annywan to buy stove polish outside iv his store, an' have it all put down to public improvemints with a pitcher iv him in the corner store.

Just as the Irish began to consolidate their power in the cities, a fresh wave of immigration—different from all those which preceded it—generated a crisis of a new and unanticipated intensity. By the 1890's, the principal source of emigration to the United States had shifted from Northern and Western Europe to Southern and Eastern Europe. The new immigrants—Italians, Slavs, Jews, Greeks, Russians, Poles—were readily distinguishable from the old. They had dark skin and dark eyes and their ways were far stranger to American culture than the ways of the Irish or the Germans. They were generally illiterate, ignorant, and poor. They did not speak English. They were not Protestants. Because the free lands of the West were all but exhausted, they were forced to settle in the cities, whether or not they wanted to. They formed substantial colonies not only in such metropolitan centers as New York, Chicago, Detroit, and Boston but in such smaller industrial communities as Paterson, Fall River, and Hamtramck. Their colonies turned forthwith into ghettos, where living conditions were appalling. Hard as it had been for the Irish, it was far harder for the dark-eyed immigrants to find a comfortable place in American society. To the social, economic, and political components of American nativism, there was now joined an element that was more purely racist than anything which had come before.

For the most part, the new immigrant deferred to the leadership of the Irish, whose adjustment to American life he admired and sought to emulate. The Irishman—as political boss, as cop, as civil functionary—was his broker with the strange American world. "The ward politicians became pioneers in social work," wrote a contemporary observer. In a few instances, the Yankee challenged the Irishman for the allegiance of the new immigrant and his vote. In some cities, in fact, Republicans succeeded temporarily in capturing Jewish or Italian blocs, if their members happened to resent Irish ways. But the immigrant rarely felt at home with the Yankee leadership, which refused to surrender any of the substance of power, while the Irish, on the contrary, learned quickly that they must make room for immigrant strength. "The Irishman has above all races the mixture of ingenuity, firmness, human sympathy, comradeship and daring that makes him the amalgamator of races," wrote a Yankee intellectual at the turn of the century. In most cities, therefore, the immigrants remained overwhelmingly Democratic, while the ruling-class Republicans continued to wane.

One by one, the big cities fell to immigrant power. New York and Boston were captured early by the Irish. As the immigrant alliance grew stronger, they were followed by Chicago, Cleveland, Philadelphia, Pittsburgh, and St. Louis. The smaller cities of the East and Midwest fell into similar patterns. The Yankee, now frequently a minority, tended to isolate himself in his well-kept ghettos, from which he continued to dominate the business and industry of the cities. But he brooded unhappily over the Irish conquest in politics. The immigrant now moved his power into a national arena, where he began to fight for ascendancy within the Democratic party. The Yankee, meanwhile, looked to the Republicans to rescue his society before it was too late.

Over the years, the Republican had showed remarkable restraint in exploiting anti-immigrant prejudice for partisan purposes. Rarely did the party yield to the temptation of indulging the Know-Nothing strain in its heritage. In 1875 Rutherford B. Hayes, running for governor of Ohio, flayed the Democrats as subservient to Catholic designs. Again, before he became President in 1876, Hayes declared: "It is owing to emigration West that Ohio and Indiana are not Republican. Catholics are taking the places of Republican farmers and soldiers." The Republican platform of 1880 contained a plank mildly reproachful to Catholics on the issue of aid to parochial schools. But anti-Catholicism was not a weapon to which Republicans customarily resorted, if only because it did not seem to be useful. When the Reverend Samuel Burchard made his celebrated charge in the campaign of 1884 that the Democrats were the party of "rum, Romanism, and rebellion," he succeeded only in provoking a reaction among New York Catholics that cost the Republicans the Presidency. To be sure, the Republicans remained the nativist party, but they were very cautious about exploiting nativist prejudices to serve their political ends.

Nonetheless, Yankee crusaders were at work, expressing in a manner not directly political the animosities that divided them from the foreigner. Their vehicle was, naturally enough, Puritan morality. Their ostensible objective was a more godly society. A more fundamental aim, however, was to establish the superiority of their own values over those of the immigrants, for cultural prestige enhances both self-esteem and political potential. The real goal of the new crusaders was the preservation, in the face of the threat from abroad, of the prerogatives of the Yankee ruling class.

It was a new cause for the Yankee to crusade for woman suffrage. Such a crusade had no precedent. The idea of political equality for women seems to have occurred to no one prior to the mid-nineteenth century. But if the Yankee had never ever recognized feminism as a cause, on reflection its relationship to the Puritan ethic emerges lucidly. Tocqueville, who understood America so well, was the first to perceive the relationship, however imperfectly. In the 1830's, he had written in his famous treatise:

> No free communities ever existed without morals; and . . . morals are the work of women. Consequently, whatever affects the condition of women, their habits, and their opinions, has great political importance. . . . In the United States the doctrines of Protestantism are combined with great political freedom and a most democratic state of society; and nowhere are young women surrendered so early or so completely to their own guidance . . . . I believe that the social changes which bring nearer to the same level the father and son, the master and servant, and superiors and inferiors

generally speaking, will raise woman and make her more and more the equal of man.

As Tocqueville suggests, the egalitarianism inherent in American Protestantism always contained the potential to break through the barriers of sex. It needed only the proper incentive, which the Yankee crusaders found in the menace to their dominance.

From its beginnings at Seneca Falls in western New York in 1848, the cause of woman suffrage was closely linked with the Puritan antislavery and temperance crusades. After the Civil War, it found its chief following on the frontiers, where the Yankee looked upon himself as a civilizing force locked in conflict with the emissaries of disorder. Inevitably, it took on a character that was both anti-saloon and Republican. As Alan P. Grimes has so perceptively noted, woman suffrage became a device for which frontier conservatives campaigned in the interests of law and order. As the movement grew, it became imbedded in the Republican party, guardian of the conventions that the ruling class considered basic to the preservation of the status quo.

Ultimately, the woman suffrage cause became openly a campaign against the outsider, in this case both immigrants and Negroes. Susan B. Anthony, the most celebrated of the suffragettes, confessed without embarrassment her disgust that:

> . . . the dangerous experiment has been made of enfranchising the vast proportion of crime, intemperance, immorality and dishonesty, and barring absolutely from the suffrage the great proportion of temperance, morality, religion and conscientiousness; that, in other words, the worst elements have been put into the ballot-box and the best elements kept out. This fatal mistake is even now beginning to dawn upon the minds of those who have cherished an ideal of the grandeur of the republic, and they dimly see that in woman lies the highest promise of fulfillment. Those who fear the foreign vote will learn eventually that there are more American-born women in the United States than foreign-born men and women; and those who dread the ignorant vote will study the statistics and see that the percentage of illiteracy is much smaller among women than among men.

In the few plebiscites taken on the woman suffrage issue before the turn of the century, the evidence made clear that the natural home for the movement had become the Republican party.

It was no coincidence that the temperance movement gathered momentum at the same time and at a comparable pace with the drive for woman suffrage. Temperance had long been a Puritan objective. In New England, the upright citizens linked the rise of drink with the decline of the Federalists. "Drunkards reel through the streets day after day, and year after year, with entire impunity," bemoaned the Reverend Beecher, Federalist to the last. "Profane swearing is heard, and even by magistrates as though they heard it not. . . . The mass is changing. We are becoming another people." In the years before the Civil War, the temperance movement became closely allied with the Know-Nothings, then with the Abolitionists. Finally, it united with the other fine Puritan causes in the Republican party. As one New Englander enjoined, nobly rejecting both persecution and ostracism as means of controlling the immigrant: "Beget about them a pure moral atmosphere, so they and their children will grow up strong in the virtues that constitute a good citizen." Another observer of the day was more candid and declared:

> The saloon fosters an un-American spirit among the foreign-born population of our country. The influx of foreigners into our urban centers, many of whom have liquor habits, is a menace to good government . . . the foreign-born population is largely under the social and political control of the saloon. If the cities keep up their rapid growth they will soon have the balance of political power in the nation and become the storm centers of political life. The hope of perpetuating our liberties is to help the foreigners correct any demoralizing custom, and through self-restraint assimilate American ideals.

Within the Republican party, temperance became just one more weapon in the Puritan's arsenal for moving his society across the nation.

As the century moved into its final decades, taboos against the use of alcohol came increasingly to serve as an article of faith among the Protestant sects. What the Yankee saw as a device for mastering the immigrant, the Southerner saw as another instrument for use against the Negro. In the doctrine of the Quaker, the Congregationalist, and the Presbyterian of the North, of the Baptist and Methodist of the South, even of the Mormon and Christian Scientist splinter sects, the movement ultimately developed to go beyond temperance to the advocacy of total prohibition. Their dogmas widened the gulf between themselves and their rivals by placing them in declared opposition to the others' way of life.

As the Protestants mobilized, so too did the Catholics and the Jews, who entered into an alliance of convenience with the powerful liquor interests. The only assistance they found within Protestant ranks came from the Episcopalians, who traced their origins to antipathy to Puritanism, and the immigrant Lutheran churches of the Germans and Scandinavians. Meanwhile, the Woman's Christian Temperance Union—campaigning simultaneously in behalf of woman's suffrage and against smoking, gambling, and prostitution—by its very vigor exacerbated tensions between the two sides. As the two contending forces lined up, there was no concealing that what was at stake was far more than a man's right to take a drink. In the words of one contemporary critic of the Anti-Saloon League, prohibition was only a disguise on the part of those seeking "Protestant political supremacy." In the anti-alcohol movement, the fight for supremacy was still being waged on a peripheral battlefield, but both sides understood the nature of the struggle.

While the Yankees, on the one hand, were taking the offensive on drinking and voting, they seemed desperately to be shoring up their defenses, on the other, against the influence of alien culture generally. Significantly, the most defensive of all seemed to be the nouveaux riches of New York and Boston, where immigrant power was greatest. Dissatisfied to be merely an aristocracy of wealth, they pressed their claim to be an aristocracy of blood as well. But throughout the North and the West, and even in the South, a drive was undertaken to endow the native-stock American with the symbols of superiority that would assure recognition of his rule.

Some set the departure date for the Yankee's aggressive caste behavior at 1877, when Joseph Seligman, a leading Jewish banker, was refused accommodations at Saratoga Springs, the most fashionable of Eastern spas. E. D. Baltzell, in *The Protestant Establishment,* discerned the trend accelerating with the invention of the country club as an exclusionary device, the establishment of Groton as a school for the rearing of young gentlemen, and the founding of the Social Register for the institutionalization of snobbery. Meanwhile, old Yankee families organized the Sons of the Revolution, the Colonial Dames, the Daughters of the American Revolution, the Society of Mayflower Descendants, and the Baronial Order of Runnymede. The upper classes, at the same time, took on the study of genealogy as the most stylish hobby. A president-general of the Sons of the American Revolution all but acknowledged the drive to establish credentials against outsiders when he wrote: "Not until the state of civilization reached the point where we had a great many foreigners in our land . . . were our patriotic societies successful."

When a serious movement to restrict foreign immigration finally began to make headway, the Yankee, oddly, was not in the leadership. The direction came from American labor, distressed by ever-growing competition from foreign workers. The native wage earner had always been the foe of the immigrant. As the union movement grew stronger, labor became more militant. But not until the foreigner threatened to undermine Yankee interests in American society did the Yankee community begin to give genuine encouragement to the anti-immigrant campaign.

Paradoxically, the Yankee became an ally of native labor largely for the purpose of confining labor's power. He had become alarmed by labor's aggressiveness and its unrest. He was uncertain of the reasons for the disquiet but he was disposed to accept the view that foreigners, with the subversive ideas they brought from Europe, were to blame. Chicago's Haymarket Riot in 1886, in which eleven were killed and a hundred wounded, appeared to have been provoked by foreign agitators. To small businessmen, white-collar workers, the native middle-class generally, the Haymarket Riot was proof that immigrants were leading the country to anarchy. The typical Yankee rallied to the anti-immigration movement when he began to feel that the immigrant was upsetting the social equilibrium.

Quite naturally, the anti-immigrant forces concentrated their attention on winning the Republican party to their views. As the end of the century approached, the party, almost in spite of itself, became a magnet for nativist sentiment. But the party leadership was not enthusiastic about such a campaign. Though Republican power at the local level was eroding, the party nationally seemed as sound as ever. The leadership detected no immediate threat in the immigrant vote. Most important of all, big business, the backbone of the party's structure, continued to oppose any legislation that might curb its labor supply. It was only by gradual steps that the nativists were able to make any progress in influencing the party's decisions.

In 1887, Republican conventions in Pennsylvania and Ohio approved resolutions favoring immigration restriction, and a powerful Republican senator, Justin Morrill of Vermont, introduced an anti-immigration bill. The following year, the California Republican convention denounced the influx of foreign radicals. The American Protective Association, an aggressive nativist lobby, blossomed throughout the Yankee Midwest and made important contributions to the election of Republican candidates. The Grand Army of the Republic, then at the pinnacle of its strength, maintained that foreign radicals were allied with "copperheads and ex-rebels, for venomous warfare against the soldiers."

Not until Henry Cabot Lodge emerged as the leader of American nativism did the anti-immigrant drive begin to make an impact. Lodge, of an old Yankee family from Massachusetts, personified the dread so many Puritans possessed at the prospect of being overrun by foreign peoples. He was outraged that the Irish and the newer immigrants had snatched so much of New England away from the Puritans who had settled it. Lodge, with his Harvard Ph.D. and meticulously trimmed beard, undertook through the devices of pseudo-science to prove that Southern and Eastern European stock was inherently inferior to the native

Anglo-Saxon population of the country. At the same time, Lodge took his convictions into politics. As a scholar, he gave nativism a measure of intellectual dignity, and as a senator, he enhanced its stature with political influence. Lodge was persuaded that unless the doors of the United States were shut to further immigration, the Yankee's leadership was doomed.

During the severe depression of the mid-1890's, Lodge mobilized behind him an impressive anti-immigrant coalition. Native labor was, as always, the most enthusiastic of the participants. But by now the Yankee middle-class, in search of a bulwark for its status, offered almost equal ardor. Hardly to their credit, the Protestant immigrant blocs—German, Scandinavian, Anglo-Saxon —gave Lodge considerable support. Regionally, the West and the South moved into line, not because they were overrun by immigrants but, on the contrary, because of a growing provincial xenophobia. When big business consented to support the coalition, however reluctantly, a victory for restrictionist legislation seemed at hand.

Lodge's device was the requirement that an immigrant had to be literate to enter the United States. He did not conceal the fact, however, that his real objective was not educational but racial. On the Senate floor he declared:

> The illiteracy test will bear most heavily upon the Italians, Russians, Poles, Hungarians, Greeks, and Asiatics, and very lightly, or not at all, upon English-speaking emigrants or Germans, Scandinavians or French. In other words, the races most affected by the illiteracy test are those whose emigration to this country has begun within the last twenty years and swelled rapidly to enormous proportions, races with which the English-speaking people have never hitherto assimilated, and who are most alien to the great body of the people of the United States. . . . The races which would suffer most seriously by exclusion under the proposed bill furnish the immigrants who do not go to the West or South, where immigration is needed, but who remain on the Eastern Seaboard, where immigration is not needed and where their presence is most injurious and undesirable.

Lodge believed his measure would be enacted if the Republicans won in 1896, but after McKinley's election he suffered a grievous disappointment. Prosperity reappeared and the reasons that provoked most of the support for limiting immigration seemed to vanish. Without warning, the coalition fell apart and Lodge's drive collapsed, but nativist sentiment was far from dead. It awaited only a more propitious moment to come forth again.

World War I became the occasion for the resurgence. It evoked an aggressive nationalism unprecedented in American history. The patriots demanded an "America for Americans" and, to discourage deviation from nativist norms, "One-hundred per cent Americanism." They roundly denounced all "hyphenates," by which they meant those groups whose origins were designated by hyphenated adjectives. The German-Americans, who tended, like the others, to identify with their former homelands, became the first victims of patriotic wrath. Then passion was directed toward Irish-Americans, who protested British repression in Ireland; Jewish-Americans, who pointed to the cruelty of the Russians; Italian-Americans, who shared Italy's grievances against a whole variety of neighbors. By the time the United States entered the war, the Yankee was more than ever convinced of the threat to the integrity of his society. Conformist pressures continued to grow. "We Americans," wrote Walter H. Page, "have got to . . . hang our Irish agitators and shoot our hyphenates and bring up our children with reverence for English history and in the awe of English literature." Over Wilson's veto, Lodge's literacy proposal swept through Congress. As soon as the war ended, pent-up tension seemed to break its dikes to generate the nativist orgy known as the "Red Scare." Its madness passed, but the long years of disorder and defense had left the immigrant groups exhausted, too dispirited to counter the legislative drive that was being mounted against them.

Meanwhile, the campaign for prohibition continued apace. At the beginning of the twentieth century, five Yankee states—Maine,

Kansas, North Dakota, New Hampshire, and Vermont—had enacted bans on liquor. From that point, the movement followed the path of nativist conquest. Between 1907 and 1915, most of the South—while completing the disfranchisement of Negroes—adopted prohibition laws. From 1914 to 1917, as anger mounted against the Germans, prohibition swept through the Yankee West, from Indiana to Oregon. In the guise of wartime measures, Congress enacted a series of anti-alcohol restrictions. Finally, at the end of 1917, Congress approved a nationwide prohibition amendment, which the requisite number of states ratified within little more than a year. In all the United States, sentiment was such that only New Jersey, Rhode Island, and Connecticut, all with heavy immigrant populations, refused to concur, and in January, 1920, the Eighteenth Amendment became part of the Constitution.

In the fervor of patriotism, in a hungering for the enforcement of a pure American identity, the crusade against alcohol that the Yankee had waged since colonial days at last met with success. It was, if nothing else, the nation's mark of homage to Puritan morality. The sociologist Joseph R. Gusfield wrote:

> The establishment of prohibition laws was a battle in the struggle for status between two divergent styles of life. It marked the public affirmation of the abstemious, ascetic qualities of American Protestantism. In this sense, it was an act of ceremonial deference toward old middle-class culture. If the law was often disobeyed and not enforced, the respectability of its adherents was honored in the breach. After all, it was *their* law that drinkers had to avoid.

What prohibition did, in symbolic fashion, was to establish the priority of Yankee values in American society.

Not surprisingly, as the fortunes of prohibition progressed, so did those of woman suffrage. Except in the South, where white supremacy had already been assured, support for woman suffrage correlated remarkably with support for prohibition. A Republican senator from North Dakota, speaking on the eve of the war, explained the reason why. "I believe," he declared, "that this Nation will soon, and that all nations must ultimately, stamp out the liquor curse, if they are not to perish from the earth. And I believe that giving the woman the vote will hasten the day when this is accomplished in the United States. I know that in my State the influence of the woman is what made it possible to banish the saloon." Bitterly, one group of proponents charged that woman suffrage referendums had been defeated in the West because the United States Brewers' Association had "organized the Russian vote against woman suffrage in the Dakotas, the German vote in Nebraska, Missouri and Iowa, the Negro vote in Kansas and Oklahoma, the Chinese vote in California." Obviously, the element of racism was as discernible in the woman suffrage issue as it was in prohibition.

By the time the United States entered the war, the woman suffrage advocates had successfully established in the public mind an identification between their cause and "Americanism." Eleven states in the West—of which eight were already "dry"—had approved woman suffrage laws. In Congress, woman suffrage followed prohibition in its steady growth, and except for the Southerners, those who voted for one almost invariably voted for the other. In 1919, the necessary margins were finally achieved in both Houses for the approval of a woman suffrage amendment. Six months after prohibition was incorporated into the Constitution, woman suffrage joined it, as the Nineteenth Amendment. It enshrined the Puritan's woman, as the Eighteenth had enshrined his drinking habits. That autumn, she joined her man to vote overwhelmingly for Warren Gamaliel Harding and Calvin Coolidge, whose triumph symbolized the restoration of Yankee power in American politics just as they had after the Civil War. Wartime emotions had served as the source of the Yankee's margin of victory.

When depression once again struck in 1920, simultaneous with the resumption of mass arrivals from abroad, it became clear that there would be no stopping Congress from enacting severe restrictions on immigration. Wilson vetoed the first bill that Congress approved. But a few months later, Harding became President, and, in May, 1921, signed into law a measure to admit annually a number of immigrants equal to 3 percent of the foreign-born in the United States at the time of the 1910 census. After two centuries of open immigration, America all but closed its doors to those who sought shelter in the New World. The nation had at last reached middle-age. In 1910, more than a third of the population of the nation was composed of the foreign-born or their children. Within a generation, the immigrant would cease to be a significant factor in the composition of American society.

Still, the nativists were not satisfied. The old anti-immigration coalition was still growing in strength. Lodge, now the patriarch of the restrictionists, was as ever a potent force. In 1924, Congress passed the bill that set American immigration policy for more than forty years. It established the principle of the "national origins" quota, which divided annual immigration—limited to 150,000—according to the homeland of the white population in 1920. Thus Britain had almost half the quota, while Northern and Western Europe as a whole, the region which the nativists regarded as the source of the finest stock, was allocated more than two-thirds. The Anglo-Saxon was by law regarded as the most desirable of Americans. Lodge, ailing and on the eve of death, was at last redeemed. The victory of the nativists was now, for all practical purposes, complete.

The newer immigrants, however, did not take graciously to their defeat. They were sensitive to its implications and they resented them profoundly. On October 30, 1926, the *Italian News* of Boston reflected this feeling vividly in a pre-election editorial directed against Lodge's successor, Senator William Morgan Butler.

> Senator Butler . . . belongs to that party which sponsored and supported the . . . Immigration Bill, that damnable measure . . . . As a result, . . . it is recorded in Congress today that the Italian people and other races from Southern Europe have had their quota reduced because they do not belong to the Nordic strain and therefore they are inferior human beings. And so . . . OUR DAY IS AT HAND. IT WILL COME NEXT TUESDAY.

Butler was, as the *Italian News* recommended, beaten for reelection. And there were many more Tuesdays in November that the Republicans had to face.

Did the Republican party's victory come too late? Had the Yankee community waited too long to close the dikes against the immigrant?

Unquestionably, the ends of the Republican party and the Yankee culture that it embodied were served by the new immigration policy. In 1903, Italy had sent 230,000 of its people to the United States; in 1913, the number was 265,000; by 1923, immigration had been reduced to 47,000; in 1933, the number was only 3,500. In 1903, there were 136,000 Russian emigrants to the United States, most of them Jews; in 1913, the figure had risen to 291,000; ten years later it had dropped to 21,000 and in 1933 it was a mere 458. As for the Irish, they had passed the peak of immigration by the twentieth century, but in 1903, there were still 35,000 immigrants; in 1913, 28,000 Irish entered the country; in 1923, the number dropped below 16,000; a decade later it was 338. Thus were the city machines deprived of their traditional troop reinforcements from abroad. The powerful showing the Republican party made throughout the 1920's certainly seemed to confirm that the Yankees had acted in time to stanch the flow of challengers from abroad.

But there were a few who foresaw trouble. In 1926, an old-stock Yankee named Daniel Chauncey Brewer wrote a book called *The Conquest of New England by the Immigrant*. In his lamentation over the growing power of immigrant blocs, he maintained:

> The least imaginative Yankee could hardly have asked better notice of the cataclysm that was to overwhelm this favored section than was offered by the incorporation of these societies. . . . Shrewd enough you were in your own conceit, you Yankees who welcomed . . . immigration, but you were coquetting with forces to which your grandchildren would pay tribute.

Throughout the 1920's, such predictions of doom were peculiarly unpersuasive. Since 1896, the Democrats had won only two victories, both under circumstances that hardly suggested permanent strength. But when the Republican party suddenly fell apart during the crisis of the Great Depression, the importance to national power of the vote now denoted, with some sophistication, as "ethnic" became painfully obvious. It did indeed suggest that immigration restrictions had come too late.

CHAPTER 7

The Lost Opportunities

Br the last years of the nineteenth century, it had become painfully evident what the unalloyed practice of the Puritan ethic had done to the country. The pursuit of riches had rendered industry oppressive, the farm impoverished, labor embittered, the city pestilent, politics base. In creating a nation of great wealth, American business enterprise and its political spokesman, the Republican party, had wrought vast human misery. But the Puritan ethic and its philosophical offshoot, Social Darwinism, taught them not to worry. Misery, it was asserted, was the misfortune of those who bore it, not the responsibility of those who created it.

Run wild, the Puritan ethic had insensitized the nation's leaders. Social morality was all but dead. As Morison and Commager, scrupulous historians, tell it:

> The manufacture and sale of impure foods, of dangerous drugs, of infected milk, of poisonous toys, might produce disease or death, but none of those involved in the process—retailers, wholesalers, manufacturers, advertisers, corporation directors, or stockholders—realized that they were guilty of murder . . . . Improper inspection of banks, insurance companies and trust companies, false statements in a company prospectus, speculation in stocks, in gold, or in grain, might bring poverty and misery to thousands, but none of

those involved in the process realized that they were guilty of larceny. Business competition might force the employment of children of eight or nine years of age in mines and in mills or dictate the use of woman labor in sweatshops, but none of those involved in the process realized that they were guilty of maintaining slavery. The purchase of votes, the corruption of election officials, the bribing of legislators, the lobbying of special bills, the flagrant disregard of laws, might threaten the very foundations of democratic government, but none of those involved in the process realized that they were guilty of treason to representative government.

But however accurately Morison and Commager describe the conditions of the day, surely they must exaggerate when they maintain that "none of those involved" was aware of any culpability. There had always been, outside the Puritan establishment, a few voices that were ready to denounce the moral indifference of business practices. As the century approached an end, a few even appeared within the Yankee establishment itself. Edward A. Ross, as thorough a Yankee as the Midwest produced, extolled Anglo-Saxon supremacy, despised Jews, and regarded American values as the hope of the future. But he learned to loathe commercial ethics and their exclusion of all sense of social responsibility. To Ross, it was total hypocrisy that "the modern high-powered dealer of woe wears immaculate linen, carries a silk hat and a lighted cigar, sins with calm countenance and a serene soul, leagues or months from the evil he causes. Upon his gentlemanly presence the eventual blood and tears do not obtrude themselves."

Quietly, there was growing throughout these years a body of thought and practice that challenged the orthodoxies of the Puritan ethic. This body had no revolutionary design, nor was it to have a revolutionary impact. Rather its tendency was to soften the harshness of a Puritanism that Social Darwinism had made even more rigid. Ultimately it was to flower in the program of the Progressive era, in the effort to modify Puritan conduct without changing Puritan goals.

It is not coincidental that the years in which this new Puritan outlook was developing were the years of the vast immigration from southern and eastern Europe. The Puritan, always disturbed a little by the foreigner, was now becoming convinced that the new immigration was transforming his society. The "safety valve," the lands of the West, was closed. The immigrants were jammed into fetid slums, and, amid signs of unrest, control of the cities was slipping from Yankee hands. Change was upsetting the old patterns of power and status, and the Puritan, in bewilderment, was becoming alarmed. The receptivity of some Puritan circles to innovation was a symptom of the alarm.

Pragmatism, presented to the Puritan by William James, was a direct assault on Herbert Spencer's Social Darwinist thinking. It challenged the Spencerian contention that man must seek his fortune within the framework of an environment that he was essentially powerless to change. In contrast to the Spencerian view that man was the victim of an inexorable evolutionary process, the pragmatists maintained that the human mind, different from any other instrument in the animal kingdom, could modify environment to make it more conducive to human development. Pragmatism taught that the exercise of human powers could make an enormous difference in the social order. In short, while the Spencerians stood on the side of collective determinism, the pragmatists restored to the Puritan ethic a belief in the power of the individual free will. To the Puritan, pragmatism represented a liberation from static dogma and an introduction to the prospect of humane experimentation. For those who would accept it, pragmatism was an invitation to social action.

Among the first to accept the invitation were a few clergymen of the Puritan churches, who had noticed that something was amiss in the practice of their faith. They could not conceal the fact that their churches served as handmaidens to the rich and ignored the misfortunes of the poor, particularly the immigrants. "The great body of rich churches," said the Reverend Jesse H. Jones, one of the first ministers to become identified with the cause of labor, "if forced to the issue would . . . deliberately set up some form of paganism, rather than submit to the thorough preaching of the truth . . . concerning property." Protestant churches had abdicated responsibility for going into the slums and tended to follow wealth wherever it settled. Characteristic was the prominent minister who, when he learned from an 1888 census that 60 percent of Protestant men came from the upper classes, took the data to mean that "evangelical Christianity pays."

The Puritan was perplexed by the vigor of the Catholic Church, which was overwhelmingly a lower class and immigrant institution. "The Catholic Church," said Richard Ely, a leader in the effort to reconcile Protestantism with the demands of the industrial era, "revealed an acquaintance with the movements of the masses —the Protestant ignorance." "Too long," agreed a conference of Methodists in 1889, "has Rome been allowed a practical monopoly of the humanitarian agencies of religion."

In the last decades of the century, a movement known as the Social Gospel grew up within the Puritan churches. It rejected the practices of the Puritan majority and promoted a doctrine of concern for human distress and social injustice. It put great effort into philanthropy and made alliances with labor unions. It called upon the state to intervene in behalf of the poor, while imposing restraints upon the rich. The Social Gospel was never more than a minority movement, but it pointed a way for Puritans willing to open their minds to social realities.

On the lay side, too, Puritans began to provide leadership in correcting social evils, often working hand in hand with the followers of the Social Gospel. The Americanization of the immigrant was normally their goal, which in its humane form meant easing the newcomer's adjustment to his new environment. Jane Addams and her disciples did magnificent work in establishing settlement houses in slum neighborhoods throughout the country. The Young Men's Christian Association was transformed from an organization purveying middle-class values to one offering valuable services to the poor. The Salvation Army was founded in the United States and gave its help to the most downtrodden members of the community. The benevolence of those who participated in these efforts stood in sharp relief against those who remained wedded to the orthodox Puritan ethic.

Perhaps more characteristic of the Puritan's response to the immigrant menace was the Americanization campaign waged by the patriotic societies. These societies had been founded during this very period as an assertion of Yankee cultural superiority. Their concept of Americanization, in contrast to that of Jane Addams, was that "obedience to law . . . [was] the groundwork of true citizenship." Their objective was nothing less than to impose a benign Yankee conformity upon the entire country. The patriotic societies' Americanization program, no less than the Social Gospel and the settlement-house movement, represented the Yankee's tardy awakening to social change. Each of these movements, in its own way, was to channel its energy and its outlook into Progressivism and become a stimulus in the drive to reform.

The Progressive movement, as a political undertaking, proceeded from the conviction of many Puritans that American business practice had become a national vice, while politics was corruption itself. It sought reform by ending the amoral impersonality that had come to characterize American institutions. It aimed to restore to them a Puritan sense of personal responsibility. It opposed the concentration of self-serving power in big business and in political organizations. It sought, nostalgically, to return to a purer era, when the individual presumably possessed greater control over his destiny, and personal ethics ruled in relations between men. Though the touchstone of the Progressive movement was social and political reform, it projected no fundamental alteration in wealth or power. Humane as the Progressive movement often showed itself to be, underneath there lay the Yankee's fear of the loss of his rank at the top of the American social hierarchy.

Brooks Adams, the pessimistic Brahmin who turned Progressive out of distaste for the crassness of business society, wrote that "privileged classes seldom have the intelligence to protect themselves by adaptation when nature turns against them and, up to the present moment, the old privileged class in the United States has shown little promise of being an exception to the rule." The Progressive movement was the American privileged class's attempt at adaptation.

Progressivism, then, was a movement that was Puritan in its

origin and its inspiration. A study of its leaders shows that they were overwhelmingly Northern urban Protestants. Naturally enough, the movement was focused in the Republican party, the Puritan's political arm, although the Democrats, almost from the beginning, came down with some of its contagious reformist feeling. Taking on momentum at the turn of the century, the Progressive movement became a major effort by the Puritan elite to streamline its methods in the legitimate interest of its self-preservation.

In the West, the Progressive movement was, basically, nothing more than a fresh surge of Populism, though it was perhaps less concentrated than Populism in the rural areas. The reforms it called for were essentially Populist in origin and flavor. It sought to undo the concentration of political power through such devices as the direct election of senators, the primary election, and the procedures known as initiative, referendum, and recall. It continued to inveigh against the railroads and the banks. When the Progressive movement made its start, most of the old Populists, save for the few that had become Bryan Democrats, swung comfortably behind it.

The East, however, far more than the West, gave Progressivism its distinctive quality. There it emerged directly out of the immigrant's presence in the cities and the threat his presence posed to the existing patterns of power. In contrast to Populism, Progressivism possessed all the sophistication of an urban movement. But more important than its style was the fact that its chief source of strength came not, like that of the Populists, from outsiders—but from genuine political insiders, those who lived in and ran the cities and were close to the levers of national power. This proximity to power, complemented by a familiarity with its processes, gave the Progressives an incomparable advantage over the Populists of the generation before. Whatever was fresh about Progressivism lay in the leadership that Eastern city Yankees, no longer content with their role in life, imparted to the movement.

Henry L. Stimson, among the noblest of the dying breed of old Yankee aristocrats, summed up the objectives of the Progressive leadership in a letter he wrote to Theodore Roosevelt. However appalled he was at the excesses of the business community, Stimson had no intention of slipping to the other extreme of letting power come into the possession of the immigrant Americans. He believed that government should be the affair of those dedicated to established values. It should be run by men of proven disinterestedness, distracted by neither venality nor poverty. In brief, he was convinced of the virtues of the Yankee elite. Stimson was a reformer, but he would reform for conservative ends, in the tradition of the British Tories. With a candor that was probably unintentional, Stimson wrote:

> To me it seems vitally important that the Republican party, which contains, generally speaking, the richer and more intelligent citizens of the country, should take the lead in reform and not drift into a reactionary position. If, instead, the leadership should fall into the hands of either an independent party, or a party composed, like the Democrats, largely of foreign elements and the classes which will immediately benefit by the reform, and if the solid business Republicans should drift into new obstruction, I fear the necessary changes could hardly be accomplished without much excitement and possible violence.

One need scarcely look further for the meaning of the Progressive movement. It was a challenge to the "stand-pat" strategy of Mark Hanna and the Old Guard Republicans. More important, it was the instrument of that segment of the Yankee community, unfriendly to the nouveaux riches of big business, which sought to maintain its position by the expedient of adjusting to change.

Politically, Progressivism largely followed the fortunes of Theodore Roosevelt, a man of great contradictions, but, like Stimson, acutely conscious of his rank within the Yankee aristocracy. It was Roosevelt who wrote in his autobiography that though his friends chose not to soil themselves in New York City's politics, "I intended to be one of the governing class." In sharp distinction to Henry Adams, for example, who withdrew gloomily from the status struggle and sat around denouncing bankers and Jews, Roosevelt intended to fight to preserve the social system of which he was at the pinnacle. It was this quality of aggressiveness, rather than any originality of mind, that propelled Theodore Roosevelt to the leadership of the Progressive movement.

As as young man, Roosevelt's ideas were conventionally, even cruelly, upper class. In 1886, when he was twenty-eight years old and in love with the West, he sounded more like Luther heaping anathema on rebellious peasants than a twentieth-century reformer. He wrote: "I don't go so far as to think that the only good Indians are the dead Indians, but I believe nine out of every ten are, and I shouldn't like to inquire too closely into the case of the tenth. The most vicious cowboy has more moral principle than the average Indian."

In 1894, by which time he should have known better, Roosevelt applauded the dispatch of Federal troops to Chicago to suppress the railroad strike, on grounds that it prevented "a repetition of what occurred during the Paris Communes." To a friend, he wrote: "I know the Populists and the laboring men well and their faults . . . I like to see a mob handled by the regulars, or by good State Guards, not overscrupulous about bloodshed." Two years later he complained that Bryan's candidacy "raised the evil spirit of revolution" and he was quoted in a New York paper as saying that radicalism should be suppressed, "as the Communes of Paris were suppressed, by taking ten or a dozen of them against a wall and shooting them dead."

But at some point, Theodore Roosevelt converted from frontier Puritanism to the Social Gospel. The reasons for his transformation are difficult to determine. His political ambitions may provide some explanation, along with his exposure to Progressive friends. But what is perhaps fundamental was his membership in an aristocracy of old and established values. Roosevelt had no commitment to the business community. He despised the business mentality and the single-minded pursuit of wealth. He found the nouveaux riches irresponsible and uncultured. "Even to dine with them, save under exceptional circumstances," he wrote in 1901, "fills me with frank horror." What they were doing, he insisted, was theatening the real values of American society by polarizing the nation into hostile classes. Roosevelt revealed much about his thinking when he said:

We stand equally against government by a plutocracy and government by a mob. There is something to be said for government by a great aristocracy which has furnished leaders to the nation in peace and war for generations; even a democrat like myself must admit this. But there is absolutely nothing to be said for government by a plutocracy, for government by men very powerful in certain lines and gifted with "the money touch," but with ideals which in their essence are merely those of so many glorified pawnbrokers.

It is interesting that Roosevelt, who enjoyed calling himself a "democrat," nonetheless extolled the virtues of "government by a great aristocracy." For it is within the framework of an aristocratic mentality that Theodore Roosevelt became the leader of the Progressive movement.

In his *Autobiography,* Roosevelt tells a revealing story about how, when he was a member of the New York State Assembly, he was converted to the support of a reform measure which, minor though it was, violated the strictures of individualism as he had learned them throughout his life. It is a story of an aristocrat's education. Roosevelt wrote:

A bill was introduced by the Cigarmakers' Union to prohibit the manufacture of cigars in tenement-houses.... I had supposed I would be against the legislation, . . . for the respectable people I knew were against it; it was contrary to the principles of political economy of the laissez-faire kind, and the business men who spoke to me about it shook their heads and said that it was designed to prevent a man doing as he wished and as he had a right to do with what was his own.

However, my first visits to the tenement-house districts in question made me feel that, whatever the theories might be, as a matter of practical common sense I could not conscientiously vote for the continuance of the conditions which I saw. These conditions rendered it impossible for the families of the tenement-house workers to live so that the children might grow up fitted for the exacting duties of American citizenship. I visited the tenement-houses once with my colleagues of the committee, once with some of the labor-union representatives, and once or twice by myself. In a few of the tenement-houses there were suites of rooms ample in number where the work on the tobacco was done in rooms not occupied for cooking or sleeping or living. In the overwhelming majority of cases, however, there were one, two, or three room apartments, and the work of manufacturing the tobacco by men, women, and children went on day and night in the eating, living and sleeping rooms—sometimes in one room. I have always remembered one room in which two families were living. On my inquiry as to who the third adult male was I was told that he was a boarder with one of the families. There were several children, three men, and two women, in this room. The tobacco was stowed about everywhere, alongside the foul bedding, and in a corner where there were scraps of food. The men, women and children in this room worked by day and far on into the evening, and they slept and ate there. They were Bohemians, unable to speak English, except that one of the children knew enough to act as interpreter.

Instead of opposing the bill I ardently championed it. . . . The governor signed the bill. Afterward . . . the court of appeals declared the law unconstitutional, and in their decision the judges reprobated the law as an assault upon the "hallowed" influences of "home." . . . The judges who rendered this decision were well-meaning men. They knew nothing whatever of tenement-house conditions; they knew nothing whatever of the needs, or of the life and labor, of three fourths of their fellow citizens in great cities. They knew legalism, but not life . . .

It is important to note that even in describing his conversion, Theodore Roosevelt did not claim that his goal was the replacement of inhuman with decent conditions for impoverished people. Progressivism was not meant to overturn the Puritan ethic. It simply was to apply pragmatism to its practice. What most upset Roosevelt was that "these conditions rendered it impossible for the families of the tenement-house workers to live so that the children might grow up fitted for the exacting duties of American citizenship." In other words, Theodore Roosevelt, like Progressives generally, was appalled not so much by the horrors of American life as by the prospect of a social revolution to sweep those horrors away. Brooks Adams believed that if Roosevelt, by his political dynamism, succeeded in thwarting the capitalists, he could assure them, in spite of themselves, fifty more years of protection. But it was not easy to persuade the ruling class that its political convictions, which were a major source of its great success, ought to be uprooted. Yankee society, as a whole, was not particularly receptive to the prospect of modifying the Puritan code.

When Roosevelt succeeded to the Presidency in 1901, he faced a Republican party that had no intention of letting him become an instrument of economic and social reform. The party not only confronted him with implacable opposition to new legislation but with the threat of abandonment in the next election. These factors fed the conservative objectives of Roosevelt's Progressivism. Energetic but intellectually uncertain of himself, contemplating Progressivism as a means to the same ends as the most "stand-pat" Republicans, Roosevelt generated during his years in office far more smoke than fire. He was strong on moralisms but weak on performance, fond of dramatizing his positions but unwilling to stand up for them over Old Guard objections, courageous in denouncing the "malefactors of great wealth" but retiring about taking any of that wealth away from them. To be sure, his dynamism revealed a new potential in the Presidential office, but on his leaving office in 1909, the trusts were more powerfully entrenched than ever. As Morison and Commager put it: ". . . after seven years of tumult and shouting had passed, many reformers came to feel that they had been fighting a sham battle and that the citadels of privilege were yet to be invested."

It was in foreign policy that Roosevelt was most aggressive, as well as most successful in finding a program congenial to both wings of the party. Building on the Republican party's tradition of involvement in international politics, Roosevelt made the United States into a power that exercised influence over global matters. Not only did he push around Colombia to build the Panama Canal and invade Santo Domingo to keep Europe out of the Western Hemisphere, but he also successfully mediated a war between Russia and Japan, for which he won the Nobel peace prize, and helped avert another by intervening between hostile European powers at the conference of Algeciras. He cemented American ties with England and France, and, at one point, even came close to making an alliance with the British. His policies pleased the Old Guard, which contemplated markets and investments, and thrilled the Progressives, who saw them as disinterested and idealistic. Furthermore, they confirmed the popular image of the Republican party as keeper of the national honor. They added much to Roosevelt's popularity and to the party's stature in the eyes of the electorate.

Led by this patrician from New York, renowned for his brave words in all manner of foreign and domestic questions, the Republican party bid fair for this fleeting moment to become the party of the people. When Roosevelt wrested the nomination from the "stand-pat" faction in 1904, he could genuinely claim a victory over the special interests in the struggle for popular government. The Democrats, by repudiating their Bryan wing to nominate the conservative Alton B. Parker, seemed to be playing into Roosevelt's hands. With the Democrats to the right of the Republicans, Roosevelt won by a record popular margin. Presumably the potential now existed for the Republican party to transform itself into a permanently progressive instrument of government. As such, the party was potentially unbeatable.

The story has often been told how Roosevelt passed up an array of proven Progressives to select as his successor William Howard Taft, a relatively obscure Ohioan of uncertain convictions. As Roosevelt's candidate, Taft easily defeated the Democrats' William Jennings Bryan, who was making his third try for the Presidency. Taft began his term promisingly enough. But when he undertook to obtain a general tariff reduction—which Roosevelt never had the audacity to attempt—he was completely outmaneuvered by big business and wound up instead with a general increase. Had Taft vetoed the bill, he would have become a Progressive hero. Had he remained silent about it, he might have restored himself ultimately to the good graces of the movement. But not only did he approve the tariff but he called it "the best ever passed by the Republican party." From that moment, Progressivism was no longer ascendant and the Republican party was back in "stand-pat" control.

The fight, however, was not over. The Progressives had strong support, often for totally diverse reasons, in different sections of the country. Throughout 1909 and 1910, it appeared that the struggle for power would be a long one, in which neither side would emerge decisive for many years to come. But then Theodore Roosevelt declared open war. In declaring that only his own restoration to the Presidency would save Progressivism, Roosevelt created a naked confrontation between the party's two wings. Against heavy odds, he determined that he must bend the party to his will or break it. With Taft as its unenthusiastic leader, the "stand-pat" wing accepted the challenge and the battle was on.

The Roosevelt who campaigned for the Presidential nomination in 1912 looked on himself as the intellectual as well as the political chief of Progressivism. He referred to himself now as a "radical," though he qualified the description by vowing his preference for conservative methods. He spoke of the "square deal" for the poor man, changing the "rules of the game," and running the government for the "welfare of the people." He was clearly talking now of a redistribution of wealth, with government as the agent. Whether his words should be interpreted as a strategem for defeating the Old Guard or as a genuine shift in convictions, Roosevelt was certainly purveying something far more potent than he had practiced only a few years before. But whatever his arguments, his personal following was so strong that he could count on a vast body of popular support.

As the nominating convention of 1912 grew closer, there was among the Republicans a feeling of impending doom. Such old friends of Roosevelt's as Stimson and Elihu Root begged him not to break up the party. On the Taft side, there were pleas for withdrawal in favor of a compromise candidate. Neither man, however, could be deterred. Roosevelt won the primary elections, but Taft, who controlled the party machinery, had the enormous advantage of disposing of the support of the "rotten boroughs" of the South, equal in convention votes to the combined delegations of New York, Pennsylvania, Illinois, Ohio, Massachusetts, Indiana, and Iowa. When Roosevelt charged Taft with "robbery and fraud" for making use of these votes, the two sides broke irrevocably apart. Since Taft had the strength to take the nomination, Roosevelt ordered his supporters to bolt and form a new party. Roosevelt took the Progressive name—though the undertaking was more familiarly called "Bull Moose"—and much of the reformist ardor within the Republican ranks.

But Roosevelt's candidacy also evoked deep hostility. Most of the old ruling elite, to say nothing of the business Republicans, felt that he had gone too far. A decade before, the party had indulged Roosevelt in his innocuous reforms. Now his program was not only radical but, more important, he had committed the unpardonable sin of disloyalty by wrecking the Yankees' political arm. Treason was unforgivable.

Francis Biddle, a Philadelphia aristocrat who was among those who made the transition from conservative Republicanism to Theodore Roosevelt, gave a hint in his memoirs of the feelings aroused in the 1912 campaign. He wrote:

> T. R. appealed particularly to youth, with its unfrayed nerves and sense of living in the present moment and dreaming of the promises of American life. . . . T. R. was not crude or raw. I saw him two or three times during the campaign. When he came into a crowded room it was like a rush of wind that at once seemed to touch everyone, and each eye was brighter, each pulse faster . . .

But Biddle's friends were not moved by Roosevelt.

> In Philadelphia among the correct and the elite it was not respectable to favor Roosevelt's campaign, and enthusiasm in that direction was greeted by a shudder of disapproval. My brother Moncure's reaction was shocked—and typical . . . he wrote me that he was sorry that I was backing a man "whom every sane citizen deprecates to the extent of using abusive language—a thoroughly unstable and dangerous demagogue." . . . Henry James shortly after the election

expressed the horror of his class for a man who had deserted it: "I must simply state to you . . ." he wrote, "that I can't so much as think of Mr. R. for 2 consecutive moments: he has become to me, these last months, the mere monstrous embodiment of unprecedented, resounding Noise—the noisiest figure or agency of any kind in the long, dire annals of the human race."

Fortune was not with Roosevelt in the 1912 campaign, for the Democrats, on the forty-sixth ballot, came up with a candidate who disputed with him the claim to the allegiance of the Progressive movement. Woodrow Wilson was far more formidable than Alton B. Parker, his conservative opponent in 1904, and even than Bryan himself, whom Taft had handily defeated in 1908. With the South conceded to the Democratic party, Wilson could concentrate his attention on challenging Roosevelt for the Northern Progressive vote. To make matters worse, Debs, the Socialist, competed for Roosevelt's labor supporters. Roosevelt campaigned with great vigor, but his defeat was foredoomed.

Still, Roosevelt did remarkably well. He outpolled Taft by a substantial margin, which suggested that among Republicans he was the more popular candidate. In the North, he fought Wilson to a virtual deadlock, although Debs won almost a million votes. Roosevelt carried California, Michigan, Minnesota, Pennsylvania, South Dakota, and Washington. In electoral votes, however, he was defeated by 435 to 88. He failed because he could not persuade nearly enough Democrats to switch their allegiance to make him President.

For the cause of Progressivism within the Republican party, the election was a disaster. The split between the two wings had been so sharp that subsequent reconciliation was impossible. Had Roosevelt won, he might have isolated the business Republicans in a political realignment. But in defeat he was powerless. The Old Guard controlled the party machinery, more than ever determined to use it to suppress the heresy. The Progressives who sought to transform Roosevelt's efforts into a long-term crusade were left without effective arms. The "stand-pat" crowd would let the apostates back into the party, but on its own terms. After 1912, the Republican Progressives, who just a few years before had stood a good chance to capture the party, were left all but impotent.

Having forced the Progressives to risk all on his candidacy, Theodore Roosevelt now seemed to lose interest in the movement. A few Progressives tried desperately to keep the cause alive, hoping to run Roosevelt as a third-party candidate again in 1916. But Roosevelt was devoting his attention to whipping up enthusiasm for American involvement in the war in Europe, perhaps with an eye to reuniting the party around his candidacy as a Republican regular. When it finally became clear that the Old Guard would have nothing to do with him, he proposed to the Progressives that they make Henry Cabot Lodge their Presidential nominee. Ludicrous as nomination of such a reactionary seemed, to Roosevelt it apparently made sense. Lodge, after all, shared with the Progressives a contempt for the capitalist rich, as well as the aim of restoring government to responsible Yankee hands. The proposal suggests strongly that Roosevelt, despite his pretensions to being a democrat, still understood Progressivism as a Yankee effort to reclaim the prerogatives of the ruling class. Finally, the Progressives did nominate Roosevelt, their only saleable commodity, against his will. When he refused to accept, they abandoned their effort in disgust, and their organization, such as it was, disintegrated ignominiously. Roosevelt, with apparent indifference, simply quit the movement he had sired and left it to die.

Ironically, it was the Democrats who absorbed the Progressive program that had gestated within the Republican party, just as they had absorbed Populism in 1896. Woodrow Wilson, middle-class scion of Calvinist ministers and as nearly a Puritan as the South might be expected to produce, was virtually forced into assuming direction of the Progressive movement. In 1912, he had denounced Roosevelt for radicalism and made no more concessions to the progressive spirit in the Democratic party than seemed necessary to retain its allegiance. As President, Wilson's dedication to reform seemed to fluctuate with expediency. It was not until the eve of the 1916 election, when he recognized that he needed Roosevelt's old supporters to win, that a great burst of social legislation emerged from his Administration. Still, the record showed that whatever the motivation, Wilson had provided the leadership for remarkable achievements in reform. Wilson had snatched the Progressive banner from Roosevelt's hands and planted it squarely in the Democratic camp.

Having been abandoned by Roosevelt, the Progressives in 1916 scattered over the political terrain. When the Republicans nominated Charles Evans Hughes, a moderate reformer, many of them found sufficient reason to return to the old party. Some of the most active, curiously, simply dropped out of partisan politics and remained in political limbo. But a third group marched directly into the Democratic party. Generally, it was not easy for them to make the change. The Yankee prejudice against Democrats remained strong. But the exodus nonetheless began, led, it is interesting to note, by those who had been active in the Social Gospel and settlement-house movements long before they heard of the Progressive party. How many hundreds of thousands of voters they brought with them it is impossible to ascertain, although computations indicate that 20 percent of those who had voted for Roosevelt in 1912 switched to Wilson in 1916. What is more certain is that the intellectual community, in overwhelming measure, transferred its allegiance from the Progressives to the Democrats, a loss the Republicans could ill afford. By the time the fuss had died down, it appeared that the leaders of progressive—later called "liberal"—thinking found the Democratic party more hospitable, while the more conventional Progressives, those of less fervent conviction, the numerical majority, were content to return to the Republicans.

In retrospect, it seems that the Progressive movement within the Republican party had always been destined to failure. As a serious political force, it was, after all, the product of the personality of one man, Theodore Roosevelt. Though the party had other luminaries more dedicated to Progressive beliefs, without Roosevelt they would never have amassed sufficient strength to challenge the Old Guard leadership. Had Roosevelt foresworn the bitter struggle of 1912, Progressivism might for many more years have stayed in the contest for party dominance. But any movement that depended so heavily on a single leader was probably too thin in resources to win a permanent victory.

Perhaps the real meaning of the Progressive's failure within the Republican party is best summed up in a chance remark that Henry L. Stimson makes in his memoirs. Stimson, the Yankee aristocrat, was an early follower of Roosevelt. In that he was nobly endowed with a spirit of public service, he was a genuine Progressive. But his Progressivism was bloodless and detached. In describing his political activity in the decade after World War I, he wrote in his timid, third-person fashion: "He was active in behalf of his favorite reform, the executive budget." Surely, any man in public life whose favorite reform is the executive budget still has not quite made his adjustment to the demands of the twentieth century. Stimson was without venality, even devoid of self-interest. But if the *reformers* of a political party look to a goal no grander than the executive budget, what then can be the objectives of the rest of the party?

It is not quite accurate to say that World War I brought an end to the Progressive era or that it extinguished the zeal for reform. The Yankee felt more acutely than ever the threat to his power and status. The war, by evoking some atavistic response within the immigrant groups to danger in the motherland, demonstrated that Yankee values remained weak outside the Yankee community. Suddenly the Americanization campaign, with all its demand for conformity, was renewed with new and solemn fervor. The Progressive spirit, always preoccupied with assimilation, turned vengefully to cleansing the immigrant of his remaining cultural differences. The most dramatic reform was, of course, Prohibition. But the drive for purification went much further. "The time and effort formerly spent by the Protestant 'church lobby' and women's organizations on behalf of labor and welfare measures," wrote J. Joseph Huthmacher about Massachusetts, "were now largely devoted to legislation forbidding Sunday movies, to warding off attempts to legalize professional boxing in the state, and to pressuring the legislature for an act to make the state's liquor laws conform with the national Prohibition code. Even when they did endorse social welfare measures in the 1920's, the old-stock groups tended to emphasize their 'Americanizing' features above all else." And so moved onward the Progressive spirit, unabashedly coercive in its postwar incarnation in behalf of Puritan goals.

As it turned away from the humane Progressivism of an earlier day, the Republican party also surrendered—more, apparently, by force of circumstances than by preconceived design—its vigorous patronage of American internationalism. The Republicans, after years of leading the preparedness fight, were cheated of the glory of commanding the nation at war by the chance presence of a Democrat in the Presidency. They then took the leadership in pressing for American participation in a postwar League of Nations. Taft, Lodge, and Charles Evans Hughes, the Presidential candidate in 1916, as well as the American Chamber of Commerce, were all on record in favor of a League. Yet so bitter had relations between Wilson and the Republicans become by the end of the war that the party chose to oppose the League organized at Versailles rather than back the Democratic President. Lodge, the party's most powerful figure after Roosevelt died in January, 1919, led the vendetta, while Wilson fanned the fury by his irritable, uncompromising response to all criticism. The final defeat of the treaty was represented as a great Republican triumph. But it placed the Republicans irrevocably on the side of isolation in international affairs, a position unworthy of their history and traditions.

Yet perhaps it was inevitable that the Puritan party take the leadership in isolationism. The exclusionary nature of the Puritan outlook made working with other nations on a footing of equality difficult at best. "From the beginning," wrote Henry Steele Commager, "Americans have thought that they were a chosen people, have insisted on New World innocence and Old World corruption, and have rejoiced in their isolationism." The imperialism in which Republican administrations engaged could scarcely be classified as foreign relations. The Puritan believed that the British and the French, chief among the powers of the day, were amoral in their diplomacy and not to be trusted. It was better to deal with nations that the United States could dominate—in Latin America, for instance. And so the Republican party maintained its claim to speak for American nationalism, only now it was a kind of ingrown, faint-hearted, negative nationalism, without a romantic quality or the capacity to fire ideals. To be sure, in the postwar era the isolationist position was popular, but it deprived the Republicans of the last positive element in the program they offered to the electorate.

By 1920, Theodore Roosevelt was dead, and the Republican image was in the hands of Warren Harding and Calvin Coolidge, the essence of Puritan conventionality. Harding called for a return to "normalcy," by which he meant Republican rule of the McKinley vintage. Indeed, his margin in the 1920 election suggested that the voters were remorseful about their experiment with the Democrats and wanted nothing more. As for Coolidge, he was all but a caricature of the Yankee Puritan. His philosophical utterances, beginning with "the business of America is business," sounded more like satire than a real expression of the Puritan ethic. Economy in government, he said, was "the full test of our national character." He opposed unemployment insurance because it would give to workers money that they did not "earn." Social welfare measures were a disservice to the country because it was better "to let those who have made losses bear them than try to shift them onto someone else." It was also Coolidge who said:

The man who builds a factory builds a temple. . . . The man who works there worships there.

And

The law that builds up the people is the law that builds up industry.

William Allen White, the Puritan who had supported McKinley before turning Progressive, recorded how the Republicans under Coolidge became what they had not been even during the long years of loyalty to business from Grant to the end of the century. Coolidge, wrote White:

gave his leadership frankly, openly, proudly, to American business by direct rather than by indirect control. Heretofore for fifty years his party had served business through the leadership of politicians. They assumed to arbitrate between capital and government, between the people and organized plutocracy—government invisible and never quite brazen. Coolidge in a few months had wrecked that political liaison. He destroyed the arbitration myth by putting much of the control of the Republican party directly into business without moderation of the political machine.

Yet this, obviously, was what the Republicans wanted. "I think what America needs more than anything else," said Dwight Morrow, a prominent Republican who had once been known as a reformer, to Thomas Lamont, the celebrated New York financier, "is a man who will in himself be a demonstration of character. I think Coolidge comes more nearly being that man than any other man in either party." It was apparent by the mid-1920's that Puritan orthodoxy had regained all the ground it had lost during the Progressive era, and perhaps then some.

But the temperament of the country was not what it had been during McKinley's years, however satisfied Harding was with the restoration of "normalcy." After twenty intensive years, full of battles first against the "interests" and then against the Kaiser, the people were tired and ready for relief. They were indifferent to the global responsibilities about which Wilson, in schoolmaster fashion, unceasingly lectured them. The immigrant groups, each in its own way, were angry at the injustices done them under Wilson's leadership.* It was tempting to try the Republican promise of prosperity and tranquility. But if the voters rose up against the Democrats, politics could not repeal twenty years of social change. The Republicans, in Talleyrand's words, had "learned nothing and forgotten nothing," and "normalcy" could not paste back together again the once-upon-a-time world that Republicans had found so ideal.

It was only the Republican party that became what it had been twenty years before. In retrospect, one can see that for the Repub-

* See Chapter 5.

licans the years between McKinley and Harding were marked chiefly by lost opportunities. They had mobilized Progressive passions, then surrendered them to the Democrats. They had sown the country's martial ardor and watched the Democrats reap it. They had championed responsible internationalism, then turned inward to timid nationalism. They came to the threshold of winning the immigrant vote, only to spurn it. The Republicans emerged from two decades of high tempo in a state of self-satisfaction, negation, and intellectual impoverishment. A pseudo-prosperity was enough to immunize them against anything as dangerous as a fresh idea. It would not be long before the party's qualities were to be tested in profound national crisis. The Republicans would enjoy their "normalcy" for very little longer.

CHAPTER 8

The Fall from Grace

IT IS not as if there were no signs of discontent in the 1920's for perceptive Republicans to discern. The indices pointed to tremendous prosperity in the nation, but the wealth was concentrated in a relatively few hands, almost all of them in the Northern business community. American agriculture was severely ill, and as early as 1922, a Populist upsurge had begun to inflict defeat upon regular Republicans in the West. The Progressive revolt in 1924 made clear that the union workingman, scarcely less than the farmer, was disenchanted with Republican rule. Meanwhile, prohibition angered the immigrant, and indifference alienated the Negro. Though the Republicans, outwardly, had never been stronger, the joyful clatter of the ticker tape was deceptive. They lived with a ferment that was undermining the foundations of their strength, though they themselves, complacent with their riches, seemed the least aware of any threat.

The election of 1928 was an ominous one. In the Democratic party, the Eastern urban wing finally emerged victorious in the long struggle for power against the rural forces of the West and South. The Democrats nominated Alfred E. Smith, the governor of New York, for President. Smith was an Irish-Catholic, the first major Presidential candidate who was not an Anglo-Saxon white Protestant. He was also a "wet" on the Prohibition issue and a Tammany New Yorker. With his brown derby and New York twang, there was little about him that endeared him to Protestant America. His Republican opponent, Herbert Hoover, did not personally pander to bigotry in his campaign, but he made no great effort to suppress it. In high station and low, those willing to resort to it were numerous. Methodist Bishop James Cannon, for example, openly merchandised his conception of the election as a holy war to maintain Yankee supremacy in American society. He declared: "Governor Smith wants the Italians, the Sicilians, the Poles and the Russian Jews. That kind has given us a stomachache. We have been unable to assimilate such people in our national life. . . . He wants the kind of dirty people that you find today on the sidewalks of New York." Smith was hard pressed to counter this kind of opposition. But such naked appeals did much to accentuate the estrangement of Catholics and new-stock Americans from the Republican party.

It was symptomatic of a persistent misreading of events that in the election of 1928 the Republicans made their first effort since the days of Reconstruction to win the white South. In the past, they had accepted the axiom that they could not get both Southern white and Negro majorities and had agreed that their Negro constituency was safer. By now, more than a million Negroes lived in the North, and in some states Negroes actually held the balance of power between the two parties. With the end of immigration from Europe, the trend was unmistakably one of increasing Negro migration to the North. Yet Hoover decided that this was the moment to go after the white South, since Smith was all the things that Southerners most disliked about the North. At the national convention he saw to it that "lily-white" delegations were seated in preference to the traditional "black-and-tan" Republican leadership. During the campaign, he mobilized lily-white organizations to get out white Southern votes. Though he tried weakly to hold on to his Negro support, he did not succeed, and for the first time the Republicans suffered substantial defections from their ranks. Subsequent events showed that 1928 was a particularly poor time for the Republicans to abandon proven old friends in behalf of dubious new ones.

But the Republicans won the Presidential election by a large margin, so huge that it insensitized them to the warnings that lay imbedded in the returns. Having split the Solid South, they failed to perceive that for the first time the Democrats had not only taken much of the Negro vote but, more important, had broken their hold on the cities. In the dozen largest cities, which Bryan could not crack and the Republicans had carried only four years before by 1.3 million votes, Al Smith emerged with majorities. Thanks to Smith's appeal among immigrant groups, the Democrats for the first time won the electoral votes of Massachusetts, ancestral seat of Puritanism. They won little else in 1928, but they had no real reason for despair. Power was shifting into new hands. Throughout the country, the results indicated that the party was stronger than its Presidential candidate. The Protestant aversion to Catholics and immigrants, as well as the nation's prosperity, had defeated Smith. But in the Smith campaign, the new Democratic coalition was being forged.

Herbert Hoover, Smith's conqueror, was not an ordinary Republican like his immediate predecessors. If Coolidge was a caricature of the small-minded Puritan, Hoover was the Puritan larger-than-life. He was a brilliant engineer and a self-made millionaire, a man of superior intellect and deep conviction. As Secretary of Commerce, he had been the dominant figure in the Harding and Coolidge administrations. He was known for his humane qualities and had campaigned on a platform to eliminate poverty. Hoover was no commonplace politician. An idealist, he was convinced that the Republican party, in remaining faithful to the Puritan ethic, had been summoned to create a higher order of society for the United States.

Appropriately for a man of orthodox background, Hoover was a believer in laissez-faire. It was he who made the expression "rugged individualism" an integral part of the political lexicon. Yet he was not averse to abandoning laissez-faire in business's behalf without recognizing any contradiction in principle. Not only did he promote high tariffs to protect American industry, but he advocated modification of the antitrust laws to encourage an end to what he considered wasteful competition. "We are passing," he said, in speaking of business, "from a period of extreme individualistic action into a period of associated activities," in which he felt government should take the leadership. But he showed no comparable flexibility of spirit in contemplating the problems of agriculture, for instance, or of labor, Negroes, or the other constituencies of the electorate. Hoover shared the party's belief that there was something sacred about business. His economic policies emerged from his faith in the Puritan ethic, which he embraced as an infallible guide to morality.

When the Depression struck in the fall of 1929, Hoover reacted with stunned incredulity that his dogma had failed him. He was staggered by the collapse of business. Left without reliable precepts, he could preach old nostrums but he could not act. His prescription for ending the Depression was government retrenchment, a balanced budget, the gold standard, the protective tariff and—out of fear of undermining the national fiber—a relentless opposition to any program that smacked of the dole. This giant of a Republican, paralyzed by the Puritan ethic's sudden irrelevance, was powerless to examine the disaster empirically. He was bitter that the Puritan ethic, having led him through so many halcyon days, had left him in an economic wilderness, naked and unarmed.

Even as the Republicans floundered, it was by no means clear that the Depression would serve to crystalize the Democratic disarray into a rational and forceful position. The Democratic party, after all, never possessed the clear sense of mission that the Republicans had. The Democratic city bosses remained dedicated to a conception of the party as a siphon for political patronage. An important segment of the party seemed determined to surpass the Republicans in generosity to business. The Southern Bourbons held steadfastly to the contention that the party was an instrument for preserving the local social structure intact. The old Wilsonians still believed in a kind of Jeffersonian, egalitarian laissez-faire. Though prohibition, by 1932, had been eliminated as a divisive issue among Democrats, there was agreement on little else—least of all on positive liberalism as a palliative of the Depression, as an instrument of social justice, and as a binding force for a national coalition.

But in New York, a young aristocrat, who was coincidentally a cousin of Theodore Roosevelt, was shaping the philosophy that was to make him the nemesis of the Republican party. A member of the Roosevelt family's Democratic branch, he moved gradually toward the welfare liberalism that Al Smith had embodied. Ultimately he stepped out beyond it. In 1926, Franklin Delano Roosevelt declared:

> If we accept the phrase "the best government is the least government" we must understand that it applies to the simplification of government machinery, and to the prevention of improper interference with the legitimate private acts of the citizens, but a nation or a State which is unwilling by governmental action to tackle the new problems, caused by immense increase of population and by the astonishing strides of modern science, is headed for decline and ultimate death.

In challenging Jefferson's dictum on small government, Roosevelt was exposing the party's foundations to the harsh light of current conditions. Painfully, he reached the conclusion that government had to adopt new methods, though its goals might remain unchanged. Elected governor of New York in 1930, he won enactment of a daring and innovative program of agricultural, industrial, economic, and social reform. In 1932, he was ready to make his bid for the Presidency.

Roosevelt's nomination by no means implied a commitment by the Democratic party to liberal policies. Though Roosevelt had attacked business and called for Federal experimentation and planning, his selection can be attributed chiefly to the base of support he had established among Western farmers, and to the division of the opposition. As for the Republicans, they renominated Hoover, who had forfeited his popularity throughout the country but who had the support, in Stimson's words, of the

"people of sobriety and intelligence and responsibility." Despond-
ent about his chance of winning, Hoover conducted a dismal
campaign, in which one of his few boasts was that "we still
have a government in Washington that knows how to deal with
the mob." The "mob" saw to it that Roosevelt won 60 percent
of the popular vote, carrying 42 of the 48 states, and that the
Democrats gained heavy majorities in both Houses of Congress.
Except for the three-way race in 1912, never in its history had
the Republican party been so soundly thrashed.

Roosevelt's election was less a mandate for the victor than
a repudiation of the vanquished. Few voters had known the new
President or the kind of leadership they might expect of him.
The voters knew the Republicans, however, and they had had
enough of them. The constituencies which, ostensibly Republican,
had in reality been floating about in search of a claimant were
at last roosting on the Democratic doorstep. Depending on Roosevelt, they might remain there or they might not. The challenge
before Franklin Roosevelt was to shape a new Democratic coalition. Few foresaw how successful he would be. But, then, few
recognized at that point how lacking the Republicans were in
recuperative powers. For some seven decades they had deferred
payment on their debts. The arrears had mounted monumentally
and now it was too late. The voters were foreclosing.

What Roosevelt succeeded in achieving was union of the
two great traditions of American reform. One, which might
roughly be called Populism, had been pregnant in the Democratic party since the days of Bryan. The other, which even
more roughly might be called Progressivism, had been planted
among the Democrats by Wilson and given important new meaning by Al Smith. One rural, the other urban, these two traditions had generally been hostile to each other throughout the
party's history. Each had looked upon the other as a rival. Only
the Depression and Roosevelt's political skills forced them into
an alliance. With price supports on the one hand, social security
on the other, Roosevelt made the Democratic party into the
repository of both. These two traditions became the foundation
of the ..ew coalition.

The urban reforms of the New Deal were the most fundamental to Roosevelt's political revolution. They made organized
labor into an adjunct of the Democratic party. They made the
immigrant Americans more solidly Democratic than ever. They
transformed the Negroes into the party's single most loyal constituency. "My friends," said Robert L. Vann, publisher of the
Negro newspaper, the *Pittsburgh Courier*, "go home and turn
Lincoln's picture to the wall. That debt has been paid in full."
Into the Democratic councils were now admitted, as responsible
partners, Italians and Jews, Negroes and union officials. "We
have participated," said Sidney Hillman of the C.I.O., "in making
the labor policy of the administration." The New Deal turned
the industrial cities into the backbone of the Democratic party.
And the industrial cities were growing into the strongest political force in the nation.

The rural reforms of the New Deal brought the Yankee farmer
into Roosevelt's camp, to join that farm vote which had been
Democratic since the days of Jefferson and Jackson. But these reforms did not succeed, willingly as the Yankee farmer embraced
them, in making him into a real Democrat. The Yankee farmer's
conversion was of the mind, not of the heart. He acquired a new
willingness to vote Democratic in times of stress, to obtain legislative relief from his troubles. But he remained fundamentally
estranged from the city Democrats, from the Negroes and the
immigrants and the others whose way of life he did not understand and with whose needs he had no sympathy. The Yankee
farmer, Puritan in his passion, tended to drift back to the Republicans whenever he had no vital interest at stake. But he was
no longer, as he had been for seventy years, a Republican by
blind faith. The Democrats offered him programs he liked, and
more often than not, he responded favorably to them.

Under Roosevelt, the South, too, functioned as a major part-
ner in the Democratic coalition. Once it had been the dominant
power in the party. Smith's nomination in 1928 signaled its
decline, yet Roosevelt would not have been selected in 1932
without the South's approval. Though the most conservative
section of the country, the South was also the poorest and most
neglected; Roosevelt paid particular attention to seeing that it

received its fair share, and more, of help from the New Deal. Yet there was a paradox in a political party, whatever its label, that could speak for the Negro, North and South, and at the same time for the Southern white. The paradox was not so evident during the Depression, when the economic crisis was so severe that it obscured long-standing status concerns. But the crisis abated, the old political considerations reemerged. So the South made a new adjustment: it stayed within the Democratic party but worked against the party's egalitarian objectives. Though turmoil continued to grow in the South, tradition tended to keep it faithful. The role of the South thus became more anomalous and its future in the Democratic party more uncertain, but it remained attached to the coalition, dedicated not to what the party was but to what it had been.

Roosevelt culminated the fashioning of his coalition with a trade that brought him an important remnant of his cousin Theodore's Progressive party, plus a substantial segment of the intellectual community, in return for the remains of the Cleveland wing of the Democratic party. Harold Ickes, Donald Richberg, Frank Knox, Henry A. Wallace, Francis Biddle, John G. Winant, and Dean Acheson were among the old Progressives who became first-line New Dealers. They were joined by prestigious figures from Harvard, Columbia, and other major universities throughout the country. At the same time such prominent Democrats as Jouett Shouse and John J. Raskob, millionaire businessmen and former national chairmen, left the party over New Deal policies. Finally Al Smith himself, now a wealthy businessman and an embittered politician, took the stump against Roosevelt. As John W. Davis, Coolidge's challenger in 1924, declared: "In some mysterious way, the whole course and direction of our party seems to have changed." He was right; it had changed. It had become an instrument of popular government and, at the same time, the country's majority party.

Roosevelt's bold programs not only attracted new converts to the Democrats but evoked from the Republicans a resistance that laid bare the full thrust of their thinking. Charles McNary, the Republican Senate leader, warned that "a party cannot gain the attention of a people distraught by business and employment worries by extolling the nobility of the forefathers and the sanctity of the Constitution, and by spreading alarms over regimentation and bureaucracy." But the best that Herbert Hoover could propose was ". . . a recall of the spirit of individual service. That spirit springs from the human heart, not from politics. Upon that spirit alone can this democracy survive."

Not since the days of William Jennings Bryan had the contrast been so great between the social objectives of the competing parties. No less vigilant in defeat than they had been in victory, the Republicans fought tenaciously for the prerogatives of the ruling class. They seemed sworn to surrender nothing of the attributes of the old order.

Yet Roosevelt, for all his reforming, was no destroyer of the existing order. His patchwork of reforms, if anything, preserved the system against the radicals who regarded it as beyond redemption. Far from confiscating fortunes, Roosevelt shored up established wealth against the vicissitudes of economic collapse. For this, Roosevelt has been characterized, with accuracy, as a conservative. Nevertheless, with each successive New Deal enactment, the old ruling elite emitted fresh howls of excruciating pain.

In *Rendezvous with Destiny*, Eric Goldman quotes the cogent observation of an unidentified member of the middle-class, who said:

> For quite a while I have lived in a commuter community that is rabidly anti-Roosevelt and I am convinced that the heart of their hatred is not economic. The real source of the venom is that Rooseveltism challenged their feeling that they were superior people, occupying by right a privileged position in the world. I am convinced that a lot of them would even have backed many of his economic measures if they had been permitted to believe that the laws represented the fulfillment of their responsibility as "superior people." They were not permitted that belief. Instead, as the New Deal went on, it chipped away more and more at their sense of superiority.

What the New Deal did was to bestow on whole new groups of Americans a share in the national decision-making process. Rule of the nation was shifted out of the domain of the Yankee elite, where it had reposed during the long era of Republican hegemony. Symbolically, the repeal of prohibition signaled the end of the Yankee's mastery of American society. In this sense, the New Deal's reforms were profound. In the words of the sociologist, Joseph Gusfield: "We have always understood the desire to defend fortune. We should also understand the desire to defend respect. It is less clear because it is symbolic in nature but it is not less significant."

If the New Deal's economic programs evoked outrage, it was scarcely because they impinged on the Yankee's pocketbook. Rather, it was because they represented a direct affront to the Puritan ethic, the Yankee's morality. Gusfield notes that "the public support of one conception of morality at the expense of another enhances the prestige and self-esteem of the victors and degrades the culture of the losers." In welcoming to power those who had traditionally been political outsiders, in inviting them to legislate in defiance of the Puritan ethic, Roosevelt struck the old ruling class a particularly painful blow. Here was a new answer to the question, as Grimes poses it, of "Whose America?" The Yankee was left no choice now but to share with others the prerogatives that once he exercised alone. He was forced to submit to the disparagement of a morality that had once reigned unchallenged. Indeed, it is understandable if he felt that his culture had been degraded. But the Yankee, an indomitable character, did not reconcile himself to his defeat. He has continued to fight, and his goal has been the restoration of the old regime.

Obviously, the means for achieving this goal lie in the Republican party's ability to win elections, particularly the election to the Presidency. This requisite has created for the party a dilemma of immense significance. If, on the one hand, the Republicans select a candidate who faithfully represents the Yankee goal, he alienates too much of the electorate to stand a chance of winning. If, on the other, the party chooses a candidate palatable enough to the electorate that he is likely to win, his goal must be so divergent from the Yankee's that his victory becomes purposeless. What appears to divide Republicans, then, is not the party's objective—which is the source of the conflict, for instance, between North and South among Democrats—but the party's order of strategic priorities.

The Republican party is split between pragmatists and ideologues. The pragmatists insist on the primacy of the means, on winning the election; they ask of a candidate that he be able to get the votes. The ideologues insist on the purity of the end, on the candidate's orthodoxy; who fails their test they see as a heretic. Ostensibly, the dispute between means and ends might be thought of as easy to resolve. But in reality, it is between worldliness and piety, expediency and devoutness. Each side looks upon the other with contempt. Each, in its Puritan fashion, heaps on the other a sectarian scorn. What appear to be differences over strategy are differences of moral conception applied to the realm of politics. Such differences are not easy to compose.

In nature and intensity, the division of Republicans since Hoover is strikingly similar to what it was in the Progressive era. One might say, in fact, that the old dispute is still unresolved, that it did no more than to go into eclipse during the party's days of high fortune in the 1920's. During neither the Progressive nor the New Deal era has the schism been over abstract questions of social justice but over the appropriate response of Puritan doctrine to the threat posed by social change. Neither the Progressives of the turn of the century nor the pragmatists of a half-century later have been proponents of social reform for its own sake. What distinguishes them from each other is that the Progressives were pioneers in behalf of reform legislation, while the pragmatists have been little more than pallid followers of the Democrats, striving breathlessly not to be outdistanced. Probably it is because, since the Depression, neither pragmatists nor ideologues have come up with a leader as dynamic as Theodore Roosevelt that the party has remained intact, although it was a very near miss indeed when Barry Goldwater was nominated for President.

If there has been a profound change in the Republican party since the Progressive era, it is that the Eastern financial interests have shifted their support from the Old Guard to the party's pragmatic wing. These interests, long the underwriters of Republican election campaigns, have confirmed that they are essentially non-ideological. One need only recall Jay Gould's confession that "I was a Republican in Republican districts, a Democrat in Democratic districts. But everywhere I was for Erie," to acknowledge that big money is moved not by doctrine but by the most carefully calculated self-interest. At one time, this big money was characterized by Vanderbilt's "the public be damned" attitude. But though its spokesmen still prefer Republican administrations to Democratic ones by far, they no longer require that these administrations be modeled after McKinley's or Coolidge's. Since the Depression, in fact, they have come to recognize that a cautious departure from laissez-faire, and some modest welfare legislation, far from impairing their profits actually contribute to the social stability that their continuing prosperity requires. This new sense of social responsibility, concentrated among the New York bankers and industrialists recently styled the "establishment," has penetrated only very little the business spirit of the American hinterland. But its influence has been substantial.

In the years after Hoover, this shift of the Eastern big money enabled the pragmatists to dominate the Republican party. The ideologues remained a powerful force, however—perhaps even a majority within the party ranks. Though they have been prevented from naming their own candidates for the Presidency, they have consistently extracted meaningful concessions in return for their support. But if the ideologues, discredited, have deferred to the pragmatists, they have looked on their condition as a temporary retreat and not as a party reform. To maintain their dominance, the pragmatists would obviously have to show results.

Alfred M. Landon, the Republican nominee in 1936, represented the pragmatists' first triumph in the internecine party struggle. Landon was a pleasant man who acknowledged that government needed to grow in response to the demands of an increasingly complex society, though as governor of Kansas he had actually reduced administrative services. His nomination did not come without a fight from the ideologues. At the national convention, it was Herbert Hoover whose Puritan caveats evoked the wildest enthusiasm. He declared: "There are some principles that cannot be compromised. Either we shall have a society based upon ordered liberty and the initiative of the individual, or we shall have a planned society that means dictation no matter what you call it or who does it. There is no half-way ground."

In the end, the Hoover groundswell was stemmed and Landon went forth, intending to tell the people that he approved of liberal reform, though he objected to its maladministration and excesses under the New Deal. His approach, however, proved intolerable to the ideologues, who put increasing pressure on him. Before long, Landon was denouncing social security and extolling the protective tariff, while proclaiming that the New Deal "violates the basic ideals of the American system." The climax of the campaign, for the Republicans, was sheer disaster. Landon took just Maine and Vermont, while losing by the biggest popular landslide in more than a century.

In the months preceding the 1940 convention, the leading contenders for the Presidential nomination were Senator Robert A. Taft of Ohio and Senator Arthur Vandenberg of Michigan, choices of the ideological wing, while District Attorney Thomas E. Dewey of New York was favored by the pragmatists. All three, however, were isolationists in their diplomatic thinking. This predilection frightened the Eastern financial interests, which were committed to supporting Britain in its war against Nazi Germany. With the New York *Herald Tribune*, the "establishment" newspaper, in the lead, the Eastern money interests suddenly undertook a tremendous campaign to promote the candidacy of Wendell L. Willkie, a Wall Street lawyer from Indiana. Willkie was, of all things, a registered Democrat, but he possessed great personal magnetism and a reputation as a New Deal foe, acquired in a celebrated court battle against the T.V.A. Somehow he appealed to the convention delegates, and with the opposition bitterly divided, Willkie won the nomination on the sixth ballot.

It came as some surprise to the Republicans, pragmatists as well as ideologues, that they had acquired in Willkie a man of genuine liberal convictions. The campaign he conducted was not only weak in its attack on the New Deal but strong in its repudiation of Roosevelt's bitterest Republican foes in Congress. Long before the campaign terminated, it became apparent that the party leadership was far from happy with its candidate. Nonetheless, Willkie did not do badly, even in defeat. Against an immensely popular President, he won ten states and received, with a total of 45 percent of the electorate, six million more votes than any Republican before him. Though Roosevelt undoubtedly lost support on the third-term issue, the results disclosed, significantly, that the Democratic coalition was holding firm. As for Willkie, his defeat was more decisive in the party than in the country. His exertions in the ensuing years to make the Republican party into a liberal instrument were totally in vain. He was equally frustrated in his attempts to turn the party from isolationism. Before his death in 1944, he had to admit that his missionary work had made no lasting impact. In the final reckoning, Wendell Willkie was a maverick, a solitary figure, unwanted by his party, unmourned, and, as a political reformer, unsuccessful.

It took the Republicans two elections to get enough of Thomas E. Dewey, the brilliant and aggressive but aloof and unappealing New Yorker. Since his election as governor, Dewey had become a favorite of the Eastern financial world. He had conducted an administration that was modern and efficient, and as 1944 approached, he was moving deliberately in the direction of liberalism and internationalism. His leadership of a pivotal state made him a natural contender for the nomination. With the opposition of the ideologues fragmented among weak claimants, Dewey became the convention choice on the first ballot. At best, his chances of election against a wartime President of Roosevelt's stature were slim. In fact, he did substantially less well than Willkie. But the party made allowance for the handicaps, and four years later Dewey was again a prospective candidate.

In 1948, unlike 1944, the Republicans expected to win. With the war over and the economy in disarray, the Democratic President, Harry Truman, was far from popular, both within his own party and in the country. The Republican ideologues had once more put forth their champion, Senator Taft, but found the field crowded with such hopefuls as Speaker Joe Martin of Massachusetts, General Douglas MacArthur, Senator Arthur Vandenberg of Michigan, and former Governor Harold Stassen of Minnesota. Stronger than any of them, however, was Dewey, who, having conducted himself discreetly since his defeat and been reelected governor of New York, had retained his preeminence among the pragmatists. In the convention fight, Dewey was nominated on the third ballot, and, as his running mate, the party chose Governor Earl Warren of California. For the first time in history, the Midwest was not represented on the Republican ticket. Perhaps equally significant, neither were the ideologues. The Republican platform was both internationalist and substantially more liberal than the party's record in Congress. But this seemed to be no time for the Republicans to worry about inconsistencies. The Democratic party had broken apart, with a faction on the left nominating Henry Wallace and the Southerners on the right nominating Strom Thurmond. Harry Truman's cause appeared hopeless and a Republican victory seemed to be a certainty.

Having adopted the theory that whatever he might say would alienate some body of supporters, Dewey scarcely campaigned. Cunningly, Truman summoned Congress back into session and requested the Republican majority to enact the liberal measures in the Dewey platform. Dewey himself had little choice but to line up with Truman, and when Congress did nothing, it was revealed just how badly the Republicans were divided against one another. Having set up the Republican Congress as his whipping boy, Truman proceeded to stage a campaign of unparalleled vigor. In the bluntest fashion, he directed his appeals to each of the member groups of the Democratic coalition—labor, Negroes, farmers, new-stock Americans. In the end, Wallace and Thurmond each polled more than a million votes, but the

Democratic coalition as a whole once again held together. Truman, to the surprise of Dewey and almost everyone else, was reelected by comfortable margins in both the popular and electoral vote.

The election of 1948 was, in many respects, a watershed in American political history. It convinced the remaining doubters that the Democratic party's strength consisted of more than the magnetic powers of Franklin Roosevelt. It demonstrated that the Democrats, in a straight fight over social issues, would beat the Republicans, even with a lackluster candidate. It provided persuasive evidence that the majority of voters preferred a vintage Democrat to a pragmatic—or "moderate"—Republican. It suggested strongly that while the Democrats could win without bowing to the conservative demands of its Southern wing, the South was fast disaffiliating itself as a Democratic constituency. The Republican ideologues were not unjustified in reasoning, in view of the election results, that the party's future lay in nominating orthodox Puritans, who could appeal not only to the bedrock of Yankees in the North but also to the white majority in the South. What they foresaw was the resurrection of the old Whig coalition of a century before.

But meanwhile, the Republicans found in the threat of communism a new issue congenial to their temperament on which to base an appeal to the electorate. For Republicans, more than for many other Americans, communism was not simply another social system, like fascism, for example. It was anathema. It was the proclaimed foe of capitalism, *their* system. It was a violation of all they believed about individual initiative, the profit system, and the right to hold property. As an enemy, it was a greater menace to the rich, whom their God had rewarded, than to the poor, whom He disfavored. It provoked class and racial antagonism to the traditional structure of society, *their* structure. It stood as a constant threat, obviously, to their own privileges and possessions. "To us," wrote Speaker Joe Martin, "the Communist menace looked more alarming than had the Hitler menace. . . ." The Democrats, with their vague egalitarian predisposition, could not claim to be as uncompromising. The Republicans had at stake in the fight against communism not only their country but themselves and their morality. With the same passion that the Federalists showed against Napoleon's revolutionary doctrines, the Republicans responded to communism. The anti-Communist crusade became their opportunity to reclaim their lost credentials as the party of American patriotism.

Not all the demagogues of the anti-Communist crusade were Republicans, nor were Republicans absent from among the foes of demagogy. But Senator Joseph McCarthy, America's most successful demagogue, was Republican, and so were most of those who followed in his trail. More important, the Republican party supported them, even if the "responsible" Republicans like Taft declined to emulate them. For years, the Republican party substituted anti-communism for the advocacy of positive programs in its appeal to the electorate. And to a considerable extent it was successful. Generating fear and bitterness and strife by their loose accusations and veiled inferences of disloyalty, they wounded the Democrats severely. Truman, who handled the issue clumsily, was much discredited and his party was put on the defensive. But, significantly, even with this powerful weapon—the most effective, politically, that the Republicans had developed since the Depression—the Democrats remained the stronger of the two parties. As the election of 1952 approached, it appeared likely that a Republican campaign based largely on anti-communism would not be enough to win the Presidency.

In 1952, the party's ideologues were determined to have a turn at the Presidential nomination. Four times they had submitted to the pragmatists, only to see Republican candidates go down to defeat. They had endured the humiliation of having their own party's Presidential nominees denounce their record in Congress. They were convinced that if they promised economy in government, cuts in foreign aid, and inflexibility toward communism, they were sure to win the election. For the first time they were united on a single candidate, Senator Robert A. Taft. Though the national polls suggested that he was weak, they were ready to fight to get the nomination for him.

The pragmatists, led by none other than Dewey himself, counterattacked by going outside the ranks of the politicians to find General Dwight D. Eisenhower, one of the great figures of World War II. Though Eisenhower had never declared any party allegiance and, in fact, had earlier been proposed as a Democratic nominee, by background and upbringing he could scarcely have been more typically Republican. Born in 1890 into a poor, devout Protestant family, he was raised in Abilene, Kansas, in the heart of Republican country. In his book of memoirs, *At Ease,* Eisenhower conveys some of the flavor of his early life.

> Everybody I knew went to church. Social life was centered around the churches. Church picnics, usually held on the riverbank, were an opportunity to gorge on fried chicken, potato salad and apple pie. The men pitched horseshoes, the women knitted and talked, and the youngsters fished. . . .

He also reveals much of the Puritan quality of his upbringing.

> Father . . . allotted each boy a bit of ground of the land surrounding our house. Each was privileged to raise any kind of vegetables he chose and, if possible, to sell them to the neighbors for a profit. . . . For my plot, I chose to grow sweet corn and cucumbers. I had made inquiries and decided that these were the most popular vegetables. I liked the thought that I was earning something on my own—and could keep it or spend it on myself. . . .

> It is fatuous to remark that a man's hometown has changed since he was a boy, but in later visits to Abilene, I have not been able to help but notice that the nights, once so quiet that the whistle and rumble of a train could be heard rising and falling away across miles of country, are now disturbed by town noises. . . . There are other, more subtle disappearances. Attitudes have gone also—or at least changed. There is a fundamental change, I think, in the attitude toward the temporal role of man—once expressed in a single word: Work—and toward the church and education. In my boyhood, most houses of worship were plain frame buildings,

without adornment of steeple and tower. The schools, too, were functional, square, two-story buildings without orna- ment, each with its bell housed in a cupola on the roof. . . . Education, in the small-town view, was intended to produce citizens who could inform themselves on civic problems. Beyond that, schools served to prepare the student for little more than the ordinary round of jobs. . . .

Eisenhower entered West Point in 1911 to begin a military career that brought no particular distinction until he was singled out during the war for great command responsibilities. He pro- ceeded to become the nation's most popular hero, thanks not only to his military successes but to a warm personality and an engaging smile that evoked confidence and conveyed a funda- mental decency. In January, 1952, while serving in Europe as commander of the North Atlantic Treaty Organization, Eisen- hower declared himself a Republican. When he made clear that he was willing to become the Presidential nominee, the organiza- tional strength of the Republican party's pragmatic wing mobi- lized behind him.

But Taft continued to gain support among the delegates to the convention. He was holding his own in the primaries and obvious- ly had no intention of giving in gracefully, particularly to an out- sider. Finally, barely a month before the showdown, Eisenhower decided to resign his commission and come home to campaign for the nomination. The ensuing weeks were filled with bitterness as the two camps struggled to capture the votes of the doubtful states. Amid charges by Eisenhower's men that Taft's side had dishonestly acquired contested delegations, the convention opened in grim humor. Taft, like his father in 1912, had control of the party machinery, but Eisenhower, like T. R., was the more popular figure and was clearly on the offensive. After days of acrid oratory, the test votes on the convention floor went for Eisenhower, which gave him control of the disputed delegations. Still, Taft battled to the very end and Eisenhower won with just a bare majority. Though Taft ultimately pledged his support to the victory, the ideologues seethed with resentment at the manner and magnitude of their defeat.

In nominating Dwight D. Eisenhower for President, the Republican party rehabilitated the hoary Whig stratagem, which it had used so successfully in Grant's day, of selecting to represent it a popular military figure who obfuscated political issues. As a politician, Eisenhower was unknown to the nation. He was considered an internationalist, who had challenged Taft chiefly out of fear that the nation might return to isolationism. But no one knew if he was a liberal or a conservative on domestic matters, perhaps least of all Eisenhower himself. His genial bearing conveyed a generosity of spirit, suggestive of a liberal outlook. His public statements, though confused and often contradictory, reinforced the impression of good will. But after a lifetime in the army, Eisenhower gave little indication that he had developed a social philosophy to deal with the nation's needs. In vain, Adlai Stevenson, the Democratic candidate, tried to focus on the issues that divided the men and their parties. Eisenhower was elected, but it was a personal and not a party victory. Though the Whig technique had worked, it hardly proved that the Republican party was any the stronger for it.

As the new President and party leader, Dwight Eisenhower spoke a great deal about developing a "modern" Republicanism. The very phrase implied a reproach to the Old Guard, and his advocacy of international policies generally regarded as liberal— reciprocal trade, foreign aid, mutual security—stamped him as a foe of the traditionalists. But in his domestic policies, his tendencies emerged only very slowly. In explaining his party objectives one day, he said: "Modern Republicanism looks to the future. . . . As long as it remains true to the ideals and aspirations of America, it will continue to increase in power and influence—for decades to come. . . ."

However sincerely delivered, words like these at best express a vague emotion, not a program of action. At one point, after it became clear that "modern" Republicanism had evoked little popular support, Eisenhower appointed a Committee on Program and Progress, to help devise a new party philosophy. Predictably, it made no impact on Republicans. Gradually, however, an Eisenhower philosophy in domestic affairs did become clear. "Modern" though it was in name, it turned out to be scarcely distinguishable from the most ancient Republican orthodoxy.

Emmet Hughes, who was one of Eisenhower's speechwriters in the White House, wrote in *The Ordeal of Power*, his gossipy "inside story," that during the preparation of the first inaugural address Eisenhower kept repeating:

> All these generalizations about freedom and history do not mean too much. What matters to the average citizen is— what can *he** do? A carpenter or a farmer or a brick-layer or a mechanic—what is *his* role? The *individual*—that's what counts. It's not just a time of crisis for the statemen and the diplomats. Every individual has got to understand and to *produce*. He's got to work harder than ever—and he's got to understand *why*.

Eisenhower, of course, was expounding pure Puritan doctrine. "Perhaps no adjective figured so prominently in his political vocabulary as 'spiritual,'" Hughes wrote, "and his spontaneous speeches were rich with exhortations on America's 'spiritual' strength." It required no conscious intellectual process but merely absorption from the Kansas plains for Dwight Eisenhower to obtain his grasp of the Puritan ethic. Yet this grasp was profound.

Ultimately, the Eisenhower Administration dropped the pretensions of "modern" Republicanism, which the Old Guard had found so offensive. Gradually, the President's views converged with those of the Republicans in Congress to produce what business had always regarded as "sound" policies. Eisenhower ignored the clamor of Negroes on civil rights, the pleas of farmers on overproduction, the warnings of labor on unemployment, the tocsins of the urban masses on the disintegration of the cities. In the interest of a balanced budget, he vetoed housing bills, and, to preserve individual initiative, he denounced medical care. In response, the electorate voted the Republicans into the minority as early as the congressional elections of 1954. And though Eisenhower remained personally popular and was overwhelmingly reelected, the party as a whole showed no further signs of recovery. In the election of 1958, conducted during a recession that Eisenhower's "sound" fiscal policies had provoked, the Republicans—still waving the "red scare" like the old

* Hughes's italics.

"bloody shirt"—suffered a stunning defeat, losing 47 seats in the House and 13 in the Senate. It was clear then that if there had been an opportunity for the renovation of the party, that opportunity had been lost. There was no "Eisenhower revolution" for the Republicans, as there had been a "Roosevelt revolution" for the Democrats. The Republican party had changed little during Eisenhower's eight years and the power of the old forces was still intact.

Long before Eisenhower retired, the old forces in the Republican party had decided that Richard Nixon, .the Vice-President, would run to succeed him. Nixon had begun his career in the pre-McCarthy era as an unabashed red-baiter, a Puritan ideologue in one of its most noxious forms. Over the years, he showed himself to be a curious jumble of partisanship, decency, expediency, intelligence, ambition, and, above all, hard work. He was such a jumble, in fact, that many Republicans, to say nothing of others, felt that he was without conviction and, therefore, dangerous. In another sense, however, this jumble was an asset, since whoever was attracted to him could find in him some likeable quality. And many Republicans were attracted to Nixon, for he was unstinting in the services he performed for party members, whatever their faction. As an aspirant to the Presidency in the last of the Eisenhower years, Nixon strove manfully to change his image from that of "Tricky Dick" to the "new Nixon," the responsible party leader and statesman. He was astonishingly successful. With connections throughout the party, Nixon performed the dextrous feat of making himself acceptable to Republican ideologues and pragmatists alike.

Nixon's only challenger for the Republican nomination in 1960 was Nelson Rockefeller, scion of America's wealthiest family. Rockefeller, after a long career in philanthropy and public service, had decided to run for governor of New York in 1958, and in the general Republican rout, he emerged a victor by more than half a million votes. A dynamic, aggressive man, there was no doubt that he expected to rise to the Presidency. His social rank and his money, as well as his family's long history in the Republican party, gave him substantial advantages over Nixon. The public opinion polls showed that he was popular, more popular than Nixon, and would probably win the election. Backed by a staff of highly esteemed strategists and political thinkers, Rockefeller set off in search of party support.

But Nelson Rockefeller had a major disadvantage. He was known as a liberal and had quit a high post under Eisenhower in a spat over the Administration's niggardly spending for social programs. Nominating him would have meant the party's repudiation of Eisenhower's conservatism. Certainly the ideological wing of the party, dissatisfied that Eisenhower had not been conservative enough, could not have been made to swallow Rockefeller, the liberal. And the pragmatists were not in the market for a candidate who would challenge the outgoing administration, which they had sired. As for the Eastern financial establishment, it was equally indifferent, though the Rockefellers were charter members. It made no effort, in Rockefeller's behalf, to do what it had done for Willkie, Dewey, and, for that matter, Eisenhower himself. Obviously it was satisfied with Nixon. In the end, the Rockefeller campaign simply fizzled out, and Nixon, practically speaking, won the nomination by default.

As for the Democrats, there was serious talk of nominating an Irish-Catholic. Al Smith's defeat had not established an immutable law, and, among the Democrats, an Irish nominee was certainly one day inevitable. The Irish had become much respected. Save for the Presidency itself, they had been accorded every honor. Only Anglo-Saxon Protestants, it was generally conceded, stood above them in the social hierarchy. They were certainly the single most dominant force in the Democratic party. As a constituency, the Irish-Catholic community had earned another chance at the Presidential office.

John F. Kennedy was an ideal Irish-Catholic to be a candidate for President. He was a fourth-generation Bostonian, son of a self-made millionaire. Educated at Harvard, he was elegant and urbane. He was a war hero. He was young and handsome. He had an accent that was engaging without sounding artificial. He went to Mass but he wore his devoutness lightly.

In short, he was everything that Al Smith was not. He was made to be pleasing to Americans, from the harbor cities of the East coast, where the immigrants had landed, to the Yankee cities of the West, where Puritan culture reigned unchallenged.

It was said, besides, that the country had become more sophisticated. Gone were the rampant prejudices that had so marred the election of 1928. There was, of course, undisguised bigotry here and there. But, for the most part, old-fashioned religious hatreds had gone out of style and had given way throughout the land to a general benign tolerance. Some even believed that religion and ethnic origin would play no significant role in the election campaign.

John Kennedy knew better. Raised in Massachusetts on "ethnic" politics, he understood clearly that his Irish-Catholic identity was a factor of major significance. Quite apart from the volatile passions known as bigotry, Americans possess a deep awareness of the role that religion and ethnic origin play in social ranking. As a factor in electoral politics, concern over social ranking—depending on the circumstances of any given election—may be no less important than economic considerations, though the two tend normally to conjoin. What the Presidential candidate symbolizes within the social hierarchy influences votes. Conventionally, the Republican stands for Yankee supremacy; the Democrat for the challenge of the "out" groups. More than any Democrat since Al Smith, Kennedy, as an Irish-Catholic, personified the aspiration of the immigrant stock to major social recognition—and Al Smith had been badly beaten. John Kennedy, himself acutely sensitive to the Irish-Catholic's rank in American society, grasped how important his origins were to others.

While Nixon campaigned without apparent strategy, spreading his efforts almost uniformly throughout the country, Kennedy directed his campaign overwhelmingly to the industrial states in the Northeast and Midwest. There the electoral vote was concentrated and the immigrant-Negro constituency was the strongest. Kennedy, like Nixon, made no appeal to bigotry. He campaigned on a platform of liberalism in economic, social, and racial policy.

But his liberalism, after the conservatism of the Eisenhower years, was understood as a challenge to the Puritan's ways. He won the key states of New York, Pennsylvania, Michigan, Illinois, New Jersey, and most of New England, while his running mate, Lyndon Johnson of Texas, succeeded in securing the South. Albeit by a very narrow margin, Kennedy's strategy was rewarded by victory.

Though the statistics are unfortunately imprecise, it is clear that the Kennedy-Nixon contest, if only slightly affected by outright bigotry, was profoundly influenced by religious and ethnic considerations. In state after state, the pattern of returns suggested city for Kennedy, countryside for Nixon, old stock for Nixon, new for Kennedy. It is estimated that as many as four out of five American Catholics voted for Kennedy. Some 70 percent of Negroes and at least an equal percentage of Jews voted for Kennedy. But Kennedy could not have won without Protestant support. More than 18,000,000, in fact, of Kennedy's 34,000,000 votes were Protestant. Nonetheless, in examining the figures, it appears that among the white Protestants in the areas of Yankee culture no more than a quarter to a third voted Democratic. In short, Kennedy did not, like Roosevelt, generate massive shifts in voting patterns. His background, rather, accentuated dramatically the patterns that already existed. No matter how one reads the returns, it is undeniable that a greater proportion of Catholics, as Catholics, voted Democratic than usual, while a greater proportion of Protestants, as Protestants, voted Republican. The election results seemed to demonstrate that religious and ethnic identity remains the most compelling of influences on the decisions of the American electorate.

The ideological wing of the Republican party, however, took the election to mean something else. The ideologues saw in Nixon's defeat another repudiation by the electorate of the party's pragmatists. In his campaign, Nixon had sought to minimize the differences between himself and Kennedy in most areas of policy. He gave little attention to exalting the Puritan doctrine. The ideologues, however satisfied they had been in nominating Nixon, felt themselves betrayed before the campaign was over. Some were convinced that his compromises had cost him the victory. The ideological wing of the party, frustrated since Hoover's day, was determined that at the next opportunity, it would get its own candidate nominated, and that, whoever he might be, he would have to be ideologically pure.

Just as it was inevitable that the Democrats would go back to an Irish-Catholic, it was a certainty that the Republicans would one day return to an orthodox Puritan. Had the pragmatists been more successful in putting their men into office, they might have delayed the day indefinitely. But after 1948 they lost their credibility and, with it, their authority. They had conducted a brilliant, rear-guard effort in keeping Eisenhower in the Presidency for two terms. They forestalled a head-on clash by accepting Nixon. But now they were in disarray, unable to make a persuasive argument in behalf of their own cause, and the ideologues were demanding that their due-bills be redeemed.

It is, perhaps, a paradox that the Arizonan who took over the leadership of the ideological wing was half-Jewish by blood, but he espoused a Puritanism which was so pristine that his origins appeared unimportant. Barry Goldwater, product of the last frontier, was a converted Yankee, more rigid than Taft, perhaps even more rigid than Hoover. He excited the ideological wing by his audacity in promoting a doctrine that, in its immaculacy, had of late so rarely been heard. The pragmatists tried to thwart him by declaring him outside the "mainstream" of contemporary Republicanism. What they failed to note was that the "mainstream" had been running underground. No less than John Kennedy among the Democrats, Barry Goldwater was the normal fruit of Republican experiences and traditions.

As an apostle of the Puritan ethic, Barry Goldwater was eloquent. He found no equivocation in the principles he took. From them, he rarely had trouble formulating his policy positions. He was a pure doctrinaire. In his book, *Conscience of a Conservative,* he wrote:

> One of the foremost precepts of the natural law is man's right to the possession and use of his property. . . . It has

been the fashion in recent years to disparage "property rights"—to associate them with greed and materialism. This attack on property rights is actually an attack on freedom. . . . Property and freedom are inseparable; the extent government takes the one in the form of taxes, it intrudes on the other. . . . But it must also be said that every citizen has an obligation to contribute his fair share to the legitimate functions of government. . . . What is a "fair share"? I believe that the requirements of justice here are perfectly clear: government has a right to claim an equal percentage of each man's wealth, and no more. . . . The idea that a man who makes $100,000 a year should be forced to contribute 90 percent of his income to the cost of government, while the man who makes $10,000 is made to pay 20 percent, is repugnant to my notions of justice. I do not believe in punishing success. . . .

As for his position on charity, John Calvin himself could not have expressed with greater clarity the Puritan conception. Goldwater said:

Consider the consequences to the recipient of welfarism. . . . A man may not immediately, or ever, comprehend the harm . . . done to his character. Indeed, this is one of the great evils of welfarism—that it transforms the individual from a dignified, industrious, self-reliant spiritual being into a dependent animal creature without his knowing it. There is no avoiding this damage to character under the Welfare State.

It is much debated how Barry Goldwater obtained the Republican nomination for President. That he was extremely personable and had always given his best for the party is generally acknowledged, but in themselves these are scarcely sufficient credentials. Some maintain that a conspiracy of right-wing extremists foisted Goldwater on an unwilling party. But if ever in recent history a minority manipulated the party, it was in the interest of the pragmatists, Willkie and Dewey. Some analysts assert, with apparent reason, that the delegates to the national convention were more extreme than Republicans as a whole, but it is doubtful that any representative body is a perfect reflection of its constituency and there is no evidence that the Republican national convention of 1964 was an unusual distortion. On the contrary, most of Goldwater's delegates had won their seats in fair fights, either in conventions or primaries. Having never concealed their intentions, their victories suggest that they had extremely widespread approval.

Among those with a particularly hopeful view of the democratic process, it has been said that the "citizen wing" of the party has consistently saved the Republicans from the "professionals" by rising up, often at the last moment, to nominate a good pragmatist for President. But the evidence hardly sustains that contention. If anything, in nominating the Deweys over the Tafts, the professionals have prevailed. In 1964, however, the pragmatists, who have been the most professional of all, approached the showdown in a state of demoralization and timidity. Their only candidate, Nelson Rockefeller, failed miserably to stir enthusiasm, most notably their own. At the convention, they made a few indecorous efforts at manipulation, but consumed by self-doubt, they mostly wrung their hands. So the "citizen wing," its designs unencumbered by pragmatism, proceeded to work its will and nominated Barry Goldwater.

In a perceptive paper called "The Goldwater Phenomenon," Professor Aaron Wildavsky of the University of California relates the text of an interview at the Republican national convention with a typical Goldwater delegate.

Interviewer: What qualities should a Presidential candidate have?
Delegate: Moral integrity.
I.: Should he be able to win the election?
D.: No, principles are more important. I would rather be one against 20,000 and believe I was right. That's what I admire about Goldwater. He's like that.
I.: Are most politicians like that?
D.: No, unfortunately.
I.: What do you like about Goldwater?
D.: I am in sympathy with many of his philosophies of government, but I like him personally for his moral integrity. I always believed that a candidate should carry out his prom-

ises [Pennsylvania's Governor William] Scranton didn't do that. But now, for the first time in my life, we have a candidate who acts as he believes. He doesn't change his position when it is expedient.

I.: Do you think that if the party loses badly in November it ought to change its principles?

D.: No. I'm willing to fight for these principles for ten years if we don't win.

I.: For 50 years?

D.: Even 50 years.

I.: Do you think it's better to compromise a little to win than to lose and not compromise?

D.: . . . I don't believe that I should compromise one inch from what I believe deep down inside.

It seems clear that Goldwater's partisans did not expect him to win. Why, then, were they so enthusiastic about him? Wildavsky maintains it was because he offered them his private conscience, unsullied by the compromises of the everyday political process. Goldwater offered them the opportunity to line up for Puritan morality. This alone, with all its implications, is the ideologue's end in politics, not public office for its own sake or even a relatively conservative economic program. Eisenhower, by constantly compromising the Puritan's ends, did almost as much to hasten the nomination of a Goldwater as did all the pragmatists who failed to win Presidential elections. After Eisenhower, the ideologues saw little to distinguish the pragmatists from the Democrats. They wanted desperately to have Goldwater elected. But they preferred to have him lose rather than to back a candidate, however Republican he might be, whose ends were less pure than their own. In nominating Goldwater, they made the Republican party the instrument of their designs. They also made it true to itself.

With Goldwater as its candidate, the Republican party could scarcely be accused—as it had been so many times—of obscuring the issues. Never before, not even by Hoover, had the country been asked with such clarity to vote for or against the Puritan ethic, along with its concomitant, Yankee supremacy. It was not a time of economic depression, nor was the party unusually split, nor was the Democratic candidate particularly popular. So there was nothing mitigating about the circumstances of the confrontation. If Goldwater had any strategy at all, it was to concede to the Democrats the large industrial states and try to build a new Republican alliance, an updated version of the Whig coalition of the Yankee West and the white South. But even this strategy was pursued without conviction, and the result, as foreseen, was a crushing Republican defeat. Goldwater did well enough capitalizing on racism in the South, but in the North, save for Arizona, he could find no more Yankee majorities. In those states significantly touched by Yankee culture, he received only 20,000,000 votes, compared to 34,000,000 for Lyndon Johnson. He emerged from the election with the hard-core Puritan vote, and no more.

The Republican party was now reduced to bedrock. It had never been more bereft of friends. Surely if Goldwater had aspired to being the apostle of God's morality, the Republican party had fallen from grace. The long journey from Ripon seemed to be over. The hope of the Yankee community to be restored to political ascendancy now appeared dead.

EPILOGUE TO
THE 1971 EDITION

On August 8, 1968, the Republican party, assembled at its national convention, nominated Richard M. Nixon for President. The prospect of a Republican victory in the fall election had, in a sense, foreordained the Nixon nomination. The party could not again indulge itself with a candidacy like that of Barry Goldwater, a purist of the ideological wing. On the other hand, it needed not consider a candidacy like that of Nelson Rockefeller, a compromiser of the pragmatic wing. At its disposal was a man who, somehow, had managed over the course of a long career to persuade the ideologues of his Republican orthodoxy, while persuading the pragmatists that he was a tough, practical politician. It didn't matter that Richard Nixon was not, in the country-at-large, the most popular of available Republicans. He had been defeated in his two previous attempts at public office and had not, on his own, won an election since 1950. Yet he was a man who had not compromised his Republican virtue and, as Republicans perceive the political cosmos, was the party's ideal choice.

The circumstances into which Richard Nixon's nomination fit so harmoniously were contained in the failures of President Lyndon B. Johnson, both abroad and at home. The country had become embroiled in a dismal, costly and apparently endless foreign war. Domestically, its peace had been shattered by crime and civil disorder, some of it political and some of it racial, but all of it profoundly agonizing. The Republican party did not have to run on a program of its own. It had no reason to test the popular reception to its Puritan principles. It had only to campaign on the record of President Johnson and the Democratic Administration.

The Republican party platform, in the following excerpts, summed up the mood which the Nixon campaign projected:

> The Administration's Vietnam policy had failed—militarily, politically, diplomatically, and with relation to our own people. We condemn the Administration's breach of faith with the American people respecting our heavy involvement in Vietnam. . . . The Administration's failure to honor its own words has led millions of Americans to question its credibility. . . . To resolve our Vietnam dilemma; America obviously requires new leadership—one capable of thinking and acting anew, not one hostage to the many mistakes of the past. The Republican Party offers such leadership. . . .
>
> Lawlessness is crumbling the foundations of American society. Republicans believe that respect for the law is the cornerstone of a free and well-ordered society. We pledge vigorous and even-handed administration of justice and enforcement of the law. We must re-establish the principle that men are accountable for what they do, that criminals are responsible for their crimes, that while a youth's environment may help to explain the man's crime, it does not excuse that crime. We call on public officials at the federal, state and local levels to enforce our laws with firmness and fairness . . .

To be sure, the platform contained a hint of Puritanism in its criticism of President Johnson's credibility. The hint was even stronger in the suggestion that whatever psychiatry and other social sciences taught, "we must re-establish the principle that men are accountable for what they do." Nonetheless, these were arguments that any party of challengers might have made. This was a platform of expediency—and perfectly fair under the two-party system. Richard Nixon, it might be noted, tended to excess in his acceptance speech by seeming, rather ludicrously, to blame the breakdown of "order and respect for law" on President Johnson's Attorney General. But, exaggeration notwithstanding, President Johnson's Administration had indeed earned its criticism, and any party which was seeking to unseat it in an election—whether or not its character was Puritan—

was playing within the rules by emphasizing the criticism of its failures over any principles of its own.

The Republican party, in fact, had been pursuing this strategy, since shortly after the Goldwater debacle, when it became clear that President Johnson's support was disintegrating precipitously. This strategy, in the Congressional election of 1966, helped the Republicans win a substantial victory. Ray Bliss, the national chairman, could then call the party "a very live elephant," and said that "after suffering a defeat in depth in the 1964 elections, the Grand Old Party surpassed even its fondest dreams by scoring a pyramidal victory in depth in 1966." But Bliss was far too honest to claim that it was a victory for a Republican approach to government. In his formal statement to the party, he declared:

> The penetrating Republican victories from the courthouses to Congress throughout the nation on November 8th have developed a solid basic foundation upon which we can build for the 1968 Presidential election. . . . Victories across the nation resulted from the teamwork and dedicated effort on the part of our candidates and party leaders at every level, the precinct workers, financial contributors, and the many thousands of volunteers who cooperated so effectively throughout the campaign.

It was noteworthy that nowhere in his victory statement— even for purposes of boosting party morale—did Bliss say that Republicans won because the voters returned to the path of wisdom and chose Republican programs and philosophy. Instead, he credited "teamwork and dedicated effort" for the party comeback.

As national chairman, Ray Bliss was responsible for rebuilding the Republican party in the years following the Goldwater defeat. He had earned his credentials as Republican state chairman in Ohio, where he had restored the party to majority status after an extended period of decline. Utterly indifferent to philosophical questions, Bliss had made his reputation as a political technician. Nothing was more alien to him than the responsibility assumed by Paul Butler, Democratic national chairman prior to the 1960 election, for forging party ideology. To Bliss, party ideology was a matter of the lowest common denominator, that point in political thought on which all Republicans could agree. He was guided by the notion that unity was more important to the party than intellectual vigor. Bliss's objective was to alienate no one. As a consequence, both the Old Guard and the pragmatists were willing to stand behind him.

It is hard, nonetheless, for a political party to admit to having no program—and Bliss, as a qualified technician, was not prepared to make that admission. The problem was that the demands imposed by the joint menace of internal disunity and popular repudiation left the Republicans with little besides a bag of rhetoric. Republicans generally called this bag of rhetoric "constructive alternatives" and, thanks largely to Bliss, they even established elaborate machinery to devise these "constructive alternatives." Invariably, however, the ideas that emerged from this machinery consisted of nothing more than minor administrative reshufflings and such ancient prescriptions for neutralizing social legislation as the transfer of responsibility to the states, the surrender of control to private enterprise and the encouragement of efficiency by the reduction of appropriations. On balance, the "constructive alternatives" turned out not to be constructive at all but rather destructive. Yet they were innocuous enough to give little public offense, while avoiding controversy within the party itself.

Senator Thruston Morton of Kentucky, a pragmatic Republican and a former national chairman himself, recognized that the party had, in the public mind, acquired a reputation for obstructionism to Democratic proposals—but even he sought to counter it only by vacuous phrases. "I am afraid," he said, "that most voters judge the Republican party as being a negative party. Nothing could be farther from the truth. Some of us don't like the Administration's program for education, yet we recognize the problems of education at all levels as one of the great challenges of our system. Some of us voted against 'Medicare,' but we are all cognizant of the health problems of the needy aged. Many of us oppose the so-called war on poverty, but we are sharply aware of the problems that face those who live in poverty. Some of us disagree with the Administration's programs to assure equal opportunity for all minority groups in getting an education, in finding a job, and in the opportunity to vote. In all of these fields we believe we have better programs in closer harmony with the American tradition. . . . We Republicans have offered programs that attack these problems within the framework of the American tradition." Morton failed to specify what these programs in the American tradition were. Perhaps his inability to find them accounts, in some measure, for his announcement prior to the 1968 campaign that he was retiring from the United States Senate.

What all the insipid rhetoric indicated was that the Republican party, face-to-face with the prospect of victory at the polls, was seeking to dissemble its Puritan character. The style contained the recognition that, outside the hard-core Yankee areas, the old Puritan clichés meant political death. For some time, only one American voter in four had been willing to identify himself as a Republican—and the trend was not improving. In more than a few instances, Republicans were running for office without citing party affiliation on their campaign literature. As the 1968 election approached, it was clear that the Democrats could be defeated—but it seemed apparent that the Republicans could be victorious not by trumpeting their Republicanism but only by submerging their own dogma in the popular wave to "throw the rascals out."

Nixon's strategy, then, was in sharp contrast, ideologically, to Goldwater's aggressive Puritanism in 1964; geographically, however, the two men ran almost the same campaign. In 1964, Goldwater virtually wrote off the industrial states of the Northeast, which had come increasingly under immigrant-black control. He reasoned that the best chance for the Republicans lay in recreating the old Whig coalition, a conservative alliance based on the white supremacist South and the areas of continued Yankee dominance in the North and West. Since 1952, the South had given its votes to Republican Presidential candidates —not necessarily because the Republicans were racists but because racism thrives on economic and social conservatism. Nixon's approach was designated the "Southern strategy," since he needed a base of Southern support, which was threatened less by the Democrats than by the avowedly racist, third-party candidacy of George Wallace. Nixon concentrated heavily on the South on the assumption that the Yankee areas of the North and West required less attention.

According to the early public opinion polls, the strategy was to give him an overwhelming victory, but a campaign that was ideologically empty inevitably cost him support. In the end, he held key parts of the South and kept narrow leads throughout most of the Yankee North and West. But his total vote was only 43 per cent, his margin over Vice President Humphrey was less than one-half of one per cent and the shift of a few thousand votes in Illinois and California would have changed the outcome. The essential fact remained, however, that Richard Nixon won—and it meant that the Republican party would probably go after the same geographical areas in much the same way in elections for the foreseeable future.

Since becoming President, Nixon has gradually abandoned his ideological neutrality to emerge as a true Puritan—not quite as purist as Goldwater, to be sure, but an authentic heir, nonetheless, to the grand tradition of Republican orthodoxy. Indeed, he started cautiously, as if uncertain how strongly his mandate justified the dismantling of the welfare apparatus created during three decades of Democratic government. Inflation, though politically embarrassing, was ideologically useful to this end. It provided him with the justification for vetoing bills to construct housing and hospitals, put the unemployed to work, increase public support of education. It gave him a reason for undermining the Office of Economic Opportunity, which President Johnson had founded to administer the "war on poverty." As much as anything, Nixon's Puritanism expressed itself in what he failed to do: devise compensatory programs for deprived blacks, provide food for all of the hungry, assist cities threatened with decay. After his first two years in office, he had not tried to destroy the welfare programs of the Democratic years, though he had severely crippled many of them. What he had achieved, however, was a change in atmosphere, so that the underdogs of society could believe no longer that the government was on their side.

Historians in a future era may determine that President Nixon's open conversion to Puritan doctrine as his guide for making policy dates from his State of the Union message of January 1971. It was in this message that he proposed his celebrated plan to share Federal revenues with the states—a plan which, parenthetically, would wipe away the entire structure of Federal programs in education, urban development, job training, law enforcement and transportation. In subsequent actions, the President announced a new taxing program to benefit business and industry, and a series of subsidies to assist troubled corporations. Meanwhile, he insisted upon impounding—on the grounds that they were inflationary—funds that had been appropriated for various social welfare programs. It was as if Richard Nixon, step by step, was seeking to move the country back to the Republican age that preceded Franklin D. Roosevelt.

To be sure, the President did devise one major new social reform, called the Family Assistance Program. It proposed, on the one hand, to set a floor under every family's income, whether or not members of the family were employed. It required, on the other, that any adult who benefitted from the program had to accept a job or train for a job. The principle that the Federal government was responsible to assure a minimum income to every family was a departure of immense significance from the old system of the dole. The work requirement seemed less important, since jobs were already scarce and, besides, a major proportion of the recipients of public assistance, according to surveys, were not really employable anyway. Throughout his early years as President, Nixon pressed gently for the enactment of this program. Not only did his fellow Republicans oppose the plan, however, but his own heart hardly seemed in it. Why he proposed The Family Assistance Program is, in fact, unclear. It was certainly the kind of program that was troublesome to the Puritan soul.

Finally, at a meeting of Republican governors in 1971, President Nixon delivered a Puritan confession about the program. It was a poignant expression of the Yankee ethic.

We have no intention of measuring the success of this Nation's welfare programs by the money spent or the number of people supported. We are going to measure it by the money saved and the number of people who are given back the incentive and the opportunity to support themselves. . . .

I advocate a system that will encourage people to take work, and that means whatever work is available. It does not mean the attitude expressed not long ago at a hearing —I read about it in the paper and heard it on television— when a lady got up at a welfare hearing and screamed, "Don't talk to us about any of those menial jobs." I am not sure what she considers a menial job, but I probably have done quite a few in my lifetime. I never thought that they were demeaning. If a job puts bread on the table, if it gives you the satisfaction for providing for your children and lets you look everyone else in the eye, I don't think that it is menial.

But it is just this attitude that makes others, particularly low-income workers, feel somehow that certain kinds of work are demeaning—scrubbing floors, emptying bedpans. My mother used to do that. It is not enjoyable work, but a lot of people do it. And there is as much dignity in that as there is in any other work to be done in this country, including my own.

In the course of reforming the welfare system, we have to re-establish the recognition of that fact—the dignity of work, any work, which will enable an individual to take care of his responsibilities without going on welfare.

Indeed, as Richard Nixon grew more comfortable with the office of the Presidency, he alluded with increasing openness to his Puritan heritage. In a memorandum dictated in February 1971 he said: "Both my mother and father were almost fierce in their adherence to what is now deprecatingly referred to as Puritan ethics. Not only were they deeply religious, but they carried their principles over into their lives in other respects and particularly in an insistence that to accept help from the government, no matter how difficult our own circumstances were, was simply wrong from a moral standpoint. . . . Not only at home but in church and school we had drilled into us the idea that we should, if at all possible, take care of ourselves and not expect others to take care of us. . . . The fact that I did not embrace the New Deal philosophy was due to a strong streak of individualism which probably was more than anything else rooted in my family background."

Some observers have raised questions about the origins of Richard Nixon's Protestant orthodoxy, since he was raised in the Quaker faith, which is generally more liberal, pious and pacifist than conventional Protestantism. The President is, indeed, a "birthright Quaker"—though he has rarely been a practicing one—by virtue of the membership of both his parents in the Society of Friends. In one interview in 1971, he got carried away with his spiritual legacy and declared: "I rate myself as a deeply committed pacifist, perhaps because of my Quaker heritage from my mother. . . . I can assure you that my words are those of a devoted pacifist." To that, the Philadelphia Yearly Meeting of the Religious Society of Friends, the country's leading Quaker organization, sternly replied that the man who presided over the American war effort in Vietnam was in no way being faithful to any Quaker convictions.

In fact, scholars have pointed out that the religious atmosphere in which the President was raised in California was much closer to orthodox Protestantism than to the pristine Quakerism of seventeenth-century England and Pennsylvania. As Quakerism moved westward across the country, it lost much of its gentleness and absorbed the grim, evangelistic piety of the frontier sects. Although the President's mother was indeed a pacifist, most Western Quakers were not, and Nixon himself did not hesitate to go off to the Navy in 1942. As a boy, his religious education was as much Methodist or Baptist in character as Quaker. In California, the Quaker values that Richard Nixon encountered were all but indistinguishable from those of middle-class American Protestantism generally. These are the values which lie at the base of President Nixon's political beliefs.

In 1972 Richard Nixon will, presumably, ask the American people to affirm these values and these beliefs. They will, of course, be mixed in the voters' minds with such issues as the Vietnam war and the Middle East, the economy and racial conflict, Presidential credibility and Presidential style. But they will be far less dissembled than they were four years before. They will, thanks to the President's pursuit of his inclinations, be clearly discernible from the values and beliefs which the Democratic party presents. More than in 1968, this will be a real test of the attraction of Republican virtue. The result will indicate how influential the Yankee and his ethic are likely to be in America's coming decades.

BIBLIOGRAPHICAL NOTES

The literature on the Republican party is, of course, extensive, but disappointingly little of it consists of sound historical interpretation. There has been a dearth of enterprise in seeking to understand the party within the framework of American social experience.

Commendable efforts have been made by Wilfred E. Binkley in *American Political Parties, Their Natural History* (Knopf, New York, First edition 1943) and Arthur N. Holcombe in *The Political Parties of Today* (Harper, New York, 1923), but both books, whatever their merits, remain the product of an earlier generation. Also of another generation is William Starr Myers's *The Republican Party, A History* (Century, New York, 1928), which is chiefly important as a document of pre-Depression Republican thinking. From our own day, George H. Mayer's *The Republican Party, 1854–1964* (Oxford, New York, 1964) is a thorough and reliable recitation of events, substantially superior to Malcolm Moos's frothy *The Republicans, A History of Their Party* (Random House, New York, 1956). Though each of these books has its inadequacies, they constitute the basic literature on the Republican party and have contributed much to *Fall from Grace.*

For general reference, I have relied on Samuel Eliot Morison and Henry Steele Commager's, *The Growth of the American Republic* (2 vols., Oxford, New York, 1950), as well as on such standard sources as the *Concise Dictionary of American Biography* (Scribner's, New York, 1964), *Historical Statistics of the United States* (Government Printing Office, Washington, 1961), *Biographical Directory of the American Congress, 1774–1961* (Government Printing Office, Kirk H. Porter, ed. Washington, 1961), *National Party Platforms* (Macmillan, New York, 1924), and countless encyclopedias, almanacs, dictionaries, textbooks, and compilations of quotations, most notably Bartlett's.

CHAPTER 1   *The Yankee and His Faith*

Max Weber laid the foundation for *Fall from Grace* in his classic innovative work, *The Protestant Ethic and the Spirit of Capitalism* (Scribner's, New York, 1958), first published in German in 1904. R. H. Tawney, in *Religion and the Rise of Capitalism* (Harcourt Brace, New York, 1926) applies Weber's analysis to the English ancestors of American Puritans. Perry Miller's *The New England Mind* (2 vols., Macmillan, New York, 1939, and Harvard, Cambridge, 1953) and Ralph Barton Perry's *Puritanism and Democracy* (Vanguard, New York, 1944) examine the political and religious ideas of the original colonists. Alan P. Grimes assesses, in *Equality in America* (Oxford, New York, 1964), the sources of religious and political tolerance. Lyrically, Stewart H. Holbrook traces the westward march from New England in *The Yankee Exodus* (Macmillan, New York, 1950). Frederick Jackson Turner's influential ideas on the pioneers appear in *The Frontier in American History* (Holt, New York, 1950).

204 : : *Fall from Grace*

CHAPTER 2 *Ancestors and Origins*

Leonard I. White's *The Federalists* (Macmillan, New York, 1948) treats the early period covered in this chapter. The Adams quote comes from Grimes's *Equality*. Charles M. Wiltse's *The Jeffersonian Tradition in American Democracy* (Hill & Wang, New York, 1960) supplies the essence of the material on Jefferson. Arthur Schlesinger Jr.'s *The Age of Jackson* (Little Brown, Boston, 1945) contains many ideas about the period. William V. Shannon's *The American Irish* (Macmillan, New York, 1963) deals in detail with the Know-Nothings. Richard Hofstadter, in *The American Political Tradition* (Knopf, New York, 1948), discusses ideas and personalities basic to the era. Binkley's *American Political Parties* is particularly good on the decades before the Civil War.

CHAPTER 3 *Metamorphosis by War*

Basic to the development of this chapter was Matthew Josephson's *The Politicos* (Harcourt Brace, New York, 1938). Benjamin P. Thomas has written a useful single-volume biography in his *Abraham Lincoln* (Knopf, New York, 1953). Hofstadter's *The American Political Tradition* presents an interesting view of Lincoln.

CHAPTER 4 *The Yankee's America*

The Logan quote that opens the chapter is from Myers, *The Republican Party,* as is the subsequent long quote about the Democrats. Josephson writes extensively about the "bloody shirt" strategy in *The Politicos,* as well as about the Republican subservience to business. The short-lived insurgency of 1872 is treated in Earle D. Ross, *The Liberal Republican Movement* (Holt, New York, 1919). Dwight D. Eisenhower quotes the Kansas City bard in *At Ease: Stories I Tell Friends* (Doubleday, New York, 1967). Richard Hofstadter's *Social Darwinism in American Thought* (University of Pennsylvania, Philadelphia, 1944) remains the eminent work on this subject. The Whitlock quote comes from Robert J. Donovan, *The Future of the Republican Party* (New American Library, New York, 1964).

CHAPTER 5 *The Lost Constituencies*

For the section on "The Negroes," Josephson once again serves as a prime source. Much material also comes from Paul Lewinson's *Race, Class, and Party* (Oxford, New York, 1932), which is rich in detail on the Negro's fate, and Kenneth Stampp's *The Era of Reconstruction* (Knopf, New York, 1965). "The Northern Farmers" draws from John D. Hicks's *The Populist Revolt* (University of Minnesota, Minneapolis, 1931), Solon J. Buck's *The Agrarian Crusade* (Yale, New Haven, 1920) and Kenneth C. MacKay's *The Progressive Movement of 1924* (Columbia, New York, 1947). The section on "Native Wage-earners" takes material from Rowland T. Berthoff's *British Immigrants in Industrial America*

(Harvard, Cambridge, 1953) and Nathan Fine's *Labor and Farmer Parties in the United States 1828–1928* (Russell & Russell, New York, 1961), as well as from MacKay.

CHAPTER 6   *Yankee and Immigrant*

The outstanding work on the rivalry between immigrant and Yankee is John Higham's *Strangers in the Land, Patterns of American Nativism, 1860–1925* (Rutgers, New Brunswick, 1955). It is a basic source for this chapter. Marcus L. Hansen's *The Immigrant in American History* (Harvard, Cambridge, 1940), as well as Oscar Handlin's *The Uprooted* (Little Brown, Boston, 1951), are rich impressionistic works on immigration. E. P. Hutchinson's *Immigrants and Their Children, 1850–1950* (Wiley, New York, 1956) provides some important statistics. Shannon's *The American Irish* is indispensable to understanding that segment of the immigrant movement. The Abram Hewitt quote, along with the material on municipal corruption, is largely from Josephson. The material on the suffragette movement comes from Alan P. Grimes, *The Puritan Ethic and Woman Suffrage* (Oxford, New York, 1967), a highly innovative work. The accounts of the temperance movement are drawn in large measure from John A. Krout's *The Origins of Prohibition* (Knopf, New York, 1925), and James H. Timberlake's *Prohibition and the Progressive Movement* (Harvard, Cambridge, 1963). E. Digby Baltzell provides useful data on the rise of overt discrimination in *The Protestant Establishment, Aristocracy & Caste in America* (Random House, New York, 1964). Joseph R. Gusfield's *Symbolic Crusade* (University of Illinois, Urbana, 1963) is particularly perceptive on the prohibition movement. The quotation from the *Italian News* comes from J. Joseph Huthmacher's *Massachusetts People and Politics* (Harvard, Cambridge, 1959), while the selection from Daniel Chauncy Brewer is from Huthmacher's paper "The Conquest of the Democratic Party by the Immigrant," written in 1967.

CHAPTER 7   *The Lost Opportunities*

The Social Gospel receives attention from Aaron I. Abell in *The Urban Impact on American Protestantism, 1865–1900* (Archon, London, 1962) and from Hofstadter in *Social Darwinism*. Hofstadter also deals extensively with Pragmatism. Higham writes in length on the Americanization campaign in *Strangers in the Land*. The literature on the Progressive movement is copious. Hofstadter's *The Age of Reform, From Bryan to F.D.R.* (Knopf, New York, 1955) is exceedingly important, in itself and as a source. Russell B. Nye's *Midwestern Progressive Politics* (Michigan State College Press, East Lansing, 1951) deals with another important facet of the era. Henry L. Stimson, who is frequently quoted, wrote his autobiography, *On Active Service in Peace and War* (Harper, New York, 1947), with McGeorge Bundy. Francis Biddle's autobiography is called *A Casual Past* (Doubleday, New York, 1961). The Democratic side of the period is recounted by Arthur S. Link in *Woodrow Wilson and the Progressive Era, 1910–1917* (Harper, New York, 1954). Otis L. Graham, Jr., considers the end of Progressivism in *An Encore for Reform, The Old Progressives and the New Deal* (Oxford, New York, 1967). Republican foreign policy gets attention from Foster Rhea Dulles in *The Imperial Years* (Crowell, New York, 1956). Higham, Huthmacher, Timberlake and Grimes deal with various aspects of the postwar reaction. William Allen White analyzed Coolidge in *A Puritan in Babylon* (Macmillan, New York, 1938).

CHAPTER 8   *The Fall from Grace*

The Bishop Cannon quote is from Gusfield's *Symbolic Crusade.* Hoover's relations with the Negro community receive the attention of Lewinson in *Race, Class and Politics.* Huthmacher's *Massachusetts People and Politics* contains many useful insights into the 1928 election, as well as on urban politics generally. Much of the material on the New Deal was drawn from Arthur Schlesinger Jr.'s *The Age of Roosevelt,* of which three volumes have appeared: *The Crisis of the Old Order* (Houghton Mifflin, Boston, 1957), *The Coming of the New Deal* (Houghton Mifflin, Boston, 1959), and *The Politics of Upheaval* (Houghton Mifflin, Boston, 1960). George Wolfskill deals with the right-wing departures from the Democratic party in *The Revolt of the Conservatives* (Houghton Mifflin, Boston, 1962). Donald B. Johnson does a commendable job on the 1940 election in *The Republican Party and Wendell Willkie* (University of Illinois Press, Urbana, 1960), as does Jules Abels in *Out of the Jaws of Victory* (Holt, New York, 1959) on the election of 1948. The classics on the two most recent elections are, of course, Theodore H. White's *The Making of the President 1960* (Atheneum, New York, 1961) and *The Making of the President 1964* (Atheneum, New York, 1965). The Columbia Broadcasting System was kind enough to furnish the statistics on voting returns compiled by its computers in the 1964 election.

EPILOGUE

Material from the Republican National Committee was supplied by the committee itself. David R. Mayhew's *Party Loyalty among Congressmen, The Difference between Democrats and Republicans 1947–1962* (Harvard, Cambridge, 1966) is an analysis based on voting records that tells much about the distinctions between the two parties.

The works cited in these notes represent only a fraction of those consulted in the course of preparing *Fall from Grace.* It is probable that inadvertently, I have committed injustices in failing to cite the source of some ideas and for this I apologize. But since *Fall from Grace* is not so much a historical narrative as an interpretation of politics, I have not felt compelled to burden the reader with exhaustive documentation.

For reading and commenting on these pages, I am grateful to Professor J. Joseph Huthmacher of Rutgers, Professor Alan Grimes of Michigan State, Professor Aaron Wildavsky of the University of California, Richard Rubenstein of the Adlai E. Stevenson Institute, Stephen Hess of the John F. Kennedy Institute of Politics, and John Anderson of *The Washington Post.* I accept, however, full responsibility for all of the content.

INDEX

INDEX

Abolitionist movement, 31, 38, 130

Acheson, Dean, 170

Adams, Brooks, 145, 151

Adams, Henry, 147

Adams, John, 20

Adams, John Quincy, 25, 26

Addams, Jane, 144

Africa, Lincoln's suggestion to re-settle freed slaves in, 54

Agrarian third-party movements, 100–105; Populist movement, 94, 95, 101–5; Granger movement, 101; Progressive party of the 1920's, 105, 113, 163

Agricultural depression of the 1920's, 105

Agriculture: change in, made by Civil War, 97–98; Department of, establishment of, 97; of nation, in the 1920's, 163

Alaska, annexation of, 81

Algeciras, conference of, 152

American Anti-Slavery Society, 45

American Chamber of Commerce, 159

American Commonwealth, The (Bryce), 73

American electorate, religious and ethnic identity as compelling influences on decisions of, 187

American Federation of Labor (A. F. of L.), 109–10; and Progressive party of the 1920's, 113

American nationalism, Republicans as champions of, 81, 82

American Protective Association, 133

American Puritanized and industrialized society, impact of Social Darwinism on, 78–79

American System, of Henry Clay, 24, 26, 29, 72

American ties with England and France, cementing of, in Theodore Roosevelt's administration, 152

Americanism: Republican party's identification with, 67; identification of woman's suffrage with, 137

Americanization: of the immigrant, 144; program of patriotic societies, 144–45; campaign in post-WWI era, 158

Anarchy, and foreign agitators, 132–33

Anglo-Saxon immigrants, 118, 134; and "national origins" quota, 138

Anglo-Saxon superiority, claims of, 111, 134, 142

Anthony, Susan B., 129

Anti-Catholicism: as political issue in the 1880's, 127–28; in 1928 election, 163–64

Anti-Communist crusade, 178–79, 183

Anti-immigrant drive, 132–35; Henry Cabot Lodge as leader in, 133–35, 138; Protestant immigration blocs in, 134; and literacy tests, 134, 135; and passage of restrictive legislation in the 1920's, 137–39

Anti-Masonic movement among Yankees, 26–27, 38, 39

Anti-Saloon League, 131

Anti-Semitism, 142

Antitrust laws, 166

Arthur, Chester, 93

At Ease (Eisenhower), 180–81

Atlanta, capture of, by Sherman, 55, 68

Autobiography (Roosevelt), 149

Babbitt, George F. (Sinclair Lewis): and Puritan-Social Darwinian ethic, 80; labor philosophy of, 107

Baer, George F., 107

Baker, James H., 4

Balanced budget, and Eisenhower's policies, 183

Baltzell, E. D., 132

Baronial Order of Runnymede, 132

Beecher, Henry Ward, 10

Beecher, Lyman, 21, 130

Bell, John, 45

Biddle, Francis, 154, 170

Bigotry, in 1928 campaign, 164

Black man: Yankee attitude toward, 39; Republican Radicals' plan to use in destruction of South's plantation system, 53, 91; *see also* Negroes; Slavery issue

Blain, James G., 72

Blair, Francis P., Jr., 69

Blease, Cole, 96

Bliss, Ray C., and task of rebuilding Republican party after Goldwater debacle, 195–96

Bosses, and the political machine, 123, 166

Bourbons of the South, 92, 93, 94, 95, 101, 102, 166

Breckinridge, John C., 45

Brewer, Daniel Chauncey, 139

Browne, Charles Farrar, 13

Bryan, William Jennings: and 1896 election, 103–4, 111, 112; defeat of, by Taft, in 1908 election, 152

Bryce, James, 70, 73

Buchanan, James, 40

"Bull Moose" party, *see* Progressive party ("Bull Moose") of Theodore Roosevelt

Burchard, Samuel, 128

Butler, Paul, 195–96

Butler, William Morgan, 138

Calvinism: and Puritan theology, 5–6; and growth of capitalism in Western world, 8; and Southern fundamentalism, 15

Campaign of 1860: candidates in, 45–46; Lincoln's victory in, 46

Cannon, James, 164

Capital and labor, struggle between, 106–7, 109, 110

Capitalism: spirit of, and Puritan ethic, 8; in America, in ascendancy in government, 72

Capitalist class: concept of Republican party as agent of, 74, 75; immigration as source of cheap labor for, 116–17, 133

Carnegie, Andrew, 78, 117

Carpetbaggers, and Radical reconstruction policies in South, 60, 90

Catholic Church: vigor of, as lower class and immigrant institution, 144; *see also* Anti-Catholicism

Charity: lack of sympathy for, in Puritan ethic, 11; position of Goldwater on, 189

Chinese Exclusion Act, 111

Cigarmakers' Union, 149

Cigars, manufacture of, in tenement-houses, legislation against, 149–50

"Citizen wing" versus "professionals" in Republican party, 190

Civil War: and establishment of supremacy of central government over states, 62–63; venality of American politics in era following, 73

Civil War Congress, legislation of, 50

Clay, Henry, 24, 25, 26, 27, 29, 30

Cleveland, Grover, 66, 67, 71, 81, 108, 114, 124, 170

Collective determinism of Social Darwinism, 143

Colombia, and building of Panama Canal, 151

Colonial Dames, 132

Colored Farmers' National Alliance, 102

Commager, Henry Steele, 1, 141–42, 151, 159

Commercial ethics, and exclusion of sense of social responsibility, 142

Committee on Program and Progress, of Eisenhower, 182

Common man: well-being of, Jefferson's dedication to, 24; Lincoln's concern for, 58; small place of, in Republican forged society of post-Civil War era, 58

Commons, John R., 79

Communism, threat of, as congenial issue for Republicans, 178–79

Compromise of 1850, 30, 33

Congressional elections of 1954 and 1958, signal defeat of Republicans in, 183–84

Conquest of New England by the Immigrant, The (Brewer), 139

Conscience of a Conservative (Goldwater), 188–89

"Conscience" Whigs, 32, 36, 37

Conservatism of Franklin Roosevelt, 171, 199

Conservative coalition of Northern Republicans and Southern Democrats, 92, 95

Constituencies of Republican

party: in years after Civil War, 87–88

Constitutional Union party, 45

"Constructive alternatives" of Republicans to Democratic Administration's war on poverty, 196–97

Coolidge, Calvin, 113, 137, 160–61

Corruption: in party politics in era after Civil War, 73–74; and the political machine, 122

Country club, as exclusionary device, 132

Craft unionism, 108

Crawford, William, 25

Culture of New England, spread of, by migrations of Yankee pioneers, 2

Daughters of the American Revolution, 132

Davis, John W., 113, 170

Debs, Eugene V., 112–13, 155

Decision-making processes of nation, and New Deal, 171–72

Deism of Jefferson, 22

Demagogues, and anti-Communist crusade, 179

Democracy of Jeffersonians, 22

Democratic party: as final name assumed by Jeffersonians, 24; and Kansas-Nebraska bill, 34–35, 36; in 1856 election, 40; ironically branded as party of treason, 47, 48; and 1864 election returns, 56; and Peace Democrats, 67–68; and 1864 campaign, 68; situation of, after Appomattox, 68–69; and 1866

congressional elections, 69; ticket of, in 1868 campaign, 69; and three decades after Civil War, 69–71; inconsistencies in policies of, 70–71; and Social Darwinism, 79; weakness of, after Civil War, as contribution to Republican strength, 88; and 1896 election, 103–4; immigrant's preference for, over Puritan party of Yankees, 115, 117, 127; as party of "rum, Romanism, and rebellion," 128; affiliation of liberal Progressives with, 157; Eastern urban wing gains ascendancy over West and South, in 1928 election, 163; and Roosevelt's coalition of Populism and Progressivism, 168; and the South of New Deal, 169–70; as country's majority party, 170, 178; and splinter parties in 1948 election, 177; unexpected victory of, in 1948 election, 178; and anti-Communist issue, 179; and "Roosevelt revolution," 184

Democratic-Populist 1896 coalition, 103

Democratic principles, reserve of Puritans toward, 12

Democratic-Republicans: as early name used by Jeffersonians, 24; and Presidency of Jackson, 26

Depression of the 1930's, 140, 166, 168, 170, 174

Dewey, Thomas E., 175, 176–78; as governor of New York, 176; as 1944 Republican Presidential candidate, 176; defeat of, in 1948 election, 177–78; as

leader of Republican pragmatist wing in 1952, 180
Donnelly, Ignatius, 102
Dooley, Mr. (Finley Peter Dunne), 3, 123, 125–26
Douglas, Stephen A., 34, 45
Dunne, Finley Peter, 3, 123, 125–26

East: Republican dominance in, and votes of native workingmen, 87; Progressive movement in, 146–47; shift of big-money interests in, to pragmatic wing of Republican party, 173–74
Economic adventurism in era after Civil War, 77
Economic programs of New Deal, 172
Economy in government, Coolidge's attitude toward, 160
Education: dedication of Puritans to, 14; undervaluation of, in Calvinist South, 15; Jeffersonians' support of, 22
Eighteenth Amendment, and prohibition, 136
Eisenhower, Dwight D., 180–81, 191; as candidate of Republican pragmatists for 1952 nomination, 180, 181; political philosophy of, 182; election and reelection of, as personal rather than party victories, 182, 183; and "modern" Republicanism, 182, 183; "sound" policies of, 183
"Eisenhower revolution," non-materialization of, for Republican party, 184

Election of 1928, warnings to Republicans in returns of, 165
Election of 1948, as watershed in American political history, 178
Election of 1960, influence of religious and ethnic factors in, 187
Election of 1968, 193–95
Electorate, Republican, 83, 84, 152
Ely, Richard, 144
Emancipation of slaves: differences between Lincoln and Republican Radicals on, 51–54; Emancipation Proclamation issued by Lincoln, 54
Equalitarianism: felt within the community, Puritans' contribution to, 12, 13; of Jeffersonian political coalition, 25; American Protestantism and suffrage movement, 129
"Era of good feelings" in Monroe administration, 25
"Establishment," of New York bankers and industrialists, 174
Ethnic origin: role of, in social ranking, 186; as compelling influence in decisions of American electorate, 187

Family Assistance Program, The, 199
Farmer: and protective tariff, 98–99; exploitation of, by railroads and banks, 99; and decreasing prices of farm products, 99; attitude of Republican party toward, 99–100; attitude of, toward Democratic party, 100,

103; Yankee, loosening of ties to Republican party, 106, 169; and labor, differences in fundamental attitudes of, 110–11; Yankee, and New Deal, 169; and problems of overproduction, Eisenhower's ignoring of, 183

Farmer-labor political coalitions, 110, 111–12

Farmers' Alliances, 101–2

Federalists: as ruling aristocratic class, 19–20, 39; economic conservatism of, 20–21, 72; loyalty of Yankee voter to, 21; and Society of Cincinnati, 21, 67; disintegration of, as political party, 21–22, 24; and War of 1812, 22; Republican party's cultural heritage from, 37, 38, 63; attitude of, toward foreigners in body politic, 115

Fifteenth Amendment, and enfranchisement of Negro, 89

Fillmore, Millard, 30, 36

Foreign radicals, 132, 133

Fort Sumter, Confederate attack on, 47

Free silver issue in 1896 campaign, 102–03

Free-Soil party, 32, 34, 37, 38, 39

Frémont, John C., 36, 40

Frivolity forbidden to the Puritan, 7, 16

Fugitive Slave Law, repeal of, 54

Garrison, William Lloyd, 31, 89

Gary, Indiana, 1967 election, 199

Genealogy, study of, as stylish hobby of upper classes, 132

George, Henry, 104

German-Americans as victims of patriotic wrath in WWI, 135, 136

German immigrants, 118–19, 134

Germans of Midwest, and Socialist party, 112

Gettysburg address of Lincoln, 48

Ghettos in cities, immigrants in, 126

Goldman, Eric, 171

Goldwater, Barry: campaign strategy of, as compared to Nixon's, 197–98; nomination of, for President, 173, 189–91; as normal fruit of Republican experiences and traditions, 188; as apostle of Puritan ethic, 188–89; 193, 197, 198; Puritan ethic and Yankee supremacy as issues in 1964 candidacy of, 191–92

"Goldwater Phenomenon, The" (Wildavsky), 190–91

Gompers, Samuel, 109, 111

Gould, Jay, 74, 174

Government: as relatively inconsequential to the Puritan, 12–13; Jefferson's concept of, as distinct from Puritans', 23; and decades of Republican dominance over, 82–86; by aristocracy, Theodore Roosevelt's extolling of, 149

Graft: by politicians in era after Civil War, 73; and the political machine, 122

Grand Army of the Republic, 66, 67, 133

"Grand Old Party," as name for Republican party, 85

Granger movement of, 101, 111

Grant, Ulysses S.: nomination of, by Republicans, 61, 62, 63, 82; profligate character of regime of, 74–75, 123
Greenback-Labor coalition, 111
Grimes, Alan P., 129, 172
Guam brought under American flag, 81
Gusfield, Joseph R., 136, 172

Hampton, Wade, 94
Hanna, Mark, 112, 147
Happiness of man, as Jefferson's criterion for action of state, 23
Harding, Warren Gamaliel, 137, 160
Harrison, Benjamin, 66, 82, 94, 108
Harrison, William Henry, 29
Hawaiian Islands, annexation of, 81
Hayes, Rutherford B., 79, 85, 91, 93, 127
Haymarket riot in Chicago, 132
Hewitt, Abram, 124
Hillman, Sidney, 169
Hoar, George F., 65
Homestead Act, 44, 45, 49, 51
Homestead strike, 108
Hoover, Herbert, 164, 165–66, 167–68, 171, 175; and Depression in fall of 1929, 166
Housing bills vetoed by Eisenhower, 183
Hughes, Charles Evans, 157, 159
Hughes, Emmett, 183
Human institutions, Jefferson's attitude toward, contrasted with Puritans', 23
Humphrey, Hubert H., 198

Huthmacher, J. Joseph, 158
"Hyphenates" as threat to integrity of Yankee society, 135

Ickes, Harold, 170
Ideologues versus pragmatists, in Republican schism, 173–174, 178; in 1948 nominating convention, 177; in 1952 nominating convention, 179–81; and candidates for 1960 Presidential nomination, 184, 185; in appraisal of 1960 election, 187–88; in nomination of Goldwater, 191; in 1968 nominating convention, 193
Immigrants: attitude of typical Yankee toward, 115, 117; settlement pattern of, 117, 126; and competition with Negro labor in South, 117; as neighbor to the Yankee, 117; estimated value of, as economic asset, 117; and the urban political machine, 121–23; Americanization of, 144; and New Deal, 169
Immigration: rise in rate of, and intensified nativist hatreds, 33; restriction of, 33, 111, 117–18, 132–35, 137–38, 140; Republican policy of open door to, 72, 117; in post-Civil War era and early decades of 20th century, 116; period of encouragement of, 116; as source of cheap labor for capitalist class, 116–17, 133; shift in source of, to Southern and Eastern Europe, 126; and anti-immigrant

drive, 132–35; as threat to Yankee's leadership, 134; and establishment of principle of "national origins" quota, 138–39

Imperialism: of America in decades after Civil War, 81–82; of Social Darwinism, 81; Democratic attitude toward, 81; Republican excursions into, 81, 159

Individual, importance of, to the Puritan, 12, 23

Industrial cities, political force of, and New Deal, 169

Industrial and commercial expansion in North, in era after Civil War, 77

Industrial revolution in America, Puritanism of New England as unifying factor in, 9

Industrial unions, 109

Industrial Workers of the World (I.W.W.), 112

Industrialist and financier, as country's new heroes, 76

Industriousness as Puritan's sign of God's favor, 7, 8

Intellect, respect of Puritan for, 14

Intellectual community of Progressive party, transfer of, to Democratic party, 157, 170

Internal improvements bill, 44, 45

International affairs: Republican party's tradition of involvement in, 151, 159, 162; isolationist position of Republicans in, after defeat of League of Nations, 159–60; liberal policies of Eisenhower in, 182

Irish-Americans as victims of patriotic wrath in WWI, 135

Irish-Catholics, as single most dominant force in Democratic party, 185

Irish immigrants: influx of, and intensification of nativism, 32–33; relations of with Yankee ruling class, 119–20; as Democratic in affiliations, 120; settlement of, in the cities, 120–21; and politics, 121; in 20th century, 139

Irish politician, and the urban political machine, 121–23, 127

Isolationism of Republican party, 159–60, 162, 175, 176, 182

Italian-Americans as objects of patriotic wrath in WWI, 135

Italian immigration, effects of "national origins" quota on, 139

Jackson, Andrew, 25, 26, 108, 171

Jackson, Michigan, origin of Republican party's charter at, 35

James, Henry, 154–55

James, William, 143

Jefferson, Thomas, 22; and strong central authority, 23; identity of Republican party with, 35

Jeffersonian concept of society, Puritan-Social Darwinian war against, 80

Jeffersonians: political tenets of, 22; and Puritans, basic differences on ultimate goals of, 22–23; as coalition of anti-Federalists, 23–24, 25; evolution of party name of, 24; power blocs within coalition of, 25; Presidential candidates of, in 1824 election, 25–26

Jewish-Americans as objects of patriotic wrath in WWI, 135

Jewish immigration from Russia, 139

Jews of New York, and Socialist party, 112

John Brown's raid on Harper's Ferry, 44

Johnson, Andrew, 55, 58; and Republican Radicals, incompatibility of goals in reconstruction of South, 58–59; and differences with Radicals on Negro enfranchisement, 59; white egalitarianism of, directed toward Northern business, 59; impeachment proceedings against, 61

Johnson, Lyndon, 187, 192, 193, 194, 198

Jones, Jesse H., 143

Josephson, Matthew, 124

Kansas-Nebraska bill: and slavery issue, 34–35, 36; as issue in 1854 election, 36; and Lincoln-Douglas debates in 1858 senatorial campaign, 42

Kelley, Oliver H., 101

Kennedy, John F.: qualifications of, as 1960 Democratic Presidential candidate, 185–86; significance of Irish-Catholic identity of, 186

Kennedy-Nixon 1960 campaign, 186–87

Knights of Labor, 109, 111

Know-Nothing party, 33–34, 37, 38, 39, 100, 108, 116, 127, 130; and 1854 election, 36; dissolution of, over slavery issue, 36

Knox, Frank, 170

Ku Klux Klan, 90

Labor: native and immigrant divisions and animosities in, 28, 33, 108, 132; votes of native workingmen, and Republican dominance in industrial East, 87; Abraham Lincoln's views on perogatives of, 106; and right to strike, 106; and capital, struggle between, 106–7, 109, 110; and tone of Republican party's relations with, 107; attitude of two major parties toward labor vote, 108; immigrant labor, and challenge of Negro labor, 108; dissipation of political power of, 108; and the farmer, differences in fundamental attitudes of, 110–11; in 1896 election, 112; and the mid-1920's, 113–14; anti-immigrant drive of native labor, 132, 134; and New Deal, 169; and unemployment, Eisenhower's ignoring of, 183

LaFollette, Robert, and Progressive party of the 1920's, 105, 113

LaGuardia, Fiorello, 124

Laissez-faire: and Republican party, 72, 79; and Cleveland, 102; and Populist party, 102; and William Jennings Bryan, 104; and A.F. of L., 110; and

Herbert Hoover, 165; Wilsonians' belief in Jeffersonian, 166–67; cautious departure of big money from, since the Depression, 174

Lamont, Thomas, 161

Landon, Alfred M., as candidate of pragmatic wing of Republicans, 174–75

Lergue of Nations, and Republican party, 159

Lease, Mary Ellen, 102, 111

Lewis, Sinclair, 80, 86

Liberal Republican movement of 1872, 75

Liberal party: formation of, in 1840 depression, 31, 39; and 1844 election, 32

"Lily-white" Republicanism in South, 96–97; delegations to national conventions, 164

Lincoln, Abraham, 41–43; factors determining political affiliations of, 41; Jeffersonian political philosophy of, 41–42, 58; and middle-class Republicanism, 42; and philosophy of the fluid society, 42; liberal capitalistic ideology of, 42; and slavery issue, 43; selection of, as candidate, by 1960 Republican convention, 44–45; and appraisal of purpose of Civil War, 48; differences of, with Radicals in Republican party, 51–52, 54, 55; attempts of, to appease Republican Radicals by half-measures, 54; Emancipation Proclamation of, 54; permanent imprint of, on Republican party, 58

Literacy, advance of, with Yankee dominance in North and West, 15

Literacy tests: and Negro suffrage, 95; and the anti-immigrant drive, 134; for immigrants, passage of law on, over Wilson's veto, 135

Lodge, Henry Cabot, 93, 133, 138, 156

Logan, John A., 62

Lowell, James Russell, 12, 14

Lynd, Robert and Helen, 80

MacArthur, Douglas, 177

Majority party of country, Democratic party as, 170, 178

"Manifest destiny," concept of, 81

Martin, Joe, 177, 178

Marxism, and Europe's industrial masses, 79

Materialistic civilization, built by the Yankee to the glory of God, 5

McCarthy, Joseph R., 179

McClellan, George B., 68

McGuffey Reader, and Puritan elementary education, 14

McKinley, William, 81, 84, 103, 112, 135

McNary, Charles, 170

Medical care as government project denounced by Eisenhower, 183

Medicare, 196

Midwest: as heartland of America's Puritan culture, 3; close relationship between Social Darwinism and Republican party in, 79–80; Republican

Presidential candidates from, during decades of Republican dominance, 83

Military nobility, and Federalists, 21

Military preparedness, Republicans as leaders in, 159, 162

Misery, creation of, by American business enterprise, 141

Missouri Compromise of, 1820, 34

"Modern" Republicanism of Eisenhower, 182, 183

Moneyed interests: gravitation of, to Republican party, 50, 51; and end to Reconstruction in South, 91–92; alignment of, with pragmatic wing of Republican party, 173–74; and nomination of Wendell L. Willkie by Republicans, 175–76

Monroe, James, 25

Morgan, J. P., 77

Morgan, William, 26

Morison, Samuel Elliot, 1, 5, 141–42, 151

Morrill, Justin, 133

Morrow, Dwight, 161

Morton, Oliver, 64

Morton, Thruston, 196

Municipal integrity, 124

"National origins" quota, as immigration policy, 138

National Republican party: formation of, by Yankees, 26; coalition of, with Southern aristocrats, to form Whigs, 26

Native American party, 33

Naturism: as political force, 32–34; and the Whigs, 33; intensi-fication of, by rise in immigration rate, 33; and Native American party, 33; and Know-Nothing party, 33–34, 36, 38; and Red Scare of post-WWI period, 113, 135; racist component of, and immigration, 126; and Republican party, 128, 133; and anti-immigrant drive, 133–34, 135, 138

Negro enfranchisement: Radical Republicans' plans for utilization of, 53; differences of Andrew Johnson and Radicals on, 59; Fifteenth Amendment, 89; and Force Bill of 1890, 93–94; in local, primary, and Presidential elections, 96

Negroes: and Republican party, 87, 96, 97, 163, 164–65; and question of land distribution after Civil War, 88–89; as tenant and sharecropper, 89; disfranchisement of, 95, 136; challenge of Negro labor to immigrant labor, 108; increasing migration of, to North, 164; and New Deal, 169; Eisenhower's ignoring of civil rights of, 183

New Deal: 201, coalition of, 168, 169, 170, 176; urban reforms of, 169; rural reforms of, 169; and the South, 169–70; intellectual community of Progressivism becomes part of, 170; and the existing order, 171; economic programs of, 172

New England: migration of Yankees from, to West and Northwest, 1–2, 16; after Yankee migration from, 3; unwavering support of Federalists in, 21; and growing power of immigrant blocs, 139

Nineteenth Amendment, and woman suffrage, 137

Nixon, Richard, as candidate for 1960 Republican Presidential nomination, 184; as candidate for 1968 Republican Presidential nomination, 193; campaign strategy of, 194, 197–98; ideology as president, 198; and Puritan doctrine, 199–200; and Puritan heritage, 200–202

"Normalcy," Harding's call for return to, 160, 161, 162

Norris, George, 7, 85

North: Know-Nothing party in, 34; reaction in, to Kansas-Nebraska bill, 34–35; industrial and commercial expansion in, in era after Civil War, 77

North Atlantic Treaty Organization (NATO), 181

Northern farmers as constituents of Republican party in years after Civil War, 87, 97

Northwest: New England Yankees as settlers in, 1–2; 16; multiple population elements in settling of, 2–3; dominance of Yankees in establishing social and economic standards in, 3

Northwestern Farmers' Alliance, 101–102

Nouveaux riches of big business, Progressivism attitude toward, 147, 148

Office of Economic Opportunity, 198

Old Guard Republicans: Progressivism as challenge to, 147; and foreign policies of Theodore Roosevelt, 152; in control of party machinery after 1912 election, 155–56; reaction of, to "modern" Republicanism of Eisenhower, 182, 183; and shift of Eastern financial interests to pragmatic wing of party, 173–74

One-party politics, 25, 26

Ordeal of Power, The (Hughes), 183

Outsiders: elitist attitude of Puritans toward, 13, 16, 117; coolness of Republican party toward, 38; inhospitality of typical Yankee toward, 115; in American society, confidence of Yankee in remaining pre-eminent over, 116; woman suffrage as campaign against, 129

Page, Walter H., 135

Panama Canal, building of, 151

Parker, Alton B., 152

Parkman, Francis, 8–9

Paternalism of successful capitalist toward labor, 107

Patriotism, exploitation of appeal to, by Republicans, 83, 179

Patronage distribution: by politicians in era after Civil War, 73; and city bosses, 166

Pattern for civilization of the North set by New England Yankee descendents, 1

Peace Democrats, 67–68

Pensions, Civil War, 66, 67

Philippines brought under American flag, 81

Phillips, Wendell, 10

Plutocracy: take-over of government by, 72–73; Theodore Roosevelt's condemnation of government by, 149

Political machine, and the Irish politician, 121–23, 127

Political party, concept of, as form of private enterprise for profit, 73

Political refugees from European uprisings, 33

Politics: venality of, in era after Civil War, 73–74; A.F. of L. attitude toward direct engagement in, 109; in a diverse society, and the Puritan spirit, 115; immigration as factor in altering quality of, 116; and the Irish immigrant, 121; honesty in, and the political machine, 122–23; conquest of, in cities by Irish, 127

Polk, James Knox, 32

Popular sovereignty, principle of, in settlement of West, 34

Populist movement, 94, 95, 101–5, 111, 163, 168; and labor, 111–12; and Progressivism, 146

Potato famine in Ireland, refugees from, 33

Poverty and the poor, Puritan attitude toward, 10–11

Powderly, Terence V., 109, 111, 112

Power: acquisition of, and Social Darwinism, 78; of individual free will, pragmatist doctrine of, 143

Pragmatism, and the Puritan ethic, 143, 150

Pragmatists versus ideologues, in Republican schism, 173–74, 178; in 1948 nominating convention, 177; in 1952 nominating convention, 179–81; and candidates for 1960 Presidential nomination, 184, 185; in appraisal of 1960 election, 187–88; in nomination of Goldwater, 191

Predestination: Puritan acceptance of doctrine of, 6, 14, 15; and Southern Calvinism, 15

Preparedness fight, Republicans as leaders in, 159, 162

Presidential candidates, and the social hierarchy, 186

Presidential election of 1824, 25–26

Price supports, 168

"Professionals" versus "citizen wing" in Republican party, 190

Profit making: Puritan New England's economy based on, 8, 9; as most moral of man's pursuits, 87

Progressive Era: growth of American Socialist party during, 112; and challenge to orthodoxies of Puritan ethic, 142; end of, and WWI, 158

Progressive movement, 145–59; as political understanding, 145; focused in Republican party, 146; in the West, 146; in the East, 146–47; meaning of, 147; and reform, 147; Theodore Roosevelt as leader of, 147–56, 157; and application of pragmatism to Puritan ethic, 150;

Roosevelt's loss of interest in, 156; under direction of Woodrow Wilson, 156–57; becomes focused in Democratic party, 157, 162, 168; failure of, within Republican party, 157–58

Progressive party ("Bull Moose") of Theodore Roosevelt, 154; in election of 1912, 155; disintegration of, in 1916, 156; transfer of allegiance of intellectual community to Democrats from Progressives, 157, 170

Progressive party of the 1920's, 105, 113, 163

Prohibition, 38, 135–36, 158, 163, 167; state laws on, 135–36; passage and ratification of Eighteenth Amendment, 136; repeal of, 172

Proletariat, dissatisfaction of, in industrial age, 77

Property: Jefferson's ideas on distribution of, contrasted with Puritans', 23; conservative approach of Whigs to, 27, 28; protection of, with army, as government function, 72

Prosperity of nation in the 1920's 163

Protective tariff, 44, 45, 49–50, 51, 72, 73, 84, 94, 166, 175; and the farmer, 98–99, 110

Protestant Establishment, The (Baltzell), 132

Protestant immigrant blocs in anti-immigrant drive, 134

Protestantism, and demands of industrial era, 143–44

Public-be-damned attitude of the industrial magnate, 77, 174

Puerto Rico brought under American flag, 81

Pullman strike, 108

Puritan codes as guides of New England Yankees, in colonizing activities, 2

Puritan crusading for good causes, 11

Puritan culture of 17th century New England, 4

Puritan education, 14

Puritan ethic: and spirit of capitalism, 8; and lack of sympathy for practice of charity, 11; Republican interpretation of, as driving force in post-Civil War industrial and commercial expansion, 77; antisocial aspects of, in industrial age, 77–78; and Social Darwinism, 78, 80, 141, 142; and Grant administration, 123; and state of the country by end of 19th century, 141; and insensitization of nations's leaders, 141–42; challenge to orthodoxies of, 142; and pragmatism of William James, 143, 150; and Hoover's economic policies, 166; and New Deal's economic programs, 172; Eisenhower's profound grasp of, 183; Barry Goldwater as apostle of, 188–89; as issue in 1964 candidacy of Goldwater, 191–92; Richard Nixon as apostle of, 200–201

Puritan faith, and elimination of conflict between material ambitions and spiritual injunctions, 5

Puritan morality, and prohibition laws, 136

Puritan response to *isms,* 11–12

Puritan school, as powerful agent in Yankee conquest of North, 15

Puritan spirit, Republican party as political incarnation of, 39

Puritan splinter groups, 38

Puritan standards, as public standards of America, 4

Puritan theology: and man's personal relationship with God, 6; and predestination, 6, 14, 15; and worldly conduct, 6–7; and demonstration of worthiness for eternal salvation, 7

Puritan womanhood, and passage of woman suffrage amendment, 137

Puritans: as described by Whittier, 4–5; and development of powerful community, feeling socially and racially privileged, 16

Racism: and craft-union movement, 108; and rural-urban estrangement, 111; as element in American nativism, 126, 133, 134; in woman suffrage issue, 137; Goldwater's capitalizing on, in South, in 1964 campaign, 192

Radicals in Republican party: Lincoln's differences with, 51–52, 54, 55; punitive plans of, toward South, 53–54; rejection of Lincoln's half-measures on emancipation, 54; and renomination of Lincoln, 55; Wade-Davis Manifesto of, 55; alliance of, with plutocrats, 58; and 1866 congressional elections, 60; reconstruction policies of, for South, 60, 90; indifference of, to fate of Negro in post-Civil War era, 61, 91; stigma of sectionalism on, 69

Railroad brotherhoods and Progressive party of the 1920's, 113

Railroads: government subsidies to, 50; land grants to, 72; and the farmer, 99

Raskob, John J., 170

Reconstruction governments in the South, 89, 90; overthrow of, by white supremacist Democrats, 91

Red Scare: of post-WWI period, 113, 135; *see also* Anti-Communist crusade

Reformers: Puritans as, 11–12, 122; in Republican ranks in Grant regime profligacy, 74–75; and the Tweed scandals, 124; and winning of New York elections, 124–25; and Progressive movement, 147

Religion: role of, in social ranking, 186; as compelling influence in decisions of American electorate, 187

Religious Society of Friends, 201–202

Religious tolerance, principle of, 13–14

Rendezvous with Destiny (Goldman), 171

Republican party: organization of, in Ripon, Wisconsin, 1, 17, 35; ancestors and origins of, 18–40; unwillingness of, to modify Puritan goals, 18; as early name used by Jeffersonians, 24, 35; origin of charter of, in Jackson, Michigan, 35; and adoption of name "Republican," 35; and slavery issue, 36, 37, 38, 39, 40, 43–44; convention of 1856 in Philadelphia, 36; early constituents of, 36–37; and belief in Yankee superiority, 37–38; as radicals in early days, 38, 100; heritage of, from Puritan splinter groups, 38; as response to integrity of Yankee community, 38; as political incarnation of Puritan spirit, 39; in first attempt at winning national power, 40; Lincoln's choice of, 41; early economic program of, 42; national convention, May 1960, 44–45; platform of 1960 campaign, 45; victory of, in 1960 election, 46; effect of Southern secession on, 46–47; ironic role of, as saviors of the Union, 47, 48; and opportunities of Civil War for changing political and economic structure of nation, 48–49; Radical group in, 49; *see also* Radicals in Republican party; reorientation of, resulting from Civil War, 50; legislation of, in Civil War Congress, 50; and new aristocracy of Civil War profiteers, 50; and renomination of Lincoln, 55; and 1864 election returns, 56–57; permanent imprint of Lincoln on, 58; and nomination of Grant in 1868, 61, 62, 63; self-evaluation of,

as party of American nation in post-Civil War era, 62; 1868 platform of, 64; as repository of respectability and responsible conduct, 65–66; and service to big business tycoons, 71–73, 83; corruption in, in era following Civil War, 73–75; alliance of, with big capitalism, 74, 75; rise of conservatism in, 75; and post-Civil War interpretation of Puritan ethic, 77; impact of Social Darwinism on, 79, 80; commitment of, to dynamic nationalism, 81, 82; and decades of dominance in government by, 82–86; constituencies of, in years after Civil War, 87–88; and 1878 elections, 93; preoccupation of, with success of business, 106–7; and tone of relations with American labor, 107; and labor, in mid-1920's, 113–14; and false sense of security from their long reign, 114; and the immigrant, 116; and temperance movement, 130; effects of immigration policy of the 1920's on, 139–40; in the Great Depression, 140; nominating convention of, in 1912, 153–54; cause of Progressivism within, after 1912 election, 155; return of more conventional Progressives to, after 1916 disintegration of "Bull Moose" party, 157; direct control of, by business in Coolidge administration, 160–61; lost opportunities of, in years between McKinley and Harding, 162; repudiation of, in 1932 election, 168; and winning of elections since New Deal era, 172–73; split in, between pragmatists and ideologues, 173–74, 177, 178, 179–81, 184, 185, 187–88, 191; Willkie's efforts to inject liberalism into, 176; defeat of, in 1948 election, 178; exploitation of anti-Communist issue by, 179; effect of Eisenhower's eight years on, 184; crushing defeat of, in 1964 election, 192; nominating convention of, in 1968, 193–94; and "constructive alternatives," 196–97

Richberg, Donald, 170

Ripon, Wisconsin: migration of New England Yankees to, 1, 17; founding of Republican party in, 1, 17, 35

Rockefeller, Nelson: as candidate for 1960 Republican Presidential nomination, 184–85; as pragmatist candidate for 1964 Republican Presidential nomination, 190; as possible Presidential candidate, 193

Roosevelt, Franklin Delano, 167, 199; as governor of New York, 167; and third-term issue, 176; *see also* New Deal

"Roosevelt revolution" for Democratic party, 184

Roosevelt, Theodore, 96, 122–23 124, 146; ruling-class attitude of, 125, 147, 149; as leader of Progressive movement, 147–56, 157; as President, 151–52; aggressiveness of, in foreign policy, 151–52; campaign of, for

1912 Republican nomination, against Taft, 153; bolts Republican party and forms Progressive party ("Bull Moose"), 154; deep hostility evoked by 1912 candidacy of, 154–55; and 1912 campaign, 155; and loss of interest in Progressive movement, 156

Root, Elihu, 153

Ross, Edward A., 142

"Rotten boroughs" of Republican party in South, 96, 153

"Rugged individualism," 165

Rural reforms of New Deal, 169

Russo-Japanese War, Theodore Roosevelt's mediation of, 151

Salvation Army, 144

Santo Domingo, invasion of, in Theodore Roosevelt's administration, 151

Scandinavian immigrants, 118–19, 134

Scott, Winfield, 30

Scranton, William, 191

Sectarian hostility of colonial tolerance, 13

Sectionalism, fanned by John Brown's raid, 44

Secular elite, belief of Puritan in his belonging to, 15

Seligman, Joseph, 132

Seneca Falls, N.Y., beginnings of woman suffrage movement in, 129

Separation of church and state, 13, 121

Settlement-house movement, 144, 145, 157

Seward, William H., 56

Seymour, Horatio, 69

Shannon, William V., 124

Shipping companies, and transportation of immigrants, 116

Shouse, Jouett, 170

Simpson, "Sockless Jerry," 102

Slavery issue: and the Whigs, 30–31; and abolitionist movement, 31, 38, 130; and Liberty party, 31; and Free-Soil party, 32; and Kansas-Nebraska bill, 34–35, 36; and Know-Nothing party, 36; and Republican party, 36, 37, 38, 39, 40, 43–44; Lincoln's attitude toward, 43

Smith, Alfred E., 163–64, 168, 169, 170, 185, 186

Snobbery, institutionalization of, by Social Register, 132

Social action, pragmatism as invitation to, 143–44

Social change: tardy awakening of Yankee to, 145; response of Puritan doctrine to, and schism in Republican party, 173

Social Darwinism, 78–82, 141, 142; challenge of pragmatism to, 143

Social Gospel movement, 144, 145, 157

Social institution, Republican party as, in post-Civil War era, 85–86

Social irresponsibility of Puritanism, 10–11, 142

Social objectives of two major parties in New Deal era, 171

Social ranking, role of religion and ethnic origin in, 186

Social Register, as institutionalization of snobbery, 132

Social responsibility, new sense of, in the "establishment," 174

Social security, 168, 175

Social welfare measures: in the 1920's, 158–59; Coolidge's attitude toward, 160; Nixon's attitude toward, 198–200

Socialist party, 112–13; alliance of, with Progressive party of the 1920's, 113

Society of Cincinnati, 21, 67

Society of Mayflower Descendants, 132

Sons of the Revolution, 132

Sound money, Republican crusade for, 64

South: and states' rights, 26; coalition of aristocracy of, with Yankees to form Whigs, 26; Know-Nothing party in, 34; secession of states of, 46; Reconstruction governments in, 89, 90; driven to Democratic party by Reconstruction policies of Radical Republicans, 90; overthrow of Reconstruction governments in, by white supremacist Democrats, 91; commercial plutocracy in, after Civil War, 92; "rotten boroughs" of Republican party in, 96, 153; and immigration, 117; and anti-immigrant drive, 134; adoption of state prohibition laws in, 136; Republican efforts in 1928 campaign, 164; and New Deal, 169–70; and nomination of Thurmond, in 1948 election, 177; disaffiliating of, as Democratic constituency, 178, 196-97

Southern Bourbons, 92, 93, 94, 95, 101, 102, 166

Southern and Eastern European immigrants, 126, 143; anti-immigrant drive against, 133, 134

Southern Farmers' Alliance, 101–102

"Southern strategy," 198

Southern wing of Republican party: after Negro disfranchisement campaign, 95–96; patronage distribution of, 95; delegations to Republican national conventions, 95–96, 153

Spanish-American war, 81

Spencer, Herbert, 78–79, 80, 143

"Stand-pat" Republicanism, 147, 151, 152, 153, 155

Stassen, Harold, 177

State of the nation in the 1920's, 163

States' rights conception of the Union, 67

Stevens, Thaddeus, 49, 88, 89

Stevenson, Adlai, 182

Stimson, Henry L., 146–47, 153, 158, 167

Strong, Josiah, 81

Success: as sign of God's approval in Puritan thinking, 8; measured by Southern Calvinist in religious terms, 15; tangible measures of, as basis of social ranking among Puritans, 15; J. P. Morgan's approval of, 77

Sullivan, Tim, of Tammany Hall, 115, 116

Sumner, Charles, 53

Sumner, William Graham, 79

Supreme Order of the Star-Spangled Banner, 33

Taft, Robert A., 175, 177, 179; as candidate of Republican ideologues for 1952 nomination, 179–80, 181

Taft, William Howard, 96, 152–54, 159

Tammany machine, 123

Tariff, see Protective tariff

Tax and property qualifications for Negro suffrage, 95

Taylor, Zachary, 30

Temperance movement, 12, 129, 130–31; see also Prohibition

Tensions generated in American society by Puritan outlook, 13

Textile mills of Puritan New England: Yankee maidens employed in, 9; millowners and overseers of, 9–10

Third-party movements of agrarians, 100–105, 113; Populist movement, 94, 95, 101–5; Granger movement, 101; Progressive party of the 1920's, 105, 113

Thurmond, Strom, 177

Tilden, Samuel J., 124

Tillman, "Pitchfork Ben," 102

Tocqueville, Alexis de, 128–29

Trade-union movement, and considerations of status, 108

Truman, Harry: unexpected victory of, in 1948 election, 177–78; and anti-Communist issue, 179

Turner, Frederick Jackson, 4, 11

Tweed, William Marcy ("Boss Tweed"), of Tammany, 123–24

Tyler, John, 29

Unemployment insurance: Gompers' denunciation of, 109; Coolidge's opposition to, 160

Union army of occupation in reconstruction of South, 60, 61; withdrawal of, 91

Union party coalition in Republican party in Civil War, 55–56

United States, recognition of, as significant power, Republicans contribution to, 81

Universal suffrage, reserve of Puritans toward, 12, 20

Urban labor vote in 1864 election, 57

Urban masses and disintegration of cities, Eisenhower's ignoring of, 183

Urban political machine: and the Irish politician, 121–23, 127; and the Puritan, 122

Urban reforms of New Deal, 169

Urban social organization of Yankee colonizers in Northwest, 2

Vallandigham, Clement L., 68, 69

Van Buren, Martin, 29, 32

Vandenberg, Arthur, 175 177

Vanderbilt, William H., 77, 174

Vann, Robert L., 169

Voters tired of party in office, given attractive alternative, 30

Wade, Ben, 58

Wade-Davis Manifesto of Radical Republicans, 55

Wallace, George, 198

Wallace, Henry A., 170, 177

Walsh, Mike, 120

War of 1812, 22, 24

Ward, Artemus, 13

Warren, Earl, 177

Watson, Tom, 102, 111

"Waving the bloody shirt" tactics of Republican campaigning, 64–65, 83, 92

Wealth: Puritan appraisal of, as measure of God's approval, 8, 77; dedication of Federalists to preservation of, 20; Social Darwinism, and accumulation of, 78; of nation, concentration of, in relatively few hands, in the 1920's, 163; and New Deal, 171

Weaver, James B., 102

Weber, Max, 8, 74

Webster, Daniel, 30

Welfare legislation, moneyed interests acceptance of, 174

Welfare liberalism, 167

Welfare State, Goldwater's position on, 189

West: principle of popular sovereignty in settlement of, 34; Republican dominance in, and the farmer, 87; and anti-immigrant drive, 134; Progressive movement in, 146

Whigs: as coalition party of Yankee and Southern plantation aristocrats, 26, 39, 178; merging of Anti-Masonic party with, 27; as rich men's coalition, 27, 28; Yankee voter as supporter of, 27–28; Southern voters for, 28; native working class as supporters of, 28; and problem of national majorities, 28; and strategy of obfuscation of issues, 28–29, 30, 182; and 1840 Presidential campaign, 29; Presidential election record of, 30; dissolution of coalition over slavery issue, 30–31; break-away of "Conscience" Whigs, 32; defections from, to Know-Nothing party, 33–34; Republican party's cultural heritage from, 37, 38; Lincoln's alignment with 41; attitude of, toward foreigners in body politic, 116–17

"White man's party," Republicans proclaimed as, 39

White supremacy: as dominating force in Southern politics, 90; restoration of, after Reconstruction, 90–91; preservation of, 94–95

White, William Allen, 160

Whitlock, Brand, quoted on Republican party, 84–85

Whittier, John Greenleaf, 4

Wildavsky, Aaron, 190–91

Willkie, Wendell L., 175–76; efforts of, to make Republican party into liberal instrument, 176

Wilson, Woodrow, 114, 135, 137; and the 1912 campaign, 155; and the Progressive movement, 156–57, 168; relations of, with Republicans, 159

Winant, John G., 170

Wirt, William, 27

Woman suffrage: crusade for, and Republican party, 128–30; correlation of support with support for prohibition, 136–37; passage of Nineteenth Amendment, 137

Woman's Christian Temperance Union, 131

Work, as Puritan's expression of submission to God, 7–8, 16

Working class, see Labor

World War I, and development of aggressive nationalism in America, 135

Xenophobia, growing sentiment of, in West and South, 134

Yankees: of New England, colonization of American Northwest by, 1–2, 16; of New England, as shapers of destiny of the nation, 4; characteristics of, 5; creation of Republican party by, 18; unwillingness of, to modify Puritan political goals, 18; faithfulness of, to political party, 18–19; and problem of transforming minority force into majority party, 19; rejection of Jefferson's ideas of democracy and deism, 22; leadership of, transferred to West, 24; reunion of Eastern and Western political wings of, 26; and formation of National Republican party, 26; coalition of, with Southern aristocrats to form

Whigs, 26; and Anti-Masonic movement, 26–27; as Whig supporters, 27–28; attitude of, toward the black man, 39; pride of, in country's expansion under Republican control and exploitation, 75–76; loyalty of, to Republican party, 84; aggressive caste behavior of, 132; restoration to power in American politics after WWI, 137; tardy awakening of, to social change, 145; and loss, through New Deal, of role of nation's rulers, 171–72; restoration of old regime as goal of, since New Deal era, 172; supremacy of, as issue in 1964 candidacy of Goldwater, 191–92

Young Men's Christian Association, 144